BETWEEN THE DEVIL AND THE DEEP BLUE SEA

BETWEEN THE DEVIL AND THE DEEP BLUE SEA

The mission to rescue
the hostages the world forgot

COLIN FREEMAN

ICON

Published in the UK in 2021
by Icon Books Ltd, Omnibus Business Centre,
39–41 North Road, London N7 9DP
email: info@iconbooks.com
www.iconbooks.com

Sold in the UK, Europe and Asia
by Faber & Faber Ltd, Bloomsbury House,
74–77 Great Russell Street,
London WC1B 3DA or their agents

Distributed in the UK, Europe and Asia
by Grantham Book Services, Trent Road, Grantham NG31 7XQ

Distributed in the USA
by Publishers Group West,
1700 Fourth Street, Berkeley, CA 94710

Distributed in Australia and New Zealand
by Allen & Unwin Pty Ltd,
PO Box 8500, 83 Alexander Street,
Crows Nest, NSW 2065

Distributed in South Africa
by Jonathan Ball, Office B4, The District,
41 Sir Lowry Road, Woodstock 7925

Distributed in India by Penguin Books India,
7th Floor, Infinity Tower – C, DLF Cyber City,
Gurgaon 122002, Haryana

Distributed in Canada by Publishers Group Canada,
76 Stafford Street, Unit 300
Toronto, Ontario M6J 2S1

ISBN: 978-178578-702-7

Typeset in Adobe Garamond by Marie Doherty

Printed and bound in Great Britain
by Clays Ltd, Elcograf S.p.A.

To my children, Daniel and Robyn, and to Jane, who somehow still puts up with me

CONTENTS

About the Author	ix
List of Key People	xiii
Timeline of Hijackings	xv
Map	xvi–xvii
Author's Note	xix
Prologue	xxiii

Chapter 1: Sinking Feeling	1
Chapter 2: It's a Sailor's Life for Me	11
Chapter 3: Maiden Voyage	17
Chapter 4: Hunted Down	27
Chapter 5: Pit of Despair	37
Chapter 6: Seafood Slaves	43
Chapter 7: Rules of Engagement	51
Chapter 8: Mother Ship	61
Chapter 9: Slaughter	67
Chapter 10: A Captain's Duty	73
Chapter 11: Son of a Pig	89
Chapter 12: The Humanitarian	99
Chapter 13: In Arrears	109
Chapter 14: The Lady Pirate	121
Chapter 15: 'Project Benedict'	127
Chapter 16: 'Captain Birdseye'	135
Chapter 17: The Gentleman Amateur	139
Chapter 18: A Lead-Lined Suitcase	147
Chapter 19: 'Not in my Children's Children's Lifetime'	159

Chapter 20: Men of Honour 173

Chapter 21: Bandit Country 179

Chapter 22: Homecoming 195

Chapter 23: Ocean Swell 211

Chapter 24: Delivery Problems 225

Chapter 25: Rat Curry 243

Chapter 26: The Odd Couple 255

Chapter 27: Pirate Conference Call 265

Afterword 279

Acknowledgements 291

ABOUT THE AUTHOR

Colin Freeman was born in Edinburgh in 1969 and has spent most of his working life as a journalist. He started his career on the *Grimsby Evening Telegraph*, before moving to the *London Evening Standard* and eventually trying his luck as a freelance correspondent in Baghdad after the fall of Saddam Hussein. From 2006–16, he was chief foreign correspondent of *The Sunday Telegraph*. He is the author of two previous books: *Kidnapped, Life as a Somali Pirate Hostage*, and *The Curse of the Al-Dulaimi Hotel and other half-truths from Baghdad*. He lives in London with his family.

Alone, alone, all, all alone,
Alone on a wide, wide sea!
And never a saint took pity on
My soul in agony.
'The Rime of the Ancient Mariner',
Samuel Taylor Coleridge

LIST OF KEY PEOPLE

John Steed: ex-British military attaché to Kenya and counter-piracy advisor to the United Nations. Leads the mission to free the *Albedo*, the *Prantalay 12* and the *Naham 3*

Aman Kumar: nineteen-year-old Indian sailor on his maiden voyage aboard the *Albedo*

Captain Jawaid Khan: the *Albedo*'s Pakistani captain

Shahriar Aliabadi: the *Albedo*'s Iranian bosun

Omid Khosrojerdi: the boss of Majestic Enrich Shipping and owner of the *Albedo*. Based in Malaysia

Shahnaz Khan: Captain Jawaid Khan's wife

Mishal and Nareman Jawaid: Captain Jawaid Khan's daughters

Leslie Edwards: an expert hostage negotiator who works alongside John Steed

Richard Neylon and James Gosling: London lawyers specialising in piracy cases, who work alongside John Steed

Ali Jabeen*: translator and negotiator for the pirate gang that hijacks the *Albedo*

Ali Inke*: chief guard for the pirate gang that hijacks the *Albedo*

---

* Not their real names.

Awale*: pirate negotiator who acts as go-between during talks between John Steed and the *Albedo* pirates

Rajoo Rajbhar: the other Indian sailor aboard the *Albedo*, later executed

Arro: female pirate, khat dealer and later investor in the *Albedo* hijacking

Omar Sheikh Ali: contact of John Steed's in Galkayo

Channarong Navara: the captain of the *Prantalay 12*

Arnel Balbero: Filipino sailor on the *Naham 3*

Said Osman: a Somali intermediary who helps Edwards in talks with pirates holding the *Naham 3*

---

* Not his real name.

TIMELINE OF HIJACKINGS

18 April 2010: the *Prantalay 12* is hijacked

26 Nov 2010: the *Albedo* is hijacked

26 Mar 2012: the *Naham 3* is hijacked

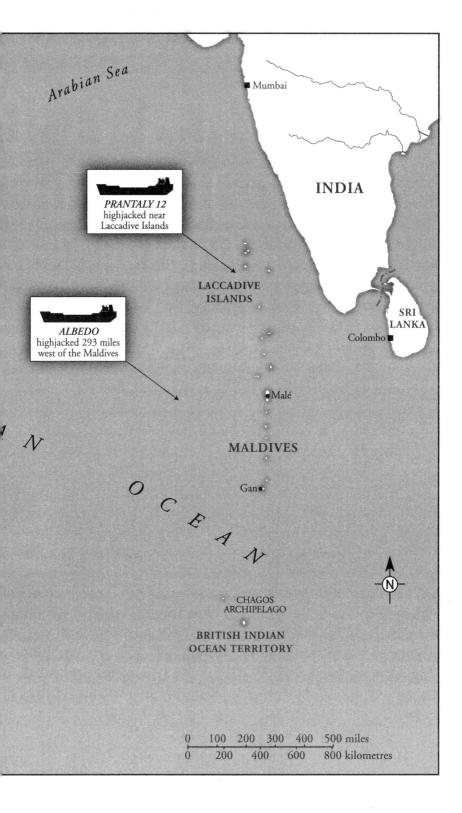

Author's Note

Any journalist seeking to find a publisher these days is usually asked: *What makes you uniquely qualified to write this book?* It's a question most writers hate, as in truth, few of us have a monopoly on competence in any particular field. For this book, though, I do for once have a fairly good answer. I was once kidnapped by Somali pirates myself, so I have some idea of what it's like.

In 2008, while reporting on the piracy crisis for *The Sunday Telegraph* in northern Somalia, I was abducted along with my photographer colleague and held prisoner in a remote mountain cave. We lived off goat meat, rice and Rothman cigarettes, and passed the time with a chess set made from cigarette foil. Several times, our captors threatened to kill us, and at one point, they had a gunfight in the cave with a rival clan.

Thankfully, we were released unharmed just six weeks later, but as an exercise in field research for this particular book, it was a reasonable primer. In the years afterwards, it also meant I became *The Sunday Telegraph*'s unofficial piracy correspondent, keeping a close eye on the mayhem off Somalia's coastline. It was during that time that I noticed that while most ships were being ransomed out, three seemed to be languishing indefinitely. The rescue of the sailors on those ships – the *Albedo*, the *Prantalay 12* and the *Naham 3* – is the subject of this book.

Much of this book is based on interviews with the sailors themselves, some of whom would not have talked to me had I not been through a similar experience. Let me stress, though, that in their company, I felt like small fry. Six weeks in captivity, after all, is a blink of an eye compared to the years of incarceration that they endured. My captors never physically harmed me, whereas they suffered regular beatings and torture, as well as seeing many of their companions die. Nor, for most of that awful time, did they have any reason to think it would ever end. Some have suffered lasting trauma. Given what they went through, I am surprised it's not more.

In return for their speaking to me, I've aimed to tell their story as best I can, although I wouldn't claim it to be perfect. This isn't a case of false writerly modesty. In retelling a trauma lasting four years or more, many of the sailors found dates and times hard to remember clearly, and sometimes events themselves. At times, accounts from one sailor tallied only vaguely with those from another.

Most of the sailors also spoke through interpreters – which, no matter how good the translation, often impacts how vividly they tell their stories. Sadly, that's also one of the reasons why these particular sailors were ignored by the world in the first place. When it comes to attracting international media attention, being non-Western and non-English speaking is still a major handicap.

Sailors and fishermen are also generally robust individuals, not overly given to soul-baring or introspection. Often, when I asked how they coped in the darkest of times, their answer was that they prayed hard, thought of their families, and told themselves to tough it out. For some, that seemed literally all they had to say on the subject – at least to me anyway. What I have tried to do, though, is convey at least the basics of their ordeals – which, in most cases, is quite horrifying enough.

Gathering the story from the viewpoint of their rescuers was rather easier. John Steed, together with negotiator Leslie Edwards and lawyers Richard Neylon and James Gosling, were all generous to me with their time, although once again, the precise details of a mission that ended up lasting more than three years had occasionally blurred. As a result of his own brush with death at the outset of his mission – more of which later – Steed finds his memory sometimes lets him down. Fortunately, he has emails and files which act as a back-up.

I also imposed limits of my own in writing this book. Some of the accounts of torture and mistreatment I have left out, as to relay them all would have felt both gratuitous and repetitive. Readers may also notice that I recount the hijacking and cruelty that took place on the *Albedo* in more detail than on the other two ships. Again, this is not to under-play what went on the *Prantalay 12* and *Naham 3*, but simply to avoid repetition. In amid the horrors, there are also acts of extraordinary courage and decency – by the Britons and Somalis involved in the rescue effort, and by the sailors too. I like to think that this is a story about humanity at its best, not just its worst.

The research for this book was often hard, as many of the hostages were still too traumatised to talk or hard to track down. Some had gone back to further long stints at sea, to make up for wages lost during their time in captivity. Those I did meet were often in remote, impoverished villages – places that they'd hoped seafaring would fund an escape from. But I'm glad they spoke out, for they also serve as the voices for a much larger cadre of seafarers who suffered at the hands of Somali pirates, whose ordeals have gone largely unrecorded.

In the five years that the piracy crisis was at its peak – roughly from 2008 to 2012 – nearly 2,000 sailors were hijacked. The vast majority were from the poorer parts of Asia and Africa, whose only crime was to seek to earn a living. Yet beyond a few paragraphs in the odd news report, very few of their stories were ever properly told.

Instead, to much of the world, pirates only existed when they captured Westerners – be they adventure-seeking yachters in the Indian Ocean, or yes, journalists like me, who'd stumbled into trouble. Hence, perhaps, the ongoing belief that modern piracy, in the best tradition of buccaneering, is a war of the have-nots against the haves. The Somalis who manned the pirate gangs were mostly poor, indeed, but so too were most of their victims – so much so that in cases like the *Albedo*, *Prantalay 12* and *Naham 3*, the world did not seem interested in buying them out of trouble, never mind in learning about their ordeal. So here – in as much detail as I can manage – is their story.

Colin Freeman
London, May 2020

Prologue

THE LUCKIEST MAN
IN EAST AFRICA

Nairobi, Kenya, August 2013

John Steed lay in the intensive care unit of Nairobi's Aga Khan Hospital, drifting in and out of consciousness. He had a drip in his arm, and a strange, unfamiliar ache in his chest. He had no idea where he was, or why he was there. Thanks to the fug of anaesthetic and painkillers pumping round his body, it was hard to separate dreams from reality. Sometimes he thought he was back commanding his old army regiment in England – he'd surprised the hospital nurses by barking drill instructions for the 33rd Signal Regiment in Liverpool.

He tried to move, but was still too sedated even to open his eyes. At the back of his mind, he knew something had gone very wrong. Like a man waking up with a monster hangover, there were vague, unsettling memories of the day before.

He'd been at a business lunch. Not a beer or glass of wine in sight. Then, just a blank, nothing. And then it got really crazy. Being wheeled down a corridor on a hospital trolley, covered in vomit. Alan Cole, his UN colleague, at his side, telling him to dictate his last will and testament, scribbling it down on a staffing rota torn from a hospital notice board. To onlookers, it had probably looked like an over-hyped episode of the hospital drama *ER*.

Onlookers there had certainly been. As news had spread around Nairobi of Steed's heart attack, dozens of friends had turned up, waiting overnight as he went into surgery. Old pals from the British embassy, where he'd worked as military attaché, colleagues from the UN and contacts from the diplomatic circuit. They weren't just hanging around to deliver get-well messages. The Aga Khan was one of Kenya's top hospitals, one of the few where heart attack victims didn't just leave via the morgue, but like many Kenyan hospitals, it had limited blood supplies. Patients' friends and relatives were encouraged to donate to replenish the stocks. The donors milled around in the hospital corridor, drinking tea to replace their missing fluids. Mobile phones rang constantly from other well-wishers.

The calls came from far and wide. In his time in East Africa, Steed had met all manner of people – presidents, ministers, clan leaders, warlords past and present. In the region's turbulent politics, yesterday's villains were often tomorrow's leaders. Some were now on the phone to his friends in the corridor, sending best wishes.

The blessings seemed to work. After a seven-hour operation, the medics declared success. The main artery to his heart, which had ripped open, had been repaired with an artificial graft. A few days later, Steed became lucid again. No more morphine-fuelled parade drills in Liverpool. A doctor appeared by his bedside.

'You had an aortic dissection. Pretty serious stuff.'

'A what?'

'A split in one of the arteries to your heart. Normally it would have killed you, because the operation to fix it is very difficult. But the same night you came, we had a specialist arrive in from London, who's here to set up a new heart clinic. He fixed you up. You're a very lucky man.'

'Right. So how am I now?'

'You should be okay. Another couple of weeks here, then home to recover.'

He tried to feel thankful. Whatever the surgeon said, it really didn't feel like his lucky day. Yet the proof was there in front of him, quite literally. Running from his sternum to his stomach was a foot-long incision, sewn up with heavy-duty, Frankenstein-style stitches, where the surgeons had split his rib cage open to get at his heart. That had been the easy part, according to the medics. The operation to repair the rupture itself was so delicate that on the four occasions it had been tried before at the Aga Khan, every patient had died. Steed was the only person in Kenya who'd survived. In fact, the only person in the whole of East Africa. The surgeon was extremely pleased, hoping it would be a good advert for the new clinic he was starting up.

The medics warned it would take a while to recover. 'Goal number one is lots of physio to regain your strength,' they said. 'Goal number two is reducing your blood pressure – watch the diet and the booze. And goal number three, most important of all, take it easy. Relax. No stressful activity.'

Goals one and two he could manage. Goal three, about avoiding stress, was going to be tricky. Just a few weeks earlier, the Luckiest Man in East Africa had begun a mission to help some of the unluckiest. Those crews of hijacked sailors, held for years by pirates on the Somali coast. It was a mission that often sent his blood pressure soaring, and sometimes made it run cold. Not ideal for someone recovering from heart surgery. But it was a mission he now felt bound to. As much as anything in his last will and testament on that scrap of hospital paper.

Chapter 1

SINKING FEELING

*Nairobi, Kenya, June 2013. Two months
before John Steed's heart rupture*

'Take a look at these,' said the caller. 'The maritime patrol aircraft took them on the dawn flyover. Not looking good.'

John Steed opened the photos attached to the email. They showed a container ship, the *Albedo*, anchored a few miles off the coast of Somalia. It was huge, with a six-storey control tower and a deck the length of a football pitch. A workhorse of global commerce, built for ferrying tens of thousands of tonnes of cargo round the planet.

For the last two and a half years, though, it had gone nowhere. In November 2010, the *Albedo* had been hijacked by one of Somalia's many gangs of pirates. Confined to the history books in most other parts of the world, piracy had become Somalia's first boom industry in recent memory. The ship was now among dozens being held for ransom up and down the coastline. There were elderly Taiwanese fishing trawlers, clapped-out Yemeni dhows, and brand-new oil tankers, some of them ten times the size of the *Albedo*, all idling like fish in an angler's keep net.

The photos had been sent by a contact of Steed's at EU

Navel Force (NAVFOR), the European Union's arm of the new international anti-piracy force. Over the past five years, scores of nations had sent naval vessels to patrol the pirates' hunting grounds, through which some of the world's busiest shipping lanes also passed. It was the first operation of its kind in more than 200 years.

They'd had little success. They were trying to police the entire western half of the Indian Ocean – an area of 20 million square miles – an impossible feat, even for modern navies armed with helicopters and spy planes. When a vessel sent an SOS saying that a pirate raiding party was in sight, the warships were usually miles away. And once the pirates were on board, guns pointed at sailors' heads, there was nothing anyone could do. Special Forces rescues, with teams of commandos storming on board, weren't an option, as there was too much risk of hostages or soldiers getting killed. Anyone who thought otherwise had read too many thriller novels.

Much of the time, the anti-piracy force found itself reduced to monitoring the progress of the hijackings. Their maritime patrol aircraft would cruise the Somali coast, checking which ships were still being held, photographing pirate skiffs as they shuttled to and from the mainland. Every so often, a ship would be released after the owners paid a ransom. A light aircraft would fly over, dropping the cash by parachute in the sea next to the ship – a couple of million dollars, sometimes more, packed into a floating plastic capsule the size of a large suitcase. After counting it, the pirates would abandon ship and speed back to the mainland, richer than most Somalis could ever dream of becoming.

Even then, though, the anti-piracy force was reluctant to pursue them. Chasing Somali pirates onto the mainland was beyond their remit. Besides, if a warship grabbed one gang of hijackers with their loot, the pirates would sometimes get their friends aboard another hijacked ship to threaten to kill the hostages there instead. Like the anti-piracy force, they showed solidarity in the face of a common enemy. A bunch of men in ragged clothes and sandals, running one of the largest kidnapping operations in modern times. Right under the nose of the combined might of the world's naval superpowers.

Most hijacks lasted about three months. Many sailors emerged traumatised, vowing never to go to sea again. They, though, were the fortunate ones. Their ship owners usually had kidnap and ransom insurance, so that if their ship did get hijacked, the insurer would reimburse the cost of the ransom. The cost of such premiums had rocketed, but no responsible owner sent a vessel into pirate waters without the means to buy it out of trouble.

That, though, was what the owner of the *Albedo* appeared to have done. The ship's fifteen crew had been stuck for two and a half years because its owner had no money to pay a ransom. Not only that, he seemed to have abandoned them to their fate, becoming ever harder for the pirates, the crew and their relatives to contact. Perhaps he hoped that the pirates would eventually give the hostages up. They hadn't. In somewhere as poor as Somalia, kidnappers didn't lightly walk away from the prospect of a fat ransom pay-out.

Yet the *Albedo*'s days as a floating jail were now numbered. Large container ships were designed to be kept in deep-water ports, not anchored in the shallows of an ocean-battered coastline. During the last few weeks of stormy monsoon weather, the ship had started to list to one side – the result, most likely, of a reef gouging a hole in the hull. The photos showed the ship's bow half-submerged in the sea, assaulted on all sides by grey-green monsoon waves. With another big storm due in coming days, EU NAVFOR reckoned it was only a matter of time before it sank.

'If it starts sinking, it could be all over in minutes,' Steed's contact told him. 'Especially in a storm at night. Could be impossible to get on the lifeboats, even if they're still working. Those hostages could drown.'

Officially, it wasn't the anti-piracy force's responsibility. Because the *Albedo* was in Somali territorial waters, they couldn't send in a rescue ship to pick the hostages up. However, it wasn't anyone else's responsibility either. Which was why his friend in EU NAVFOR had come to him – Colonel (Ret'd) John Steed, formerly of the British Army, now Head of Maritime Security and Counter Piracy for the UN Political Office for Somalia, known in the trade as UNPOS.

It was a grand-sounding title, with not a lot of power attached. What UNPOS did have, though, was a 'Hostage Support Programme'. Steed had set it up a few months ago himself, to help sailors who'd got stranded after being freed from pirate captivity. He'd help get them home, sorting out new passports, arranging flights, using the UN's name to barge through what often felt like ludicrous amounts of red tape.

The *Albedo* sailors, though, weren't ex-hostages. They were *current* hostages. And, if his friend at EU NAVFOR was correct, soon-to-be-drowned hostages. How the hell was he supposed to help them?

The *Albedo* wasn't the only hijacked ship that seemed to have been left to fend for itself. There was also the *Naham 3*, a Taiwanese trawler moored just next to the *Albedo*, now in its fourteenth month in captivity. And further down the coast was the Thai trawler *Prantalay 12*, whose crew had now been hostage for more than three years. They had the dubious distinction of being the longest-running hijacking case in modern history. Their plight ought to have been a global scandal, yet there was barely a mention of them in the international media, other than a few brief lines in the shipping newspaper *Lloyd's List* when they'd first been hijacked. Steed wasn't surprised. Piracy cases only attracted much attention if they involved Westerners. Like the *Maersk Alabama*.

The *Maersk Alabama* was the one everyone remembered. A US-crewed cargo ship, hijacked by four pirates in early 2009. The crew turned the tables on the hijackers, ambushing one of the pirates in the engine room and taking him hostage. The other three pirates then fled in a lifeboat with the ship's skipper, Captain Richard Phillips, as a captive. A stand-off ensued with a US warship, all over in a split second, when snipers on the warship killed all three pirates with synchronised shots to the head. The good guys had won – Hollywood got interested.

A blockbuster movie version of the hijacking, *Captain Phillips*, was due out that autumn, yet most hijacked seafarers got no media spotlight at all. They were men from the poorer parts of Asia, from villages in Thailand, India, Bangladesh, Cambodia. Most didn't speak English – not the kind of people who worked well on CNN, or captured the imaginations of Hollywood producers. Likewise, just as most hijacks didn't end up as movies, most hijacks didn't end up with the cavalry coming to the rescue, as they'd done in *Captain Phillips*. America, Britain and several other countries on the anti-piracy fleet had Special Forces soldiers on standby, ready to carry out rescues by force; but they'd normally only use them to rescue their own citizens, and only if there was an imminent threat to life. There'd be no good guys coming in to help the *Albedo*, the *Naham 3*, or the *Prantalay 12*.

Steed had recently tried contacting the ships' owners, hoping to shame them into action. It was bad enough that they weren't properly insured, but couldn't they try to help anyway? Borrow some money from somewhere? Rather than leaving their sailors to rot? He'd got nowhere. The *Albedo*'s owner had already cut off his phone and email accounts, blanking even the sailors' relatives. He'd been unable to get hold of the owners of the *Prantalay 12* or *Naham 3* either. There were rumours that the *Naham 3* owners were in financial trouble.

Nor had the sailors' governments been much help. Several had smart embassies in Nairobi's diplomatic quarter, complete with retinues of house staff and chauffeurs. Steed had rung round them, but most simply never returned his calls, or flannelled: *It's a civil matter, sir, nothing to do with us. Can you put this request in writing to our foreign ministry? Have you contacted the police in Somalia? Sorry, what sailors?*

All of which meant that neither Steed nor anybody else had any idea how the hijacked sailors were faring. All three ships were entirely incommunicado. It wasn't even clear if the hostages were still alive or not. Steed had put out feelers among contacts in Somalia, locals who were tuned into the gossip on the pirate coast – the word that came back was not good.

The pirates on all three ships, by all accounts, didn't believe the owners' pleas of penury. Instead, they'd assumed it was just a particularly callous negotiating ploy, and they'd responded in kind. They were now torturing their captives, to heap pressure on the owners. Not just the odd beating, but lashings, scaldings, thrashings and even executions, harking back to the brutality of piracy's medieval heyday. Several sailors were said to have starved to death after being put on punishment rations. Of those still alive, many were slowly losing their minds, or suicidal.

Somali pirates weren't supposed to be like this. As a rule, they treated their hostages reasonably well. They styled themselves as Robin Hood characters, stealing from the world's rich to give to its poor. Just a tax on passing seafarers. Businessmen with guns, as they called themselves.

Steed had asked his contacts if it could be just exaggeration. Might the hijackers be putting out stories to frighten the owners? Maybe, yes. But the piracy game was attracting some bad people these days.

Steed had spent most of his life in the British Army. After officer training at Sandhurst, he'd joined the Royal Signals, the service's communications experts. He'd spent the last decade as a military attaché, first with the British embassy in Dublin, then at the embassy in Nairobi. People thought he spent his time watching military parades and cruising the cocktail circuit. The Canapé Corps, they called it. If only.

For his final job in uniform, he'd been seconded to UNPOS, to help run international efforts to start a new national army in Somalia. The last one had collapsed back in 1991, when Somalia's civil war had begun. More than twenty years on, the new one was still very much a work in progress. Every so often, he'd fly to Mogadishu, skimming in on a plane low across the sea to avoid rocket fire, before heading for what passed for the British embassy – a Portakabin in a fortified diplomatic compound. Then he'd take an armoured personnel carrier to the president's villa for the latest security updates. The news was seldom good. It reminded him of films he'd seen about Vietnam in the run-up to the US evacuation of Saigon, only everyone was sticking around for the storm to come.

Yet the work – part soldier, part diplomat and part aid worker – had been rewarding. So much so that when he'd reached his 55th birthday – the official retirement age for the army – he'd taken a new job with the UN as a counter-piracy advisor. He'd worked on a range of carrot-and-stick measures to try to curb the problem. There were legal measures to prosecute pirates caught in international waters, and job creation schemes for Somalia's coastal villages, to give young men money-making options other than hijacking.

It was easy to tell himself that he was doing some good. Yet as long as those poor souls on abandoned ships like the *Albedo* were languishing indefinitely in captivity, it all seemed slightly beside the point. He'd wanted to do something to help them himself: at least to establish contact with them, to find out how many were still alive, and whether any needed medical help. But with the crew of the *Albedo* now at risk of drowning, he might already be too late.

He got up from his desk, staring out of the window of his flat in Nairobi. He lived on the tenth storey of an apartment block, home mainly to UN-types like himself, and bureaucrats from aid organisations. Nairobi was the hub for aid agencies for the whole of East Africa. There were countless aid missions based here: education; health; empowerment; human rights. A global capital for the caring and concerned. Why, he sometimes wondered, with so many benevolent organisations on the doorstep, was nobody shouting about these forgotten sailors? Where was the public outcry on their behalf? Why, in an age when charitable appeals could direct billions of dollars around the world, were a bunch of hostages stuck in limbo for want of a ransom payment? And, God forbid, what was life like for them on those ships?

Chapter 2

It's a Sailor's Life for Me

Kardial village, northern India, 2009

'Seafaring opens up a universe of
opportunities for achieving different
landmarks as successful human beings.'
Brochure for the Trident Maritime College, Calcutta

The farming village of Kardial in India's far north is not a
place where many locals consider a career in seafaring. It lies
in the foothills of the western Himalayas, 700 miles from
the Indian Ocean and more than 2,000 feet above sea level.
In the days of the British Raj, the surrounding valleys were
a favoured summer retreat for sweating colonial envoys, desperate to escape Delhi's ferocious heat. Today, they're better
known as a picturesque backdrop for Bollywood movies.
Big-eyed starlets go on the run in the forested glades, fleeing
thwarted suitors and scheming uncles.

While outsiders seek sanctuary here, locals dream of
leaving. In Kardial, few were keener to see the wider world
than Aman Kumar Sharma, a restless, boyish-faced teenager
often seen cruising his motorbike up and down Kardial's

main street. At one end was a new electricity substation and a shop selling the latest smartphones. At the other, a tailor still knocked out suits on a pedal-operated sewing machine.

Kardial, like the rest of rural India, was slowly being dragged into the 21st century. Youngsters now had a choice of career beyond tilling the fields. As he reached his seventeenth birthday, though, Aman had already decided on one thing. Whatever he did when he left school, he was *not* going to become a bloody engineer. In Kardial, it seemed like nearly every family wanted at least one son to be an engineer. Most of Aman's friends had had the pep talk: *Engineers built the roads that connected this village to the outside world, son. And who do you think built that hydroelectric power station in the valley? The one that brought us electricity. Engineers, that's who.*

If it wasn't engineering, it was some other profession. Accountant, doctor, lawyer, whatever. Modern India was obsessed with social mobility. The pressure wasn't just at home. On Kardial's main street, the billboards were festooned with adverts for engineering colleges, most run by ex-army officers boasting long rows of medals and even longer rows of B.Eng's, MScs and PHDs. The message was always the same: letters at the end of your name equates to zeros at the end of your salary. Yet it fell on deaf ears with Aman. By his final year of school, when most of his class were sitting exams to become engineers, he'd already set his heart on joining the merchant navy.

As with most life-changing decisions, it had come by chance. He'd been out on his motorbike when he'd spied another rider on a 200cc Honda, the most expensive bike he'd ever seen round Kardial. Its owner looked barely older than him.

'What do you do for a living, man?' Aman asked.

'I'm a sailor. Merchant navy. It's a good living, my friend – $1,000 a month, if you get on the right ships. Buy yourself a bike like this, visit the USA, whatever you want.'

This was how men had been lured into merchant sailing for centuries. Not through adverts or recruitment drives, but through sailors flashing their money around. Richard Phillips, the hero of *Captain Phillips*, had fallen for just the same patter in 1970s Boston. He'd been driving a cab, his life going nowhere, when a merchant seaman clambered into his car one morning and declared: 'I want booze and I want broads.' The seaman tipped him $5 for the $5 fare to the nearest flesh-pot. A year later, Phillips enrolled in Massachusetts Maritime Academy.

Unlike Phillips, who grew up in one of America's biggest port cities, Aman had never even seen the sea before. But so what? If nothing else, joining the merchant navy would get him out of Kardial – away from the village gossips, always wondering how so-and-so's son was doing, and when they were going to do their family right by getting onto a good college course. It wasn't as if that guaranteed you a job anyway. Aman knew plenty of engineers in Kardial who were working as cabbies. The more he thought about it, the more a life as a merchant seaman appealed.

The job had a good reputation, judging by the comments posted on Indian jobseeker websites. Sure, you could be away at sea for nine months at a time, but you could take as much holiday as you wanted in between. Not like those call centre jobs, having to be polite all day to whingeing Europeans, where the bosses tutted if you even asked for time off to get married. And while it wasn't quite up there with being a doctor, it still had a certain cachet. That crisp white sailors' uniform made a good picture for the family to hang in the parlour, stopped the relatives asking why you hadn't become a bloody engineer.

'No, I don't think so. Why don't you apply to be a vet instead?'

Aman's father, Kewal Krishan Sharma, looked like he could have stepped out from one of the college adverts on Kardial's main drag. An army veteran, he'd fought in India's war with Pakistan in 1999, when for three scary months, the two nuclear powers had battled over the disputed territory of Kashmir. That made him a respected man in Kardial. He wasn't insistent on his son following him into the military, but he had his doubts about the merchant navy. Not least because maritime college was going to cost $6,000.

Aman didn't want to be a vet any more than he wanted to be an engineer. He'd had enough of farm animals around the family home, where water buffalo still grazed in the back yard. The more his father pushed back, the more he wanted to go to sea. Eventually, he got his way. In 2008, shortly after his eighteenth birthday, Aman headed for a private maritime college in Calcutta, 1500 miles south-east on the Bay of Bengal.

The college was one of dozens in Calcutta, feeding what was now one of the largest merchant navies in the world. Cadets lived in dorms, and wore a uniform of neatly-ironed shirts, shorts and socks pulled to the knees. They studied container ships and oil tankers, and how to load them to keep them stable. They were trained in how to climb ladders and masts, practising on a ten-metre tower, and they learned knotting, a skill that even Boy Scouts no longer bothered with, but which sailors were still expected to perform with their eyes closed.

Yet Able Seaman Sharma, as he became a few months later, found himself unable to become a seaman. By the time he graduated in 2009, the global recession was kicking in. Shipping was one of the first casualties. Around the world, businesses were trimming orders back, be it for boxes of Sony PlayStations or 100,000-tonne consignments of steel. Container ships were idling in port, and so too were the men that crewed them. In Calcutta, the seamen's hostels were full of jobless sailors, yet the maritime colleges were still churning out another 50,000 sailors every year. With no prior experience, they had no chance against the older hands.

'Give me $6,000, and I can get you a job on a ship around the Gulf,' the agent told Aman. 'A nine-month contract.'

The naval college had warned him about guys like this. The backstreet shipping agents, who operated out of shabby offices around Calcutta's docks. Men with connections here, friends there. Men who somehow always knew of jobs going somewhere – so long as you paid a 'recruitment fee'. The 'fee' was often just a bung to some disreputable captain, the kind whose ships were best avoided anyway. But after six months languishing back in Kardial, Aman was desperate. The agents spun it as a kind of paid-for internship – get the experience you need, then get a better job next time. Even though the

$6,000 they wanted was the same amount he'd paid for maritime college.

He did the maths. On the ship the agent was offering, his wages would be just $200 per month. So much for the $1,000 a month that his pal with the smart Honda back in Kardial had boasted of. At $200 a month, it would take three years just to pay off the recruitment fee – not much better than bonded labour. His father thought it was throwing good money after bad. Or rather, bad money after good, given the stories one heard about these agent types. Still, anything to help his son.

Chapter 3

MAIDEN VOYAGE

Jebel Ali Port, Dubai, October 2010

On 16 October 2010, Aman flew to Dubai to start his new job. His first time on a plane, taking him to his first time at sea. He spent a night in a hotel downtown, surrounded by skyscrapers and construction sites. Looking out of the window, it was hard to believe there was a global recession in full swing.

Dubai is the Arab world's Hong Kong, a hot, humid city that lives by its wits. An oasis of prosperity in a tough neighbourhood, its banks are stuffed with the life savings of half the Middle East's people, from war-weary Syrians to sanctions-wary Iranians. With no shortage of willing investors, it always looks busy, even in an economic downturn.

There was even more bustle down at the port of Jebel Ali, Aman's destination the next day. The largest manmade harbour in the world, it was twice the size of Manhattan island. As Aman came through the gates, he saw endless piles of oblong cargo containers, stacked up like gigantic Lego bricks. He'd learned about them in maritime college: the standard delivery box for world trade; super versatile; designed to be stacked ten-high on a ship, loaded end-to-end on a train, or carried solo on a lorry.

Next to them were fleets of huge container ships, some a quarter of a mile long. Behemoths that transported 90 per cent of the world's trade, be it shoes, food, steel girders or flat-screen TVs. Without merchant sailors, the planet's shop shelves would be empty.

Against these giants, the ship Aman was now clambering onto was a minnow, yet still massive to a newcomer. The *Albedo*'s main deck was bigger than a full-sized football pitch. At the stern was a khaki-painted tower block six storeys high, housing the living quarters, the engine rooms and the bridge, or control room. The ship's bow was 30 feet above the water, but was sinking lower as 10,000 tonnes of cement and rice were loaded onboard. Aman's first voyage on the *Albedo* would be to haul the cargo to ports in Pakistan and Iran, and then back to Dubai. Beyond that, he knew little about his employers for the next nine months, the Majestic Enrich Shipping Company. The founder of Majestic was an Iranian, Omid Khosrojerdi, who worked out of offices in Malaysia, where the *Albedo* was flagged. Had any crewman searched the internet to learn more, all they would have found was a brief entry in an online shipping registry giving Majestic's office address, and the *Albedo*'s International Maritime Organisation number, the equivalent of its number plate. It had the corporate profile of a back-street mini-cab firm.

This wasn't unusual in the world of international shipping. In an industry that has been globalising since the age of sail, ships were often owned in one country, flagged in another, based in a third and crewed from a fourth, fifth, sixth and more. Operated through networks of agents, charter firms and middlemen, the set-up could be as opaque as a shell company in a tax haven. Things were not always what they seemed.

Majestic Enrich, for example, was neither majestic nor rich. The firm had aspired to be a major player on the Asian trade routes, but the recession had reined in its ambitions. Now, rather than a fleet, it had just the *Albedo*, an ageing journey-man that had already had several previous owners and several different names. In eighteen years at sea, it had operated as the *Universal Bahana*, the *Silver Dawn*, the *Mumbai Bay*, and most recently, the *Cape Ann*.

Still, Aman felt overawed as he walked up the gangway. The hatchways, corridors and stairwells seemed to stretch forever. There was the smell of diesel and cleaning products, levers, lights, buttons and warning signs everywhere, the sense of being inside a giant machine. It was going to take him weeks just to learn his way around the rear tower. Now he realised why they'd practised gangway guard at naval college: if stowaways sneaked on board, it would be impossible to find them.

After being shown his cabin, a small shared bunk room, he took a wander. There was a dining room, a kitchen and a small lounge, where the crew could watch TV, play video games and socialise. At the top of the tower, fitted out with tinted panoramic windows like an ocean-going penthouse suite, was the bridge where the captain sat.

As he made his way around the ship, Aman saw men from all over Asia. Westerners were a rare sight among big container crews these days, the jobs long outsourced to countries with cheaper labour. The *Albedo*'s captain, Jawaid Khan, was Pakistani, as was the chief officer, Gulam Mujtaba. The ship's bosun, the officer in day-to-day charge of the crew, was Shahriar Aliabadi, from Iran. Of the nineteen other sailors on board, there were six more Pakistanis, six Sri Lankans, three

Bangladeshis, and an Egyptian. Plus, Aman was pleased to learn, one other rookie Indian about his own age.

The newcomers weren't the only ones feeling a sense of occasion. Ahead of a long stint at sea, even the experienced sailors would find themselves in a reflective mood. Like soldiers embarking on a tour of duty, the start of each trip to sea was a marker in life, a time to take stock. They'd ponder the state of their marriages, their finances, the ever-present gap in life between where they were and where they wanted to be. There'd be resolutions to spend more time with the children, to treat the wife better, to divorce her; to find a better ship to sail on; to quit sailing altogether.

While Aman was contemplating the start of his days at sea, the *Albedo*'s captain, Jawaid Khan, was contemplating the end. A 63-year-old career sailor from the Pakistani port of Karachi, he'd spent most of his adult life on the oceans. Probably more time than he'd spent on land. He was slim of build and save for a few strands of swept-back hair, it was as if his scalp had been worn smooth by decades of ocean breeze. With his crisp white captain's shirt and well-spoken, lightly-accented English, he could have passed for a Greek shipping magnate.

Yet the bags under his eyes and the lines across his face betrayed a certain frailty. Or so his elder daughter, Nareman, had told him just days before. She'd noticed that the father who'd always seemed so sturdy, who'd spent his life as a leader of men, was now looking rather old. Her words came back to him now as he did the final paperwork for the *Albedo*'s journey: *'Why don't you retire soon, father? Please make this your last journey. Come home and spend more time with the family.'*

It was always hard to ignore his daughters' wishes. Even though that was what he'd had to do for half his life. He'd been away when Nareman was born, and had seen her and her sister Mishal grow up in snapshots. Whenever he came home on shore leave, the girls who ran into his arms were at a different stage in life. First as toddlers, then as boisterous, gap-toothed young kids, then as shy teenagers, and now as self-assured young women. Self-assured enough to start telling him what to do.

Nareman, now 21, had recently finished university, and had moved to Dubai to work as a consultant. She'd come down to Jebel Ali to see him off on the *Albedo*. Aware that he owed her some time in his dotage, he'd agreed to make it his last voyage. He'd hugged her and said goodbye, wondering what retirement with his family would really be like.

On 30 October 2010, the *Albedo* set sail, and Dubai's sky-scrapers receded as they made their way towards the Gulf of Oman. Aman began duty, eight-hour shifts day and night. Like housekeepers to a huge stately home, much of the job was maintenance work. There were lifeboats to be tested, cables to be repaired and spliced, rust to be removed, fresh paint to be re-applied. There were also workmates to get to know. In the rec lounge, there was the usual guarded banter between strangers who knew they faced a long time together, participants in a floating *Big Brother* show that would run for months. They talked about past trips, captains good and bad,

wives and partners. Aman mentioned his girlfriend in Kardial, who he was hoping to get engaged to when he got back.

After nine days of sailing, *Albedo* stopped for two nights in Karachi, and then headed on to Iran, arriving at the port of Bander Abbas on Nov 12. There, Captain Khan received new orders from Majestic Shipping. They were to return to Dubai, and then head south, to Mombasa in Kenya. First, though, there was a staffing problem to sort out. The ship's electrician, an Egyptian named Magdy Muhammad, wanted to quit.

A tall, highly-strung man, Magdy was an observant Muslim, who wore a beard and prayed five times a day. On the way back to Dubai, he claimed to have had a premonition that the journey ahead to Kenya would bring bad luck. The sense of foreboding had got so strong that one day, he'd asked God for a sign. God had got back to him that very evening. Just after midnight, he'd woken in his bunk, sweating and terrified. He'd dreamed that a malign force had scooped the *Albedo* out of the sea, hurling it onto a sandy beach, where it lay stricken.

'Believe me, it's an omen of some kind,' he told Aman, and any other crew member who would listen. 'It's better to get off when we get back to Jebel Ali.'

Superstition comes naturally to sailors. The open ocean is a perilous place, where acts of God are not just some abstract clause on an insurance form, but an occupational hazard. To this day, some sailors still refuse to say 'goodbye' to their loved ones, preferring something more non-committal like 'see you soon'. Magdy, however, got short shrift from his shipmates. Some politely ignored him, others laughed in his face. Some wondered why he'd been allowed on board in the first place. Container ships were dangerous enough as they were, without religious types jabbering about imminent disaster.

Sane or not, though, electricians were hard to replace. Suspecting it was just a ruse to get more money, Majestic, the ship's owners, offered to double his wages. He wasn't interested. 'I will not go on that ship if you give me $10,000 per month,' he said. At Dubai, Magdy wandered down the gangplank with his trolley bag. It was the morning of 17 November 2010. Shortly afterwards, the *Albedo* cast off for Kenya.

Captain Khan, too, had a bad feeling about the journey ahead to Mombasa, although his misgivings were rather more specific. He was worried – very worried – about pirates.

They'd been a hazard off the Somali coast ever since the early 2000s, when local fishermen had begun attacking foreign trawlers poaching the country's vast, unpoliced fish stocks. Holding crews to ransom allowed the fishermen to press home Somalia's one competitive advantage – that in a country as lawless as theirs, nobody dared come after them. As news of generous ransom payments spread, militiamen from all over Somalia had got in on the act. Some were less than discriminating about their targets.

Today, they didn't just hijack marauding trawlers, but any vessel they could grab. At first, commercial shipping had been able to stay safe by staying 70 miles off the Somali coast. The pirates, operating in wooden skiffs with high-speed outboard engines, couldn't reach that far out from shore. But by 2010, merely giving Somalia a wide berth was no longer enough. Using trawlers captured in previous hijackings, the pirates now had 'mother ships', floating operation centres that allowed them to range thousands of miles out into the Indian

Ocean. They could go stalking for weeks at a time, towing their skiffs by their side like a hunting caravan with a pack of hounds. The entire western Indian Ocean was now categorised as a 'High-Risk Area' by insurers. It was a hunting ground twice the size of India itself. And the *Albedo* would be going right through it.

They could not have picked a worse time. The international anti-piracy force was urging shipping to stick to set routes so that they could protect them more easily, but in an area so vast, the combined might of the world's navies was still like a few lone traffic cops on an inter-state highway. In late 2010, as the *Albedo* began its journey, Somali pirates were holding around 700 sailors hostage on 30 hijacked vessels, their greatest number ever.

Khan knew that old, slow-moving craft like the *Albedo* were likely targets. Ships capable of more than eighteen knots (21 miles per hour) were generally safe from pirates, as they moved too fast to make a boarding easy. The *Albedo*, laden with cargo, would probably struggle to reach fourteen. She also failed the 'freeboard' test, which held that ships with a deck more than eight metres above the water were too high for the pirates to climb up. The *Albedo*'s was barely half that. They were easy prey, no doubt about it, like an elderly wildebeest being stalked by lions.

When Majestic had first told Khan about the *Albedo*'s new route, he'd asked if the ship could have armed guards. He'd been refused. While armed guards gave captains peace of mind, they made ship owners anxious. Too expensive, for a start, and too much risk of legal hassle. Guards licensed to carry a gun in one country's port might be arrested in another. And what if they shot the wrong person? An owner might end up in court with them.

Like Magdy, the Egyptian electrician, Khan had contemplated quitting the ship altogether back in Dubai, but he knew it would ruin his chances of more work, from Majestic or anyone else. Despite telling his daughter that this would be his last journey, he didn't want to make himself unemployable. Instead, he'd pressed ahead, keeping a close eye on the ship's radar at all times. The typical warning sign would be two or more tiny dots advancing quickly across the screen. He also wrote a draft SOS email to the Maritime Trade Operations centre in Bahrain, which would alert foreign naval patrols if he hit the 'send' button.

He reminded himself that statistically, the chances of being attacked were still low. Every year, nearly 100,000 vessels travelled through these waters. So far in 2010, only 28 had been taken. As shipping firms were keen to point out, that made the chances of being hijacked on the Indian Ocean less than those of being mugged on the streets of London.

Indeed, few of the other sailors on the *Albedo* had even thought about pirates. They hadn't featured in the syllabus at Aman's maritime college, the first he heard about them was during a brief counter-piracy attack drill in Dubai. If pirates tried to clamber aboard, the crew would repel them by firing high-pressure water hoses at them. The *Albedo* also had an electric cable that could be lowered around the deck, which would give a strong but non-lethal shock.

It almost sounded fun, like defending a castle from invaders, but it seemed no more likely than the ship catching fire or sinking. The crew's thoughts were mainly about what they'd do on their shore leave in Mombasa. There was talk of going on one of Kenya's famous safaris.

Chapter 4

HUNTED DOWN

The Albedo, *west of the Maldives, 26 November 2010*

The *Albedo* was nine days into its journey to Kenya. Rather than taking the quickest route and approaching direct from the north, Khan had headed out to the middle of the Indian Ocean first, planning to loop around and approach Kenya from the south-east. The detour had taken several extra days, but kept them further away from Somalia. It wasn't far enough, in the view of Shahriar Aliabadi, the Iranian bosun. He was convinced the route was still risky, and had made his objections known. 'We are in a sea of sharks here,' he told Khan. The captain, he suspected, was trying to get in the owners' good books by using less fuel.

The *Albedo* was now just west of the Maldives, a speckle of coral atolls in the middle of the Indian Ocean. Slumbering in his bunk that morning, Aman drifted in and out of sleep, thinking about breakfast. He barely even registered the announcement that suddenly blared its way into his dreams just after 7.20am.

'ATTENTION ALL CREWS! PIRATES ARE COMING!'

He rolled over in bed. It was coming from the ship's PA system, piped into every room. The voice was that of Mujtaba, the chief officer. It couldn't be a genuine alert, surely, as right now they were nearly 2,000 miles from the Somali coast. Mujtaba was probably just testing the PA, or doing some kind of drill. Not worth getting out of bed for. He shut his eyes and tried to drift back to sleep, but Mujtaba's announcement continued, and the ship's vibration felt odd, as if the engine was straining.

'PIRATES ARE COMING! STAND BY WITH FIRE HOSES!'

The noise stopped him getting back to sleep. He pulled on trousers and a shirt, and wandered into the corridor outside. Nobody was around. He headed out on deck, squinting in the morning sun. Rajoo Rajbhar, the other Indian sailor, was staring at the horizon.

'What's going on?' Aman asked.

'They say a small boat is coming. Five nautical miles away.'

Was this for real? Aman tried to follow his gaze. They'd been taught that from a distance, an approaching pirate skiff would often look just like a fast-moving crest in the water, snaking towards the ship like a torpedo. Right now, Aman could see little because of the sun's glare. Perhaps the pirates – if that was what they were – were coming on that side deliberately.

The crew began the anti-piracy measures. They powered up the hoses, giant automatic sprinklers that sent heavy curtains of water down the ship's sides. Aliabadi ordered the engine room staff to start charging up the electric cable that ran round the deck. Every door in sight was locked; emergency exits, side ports, deck doors – anything that led from out to in.

As they did so, they could feel the *Albedo*'s elderly engine, normally calm, pulsing as never before. It was on full throttle, straining like an overweight smoker. Khan, up in the bridge, was making the ship zig-zag, trying to create enough churn in the water behind him to slow any pursuers down. Heading up to the bridge, Aman caught his first glimpse of a skiff. No more than half a mile away, a flimsy wooden narrowboat with two big outboard engines at the back, like a dinghy on steroids. It was doing at least 25 knots. On board he could make out four dark figures. The skiff was bouncing wildly over the waves created by the *Albedo*'s wake, yet they clung on languidly, like workers on a fairground ride. One carried an assault rifle, another had a larger machine gun with an ammunition belt. A third brandished a stick with a diamond-shaped head on it. It looked like rocket-propelled grenade. *Shit. If that hit the* Albedo'*s fuel tanks …*

What really struck him, though, was not how the pirates were armed. It was how they *looked*. Wild and unkempt, with barely any clothes on, save for a pair of shorts and the odd ragged vest. Skinnier than a slum kid in Calcutta, yet muscular, not frail. There were people like this in the 21st century? They looked like they came from the Stone Age.

He could hear shouts from his fellow crewmen, curses in different languages. Mujtaba, the chief officer, was still repeating his alerts over the PA.

From the bridge, Aman could clearly see down to the skiff below. Ten minutes must have passed now since the alarm first sounded. The skiff had circled the ship a few times, now it was pulling up alongside. The pirates were brandishing a long ladder with grappling hooks, trying to get it over the ship's deck rails. The hoses were soaking them every now and then, but it wasn't stopping them.

Boarding a ship is the hardest part of any hijacking. With

the skiff bouncing on the waves, the chances of falling off half-way are high, as are those of a messy landing somewhere in the gap between the skiff and the ship. A good boarding man usually gets a higher share of any ransom, and not for nothing.

Yet when a boarding party is successful, it sends out a powerful psychological message, every bit as intimidating as the guns shoved in the crew's faces. It says: *'We are desperate enough to try anything, and we have succeeded. Do not underestimate us.'*

Up on the bridge, the crew watched as one of the pirates finally hooked the ladder to the ship's side. He was now scaling up it, an assault rifle slung over his back. *Why the hell had nobody pulled the ladder away?* Aman wondered. Then he noticed that the pirate with the rocket-propelled grenade was pointing it towards the deck, covering the spot his comrade was reaching for. If anyone had gone near, the grenade would have come their way.

Still, the pirate had the electric fence to contend with. Aman watched him draw near it. Would he be hurled backwards in a puff of smoke? Or would he be glued to the spot, frying like meat on a grill? Neither. The pirate simply clambered over it. It wasn't working. Later, they'd learn that the panicking crewman assigned to switch it on hadn't connected it properly.

Two more pirates swarmed up the *Albedo*'s side. They clambered straight through a coil of razor wire, looking untroubled as blades tore into their clothes and skin. The crew watched, horrified. Still, the bridge was safe for now. All the doors to the tower's lower decks had been locked. Then Aman remembered the steel escape ladder welded to the tower's outside wall. It led directly from the deck to the bridge.

Khan was hunched over one of the bridge's computer screens, trying to send an SOS email to the reporting centre in Bahrain: *'Pirates are on board, if you can save us, please come.'* There was a thud, as a patch of the glass on the bridge's window suddenly frosted. Then another, and another. Fragments of shatterproof glass scattered across the *Albedo's* control panel.

'They're shooting!' shouted Shahriar Aliabadi, the Iranian bosun. 'Get out of here. Go to the engine room!'

They charged down the stairwell, shoes thumping on the metal stairs. The engine room was several floors below the main deck, isolated from the rest of the vessel to stop any fire spreading. It was as hot as a stoking room on an old-fashioned steamship, but there was plenty of room to hide. The engine alone was the size of a tennis court, surrounded by endless corridors of pumps, levers, air compressors and generators.

As bosun, Aliabadi had had more counter-piracy training than the ordinary sailors. He remembered being told that the engine room was the place to hold out in. Pirates, apparently, didn't like going into them. They were cramped, dark and noisy, full of narrow gaps and blind corners. A pirate clutching a rifle could find it hard to manoeuvre, and nor would he know if there were a few sailors hiding round the next corner, ready to plant a twelve-inch spanner in his skull.

Aliabadi knew that if the crew could barricade the engine room doors properly, they could turn it into a citadel, where they might hold out until help arrived. Some newer ships now came with purpose-built hide-outs with specially-strengthened walls, food supplies, and a phone line. On an old hulk like the *Albedo*, the engine room was the next best thing. Isolated from the rest of the ship by thick metal walls, it also gave the crew some protection if a naval ship arrived and started a shoot-out.

The crew regrouped by the engine room door. Their eyes were wide, their chests heaving, breathing in hot, diesel-filled air.

'Be calm, everyone,' urged Aliabadi. 'If we can hold out here for a day, we might stand a chance.'

Then an announcement came on the PA: 'Attention all crew! Please come here on the bridge.'

It was Khan. When they'd last seen him, he'd still been trying to get the SOS email out. Why hadn't he come down to the engine room with everyone else?

'Attention all crew! Please, for the sake of our lives, come here on the bridge!'

The crew stared at each other.

'Should we go back up?'

'Are you crazy? The captain should have come with us in the first place!'

'Hang on, maybe he got that SOS email out? What if the navy is on the way already?'

'All the more reason to wait down here!'

'AAAAGH!'

A cry of pain came from the PA, echoing around the engine room like a banshee. It was followed by the sound of two gunshots, the noise distorting through the speakers. Then came Khan's voice again, this time thick and mucus-filled, as if he was choking on tears.

'*Please come!* Or they will shoot me and the third officer.'

'We should go up!'

'What, and get killed ourselves?'

'Do you want the captain's blood on your hands? He was trying to get that SOS out! To save us!'

Mujtaba, the chief officer, spoke up. Just as a captain should not desert his crew, he argued, a crew should not desert its captain.

'We all here are like a family,' he said. 'We will go to the bridge and be ready to face these pirates' torture. Or any other situation.'

Aliabadi backed him. He knew it was a big ask – to hand themselves to the same men now roughing up their captain; the same men they had tried to swamp with water, and then electrocute, but they had no choice. He glanced round the crew, and sensed agreement. Some looked angry, some resigned. Others just looked blank, not listening properly, unable to register what was going on. 'Brain freeze' – he'd read about it in an anti-piracy training manual. A state of shock in which people became passive, unfocused. If they went upstairs like that, they might not be able to follow the pirates' orders. That might lead to a gun butt in the head. Or a bullet. He quickly gave a pep talk, trying to remember what else he'd learned in the manual: 'Don't look the pirates in the eyes. Do exactly what they say. No sudden movements, and no heroics. These guys will just be after money. Not worth getting killed over. In case of 'brain freeze', breathe deeply for four seconds, hold, then breathe out. That tricks the body into thinking you're calm. Clarity of thought will return. Or so the manual says …'

The crew opened the engine room door, half expecting to find a gun in their faces. Nothing. They clambered up the decks, hands already above their heads. They reached the second floor – nobody. Third floor – nobody. Fourth floor – nobody. Now the bridge.

'*GACMAHA KOR U TAAG! ISTAAG AMA WAA KUGU DHUFANEYNAA!*'

Three men surrounded them: dark, angry faces; very white teeth; red, bloodshot eyes. A mixture of guns and rags, yelling and jabbering, pointing weapons. Khan was sprawled in a chair, his face a mess, bloodstains on his white captain's shirt.

As Aman looked round, a pirate raised the butt of his gun and hit him on the head. Not quite a baseball bat swing, but not a gentle rap either. Even with the adrenaline surging through his body, it hurt. A lot. *Fuck! What was that for?* Hands grabbed him, spinning him around. A gun barrel was poked in his back, shoving him to one wing of the bridge. Other crew members were already crouched there, hands on their heads. Aman was shoved down with them. As he looked up, a hand slapped him hard across the face, as if he was no longer a threat, could be subdued like a child. On the other side of the bridge, he could hear Khan was getting beaten again. Aman prayed: *My life is finished today. Please save my life.*

Someone prodded him into a kneeling position, his hands in the air. After a few minutes, his knees were hurting more than his head. He tried to move to get more comfortable, but a gun butt rapped the back of his head. Aman snatched a few glances at the pirates. One seemed to be the leader, judging by how he barked orders at the others. An ugly fucker. Teeth all black and broken, rows of stumps and points; arms covered in scars; his left eye mottled and cloudy, swivelling uselessly in the socket. *You could barely count this guy as a member of the human race*, Aman thought. *More like a Neanderthal.*

The pirate grinned and pointed to himself.

'Somali. Somalia.'

He gestured at the crew.

'You no problem, Somalia no problem. You make problem, Somalia too much problem.'

The pirate pointed through the bridge's shattered windows. A clapped-out Arab dhow was sailing alongside. From it, eight more pirates had swarmed onto the *Albedo*'s deck. One came up to the bridge. He was older, dressed in shirt and trousers, unarmed. Compared to the others, he looked like a visiting university professor.

'My name is Ali Jabeen,' he said in fluent English. 'I am not a pirate, I am just the translator for these men. If your ship owner pays us money, you will not be hurt.'

His tone was patient, and slightly bored. As if he'd been through all this many times before, and had better things to be doing.

'You are going to come with us to Somalia. You are going to take us there in your ship.'

Jabeen pointed to the dhow, now tied up alongside the *Albedo*.

'You see that? It is a ship from Iran. These men here caught it. When they asked the chief engineer of that ship to sail to Somalia, he tried to say the engine had run out of fuel. He was lying. So do you know what these men did?'

He paused, watching the effect of his words.

'They killed him. So don't you dare to cheat us. Don't you fucking dare. Otherwise these men will shoot you.'

Another pirate handed what looked like a large green mobile phone to Khan. It was a GPS device, with two sets of co-ordinates on it.

'Somalia,' said the pirate, pointing at the co-ordinates. So maybe that was how these Stone Agers could sail out so far to sea without getting lost. They had a pirate satnav.

Khan entered the co-ordinates into the ship's GPS. Latitude 5°21′05′N. Longitude 48°31′32′E. Somewhere called 'Hobyo' flashed up on the GPS screen. Halfway down the Somali coast, 200 miles north of Mogadishu. About six days' sail from here.

'May I go to talk to my crew first, please?' asked Khan.

He was recovering his composure. He'd always known that as captain, he'd be the first up for a beating. It was a power game. The pirates would show him who was in charge, then use his authority to boss the crew around.

'Go ahead,' said Jabeen. 'Talk to your men.'

'Okay, crew, listen to me. We are going to this place Hobyo. Then we will contact the owner. We just all need to stay calm till then.'

By 10am they were off. Under pirate supervision, the chief engineer and the oiler were allowed back down to the engine room.

'Get one of your guys to make the crew some food,' said Jabeen a few hours later. 'And some for us too.'

The crew ate where they were sitting. Trips to the toilet were allowed grudgingly, one by one, with the added pressure of trying to piss while a pirate pointed a gun at them. To his embarrassment, Aman found himself fighting back tears. *Fuck! He should have listened to that guy Magdy. Not so crazy after all.*

As night drew in, he tried to get some sleep on the floor. Anything to switch this nightmare off for a while. Be strong, he told himself. Get to this place Hobyo, or whatever it was called, then Captain Khan could call the ship's owner. That should sort things out.

Chapter 5

PIT OF DESPAIR

The Albedo. *Off the coast of Hobyo, Somalia,*
March 2011. Four months into captivity

Like many container ships of its size, the *Albedo* had a tiny
open-air swimming pool on the deck. It wasn't much larger
than a ping-pong table, and for as long as anyone could
remember, had lain drained and empty.

In the four months since the *Albedo*'s hijacking, it had
been repurposed as an outdoor toilet for the pirates. They
treated the entire ship as one gigantic commode, shitting in
cupboards, storerooms and any other recess that took their
fancy, but the pool was a particular favourite. It was now
a huge, festering latrine, the floor covered in urine, faeces,
and banqueting flies, and was the perfect place to teach the
hostages a lesson.

Sitting on the pool's tiled floor, Aman tried not to retch.
He'd been in there for two days, along with twenty of the
23 other crewmen. The smell was horrendous, the heat
unbearable. When the midday sun was directly overhead,
the temperature hit 45°C. They were in a human pigsty, only
pigs had the privilege of wallowing in their own filth, not
someone else's.

Above them the pirates circled, snarling and laughing. Every so often, they'd relieve themselves on those below. It was all Aman could do not to add the contents of his own stomach to the toxic mix on the floor. Not that his stomach had much left in it. They'd had nothing to eat or drink for 48 hours.

Their throats were now so dry that when they swallowed, it felt like salt on raw flesh. They craved liquid, dreamed of it. Even a stream of pirate piss was a painful reminder of what they were missing. Pleas for water were met with laughter, and more salvoes of piss and shit. Arguments broke out among the crew, as some of the sailors, feeling the call of nature themselves, squatted over the pool's drain.

'Don't do that here, man, we have enough shit in here as it is!'

'I can't hold on any more! We could be in here for weeks!'

Squabbles apart, the crew sat in silence, not wanting to talk. Beatings were one thing, but this was degradation. Not the kind of merchant sailors' tale they'd ever want to tell. Still, other people on the *Albedo* were having it even worse. Screams from the ship's chief officer, coming from somewhere further along the deck, told them that.

The *Albedo* was anchored seven miles off the port of Hobyo. 'Port' was perhaps too grand a word. Hobyo was a scattering of tin-roofed shacks, squatting amid sand dunes on a vast, empty beach. An Italian-built fort, ramparts slowly crumbling, was the sole reminder of Mussolini's attempts to turn

Somalia into a colony a century before. Several big container vessels, plus assorted dhows, barges and trawlers, were moored offshore.

'All ours, all hijacked,' Jabeen declared proudly, when they first sailed in.

Upon their arrival, skiffs full of new pirates had headed over from the beach, bringing live goats and other food supplies. Sacks of rice for breakfast, lunch and dinner, sacks of sugar for never-ending rounds of hot, sweet, Somali tea. They seemed to be settling in for a long wait.

Yet the *Albedo* wasn't designed to be a floating prison. Four months on from the hijacking, it was running low on diesel for the generator that provided electricity, air conditioning and running water, including the desalination plant for drinking water. Without these things, life on board would become even more uncomfortable. That, though, was not the only thing that concerned Ali Inke, the pirates' boss-eyed commander. Without electricity, the ship would also be pitch dark at night. That would make it harder to keep watch on the crew, and easier for foreign navies – or other pirates – to creep up on them.

To add to Inke's frustration, the ransom talks were going nowhere. Not long after the hijacking, he and Ali Jabeen, the pirate translator, had used the ship's satellite phone to contact Omid Khosrojerdi, the boss of Majestic Enrich and the *Albedo*'s owner. Inke had made an opening ransom demand of US$20 million. The word was that another ship in Hobyo bay had just been ransomed out for $10 million, so Inke wanted to go somewhat better. Khosrojerdi, had come back with a counter-offer of just $300,000. To Inke, that wasn't just low, it was an insult.

Since then, Khosrojerdi had upped his offer to $1.25 million, but that was still nowhere near enough for Inke. Settling for anything less than $10 million would now look like failure. Other pirates would think he was a lightweight. But Khosrojerdi had refused to budge, or even take his calls – another insult. It had fallen to Nalindre Wakwela, the *Albedo's* chief officer, to tell Inke yet more news that he didn't want to hear.

'The diesel is all gone,' he said.

Ali Jabeen, the interpreter, replied on Inke's behalf. Normally, he tried to be Mr Nice Guy, or at least Mr Reasonable. Now, speaking for Inke, his persona changed.

'You fucking liar. You remember what happened to that guy on that Iranian boat we hijacked? He told us there was no diesel too. We killed him.'

'Please. We promise you,' pleaded Wakwela.

'*You think we are fucking stupid?*'

That was when Inke had ordered the crew into the swimming pool. The chief officer had been kept behind and stripped of his shirt. The pirates had made him lie on one of the deck's metal floor hatches, a giant hotplate in the midday sun. His screams had echoed round the ship.

Then they'd tied him up, and hit him with everything they could get their hands on. Gun butts, brass fire hoses, tools. From the pool, the crew could hear Jabeen yelling: 'Where is the rest of the fucking diesel? Bring it out!'

The chief engineer was dragged back to the pool unconscious, white-red foam leaking from his half-open mouth. Two crewmen were allowed out to look after him. Aman watched as they checked for a pulse. *Oh my God, what have these people done to him? Next it will be my turn.*

The chief engineer stirred, and the crewmen looking after him were told to take him to his room. Aliabadi, the ship's Iranian bosun, tried to calm those left in the pool. Normally he told them to be thankful they were alive. Now he urged them to make their peace with death.

'God gave us life,' he said, 'but one day, he will come to take it.'

Now Daoud, the second engineer, was hauled out of the pool. Jabeen's interrogation resumed.

'Where is the fucking diesel?'

'There is none!' Daoud screamed. 'Why would we hide it? We want electricity as much as you do!'

BANG! BANG!

The pirates opened fire on the deck floor, aiming just inches from Daoud's feet. Each shot made him dance desperately on the spot, the bullets sparking on the metal floor. The pirates laughed and the shots got more frequent, Daoud's pirate hornpipe more frenzied. It went on and on, other pirates joining in the fun. Eventually, exhausted, Daoud gave up altogether and stood still. A pirate advanced towards him, gun pointed. Daoud raised his hands. *Enough, please, I've had enough.*

BANG! Daoud's hand exploded, blood sprayed the deck. A bullet had gone through his palm.

A few crewmen were summoned to look after him. They took him back to the bridge, blood dripping up the stairs. Then they put him in a bedroom with the chief engineer, watched over by a pirate. The chief engineer made not a sound, he was pretending to be out cold.

Chapter 6

SEAFOOD SLAVES

Bangkok, Thailand, April 2010

Anyone who asked Captain Channarong Navara what had happened to his left hand got the fisherman's tale to end them all. Sticking out from the back of his stubby, sun-darkened wrist was a strange, dome-like swelling. It looked like someone had cut a tennis ball in half and grafted it under the skin. Most people assumed it was the result of gangrene, scurvy or some other long-forgotten ailment that only seafarers had to worry about these days. The truth was even more bizarre. It was part of his left breast.

Back in 1985, Channarong had been fishing illegally off the coast of Burma when his trawler had been spotted by a Burmese navy gunboat. The Burmese navy didn't mess about with warnings, they'd machine-gunned the trawler straightaway. Channarong was hit in the back, the skull and the left hand.

Somehow, he'd survived until his bullet-riddled vessel got back to Thailand, where he spent the next few months in a hospital run by a seafarers' charity. To repair his hand, doctors had taken a skin graft from his left breast, where he happened to have a chest tattoo of a tiger. What looked like thick veins on the back of his hand were actually the tiger's stripes. Why the graft bulged out so much, Channarong had no idea, although the surgeons who treated impoverished fishermen weren't known for their cosmetic skills. The way he saw it, he was lucky he hadn't ended up like Captain Hook.

Yet despite his disfigured wrist – and the missing patch in what had been an expensive tiger tattoo – Channarong had carried on poaching. Lots of Thai fishermen did it back then, getting caught was an occupational hazard. Normally all it led to was a few nights in the cells. Only Burma, with its hard-line military dictatorship, would just machine-gun a bunch of poor fishermen like that.

Bullet wounds aside, fishing wasn't that bad a job, especially when you were poor. When Channarong had been born in 1950, in a village in the hills outside of Bangkok, life in Thailand had been as hard as anywhere in Asia. No tiger economy, no tourism, no backpackers. After leaving school aged nine, he'd been destined for a life on the paddy fields, just like his parents and grandparents. Farming methods hadn't changed in centuries – ten hours a day from dawn till dusk, ploughing by water buffalo, harvesting by sickle, carrying the crop on one's back. Channarong decided to try making his living from the sea, not the land.

By his teens, he was a hired deck hand at Samut Sakhon, the sprawling fishing port south-east of Bangkok. He learned fast, moving from small inshore boats to the 150-tonners that cruised the ocean for squid and mackerel. Eventually he became a skipper, earning enough to rent him and his wife a modest single-storey home near the docks. On the mantelpiece sat a Buddhist shrine, complete with a model ship to ensure that every time he went to sea, he came back alive.

So far it had worked. At 59 Channarong was at the age when many skippers would be looking forward to retirement. Fishing at sea was a rough, dangerous business, one of the few occupations where men still hunted a quarry in the wild. Crews often worked 36 hours in a stretch to catch, gut and refrigerate as much fish as possible. It wasn't really an old man's game.

Yet Channarong had no money to retire on. The year before, in a bid to save him having to go to sea again, he and his wife had started a fish sales business. They'd hoped to export squid for dining tables in Japan and South Korea, but so far, they'd lost money on every batch they'd sent abroad. Channarong was now looking at years more at sea just to repay what he owed. In early April 2010, he prayed once more to his ship-shaped Buddhist shrine, and headed back to the docks at Samut Sakhong.

Down at the docks, the muggy sea air mingled with fresh and not-so-fresh smells from the fish market. Rickshaws carrying pungent stocks of dried seafood rode past stalls selling the catch of the day, baskets brimming with octopus tentacles and taped-up crab claws. Much of it would eventually find its way into sushi bars, restaurants and supermarkets in New York, Tokyo or London. It would be sold as authentic Thai seafood.

That, though, was only telling half the story. These days, much of the fish that came out of Samut Sakhong was actually caught by Burmese fishermen, not Thais. There were thousands of them at the docks, mostly illegal migrants who'd smuggled themselves over the vast, jungle-covered

Thai–Burma border. Their gamble was that life as a twilight citizen in Thailand would still be better than life as an ordinary citizen in Burma. Burma's military rulers had started a reform programme in 2010, holding proper elections for the first time in 50 years, but after half a century of dictatorship, no-one expected things to change overnight. The flow of migrants was as big as ever, the Burmese taking the jobs that Thais no longer wanted to do.

The fishing industry was a case in point. Most young Thais no longer wanted to spend months at sea, or work in a gutting factory where they'd come home stinking of fish, and so the Burmese made up the shortfall. They didn't move up the ranks to become skippers, like Channarong, but worked for $1.50 a day as deckhands and as gutters in the backstreet factories around Samut Sakhong. They rarely complained. Any Burmese stupid enough to do that would find the Thai immigration police waiting for them at work the next day, tipped off by whichever ship or factory owner they'd tried to challenge.

With such a compliant labour force on tap, the owners often took advantage. Many of the fishing crews were now majority Burmese, with a few Thais as skippers, bosuns and engineers. Some captains, like Channarong, felt pity for their Burmese crewmen, and tried to look after them. Others didn't. There were stories of men being beaten, imprisoned and even killed if they questioned their superiors.

The ship that awaited Channarong was the *Prantalay 12*, an ageing 150-foot trawler. It was a floating advert for its owners,

Union Frozen Products, which made a range of seafood meals under the brand name 'Prantalay'. Along with two sister ships, the *Prantalay 11* and *Prantalay 14*, they would be sailing across the Indian Ocean to Djibouti, and the rich fishing grounds of the Red Sea.

In all, there would be 70 sailors in the fleet, 26 of them on the *Prantalay 12*. Of those, only four, including Channarong, were from Thailand. The rest were Burmese. Channarong hadn't worked with any of them before, but he'd have plenty of time to get to know them. Under the contract they'd just signed up for, they'd be at sea together for two years without a break. Owners didn't usually pay for R&R flights home.

For Kosol Daungmakkerd, one of the other Thais on board, two-year stints were normal. Aged 39, he'd been at sea almost constantly for the last two decades, once for nearly four years with hardly any shore visits. When he finally set foot on land, he'd stagger around like a drunk, nauseous as a rookie sailor in his first storm. Like Channarong, fishing offered a better life than he'd otherwise have had. He'd grown up in a remote village in the jungle near the Cambodian border, in a wooden slatted house on stilts. The family worked the rice paddies, earning extra by farming frogs for local noodle restaurants. When Kosol left school aged twelve, having learned to read and write but little else, his older siblings had told him not to follow them into a life on the land. 'Take our word for it, go and work on the seas,' they said. 'It will be better for you.'

It had been sound advice. Kosol's grasp of basic numeracy and literacy had allowed him to graduate from deck hand to mechanic, and finally to chief engineer. On the *Prantalay 12*, he'd be on $800 per month, decent money by local standards.

And the firm that owned the ship seemed like a good one – he'd even seen the adverts for Prantalay frozen meals on TV.

The month-long journey across the Indian Ocean towards Djibouti was dull as it was long, 5,000 miles of sailing with little to relieve the monotony. Meals were a non-stop diet of Prantalay Frozen Food. Kosol had brought a portable DVD player, sharing his *James Bond* and *Rambo* movies with the rest of the crew. Otherwise, the only excitement was the odd fight among the Burmese over who'd eaten more than their share of the food.

By 8am on 18 April 2010, the ship was more than a week into its journey and sailing just west of India when a shabby fishing dhow appeared. Channarong, up on the bridge, barely gave it a second glance – probably other sailors from India or Sri Lanka. The dhow sailed past at a distance, then it U-turned, showing obvious interest in the *Prantalay* fleet. Four wooden skiffs that had been towed behind the dhow were now approaching from different angles. Each one was full of dark figures.

THUD! THUD!

Channarong remembered the sound of gunshots from his run-in with the Burmese navy. He looked out at the men on the skiffs, now just a few hundred metres away. Must be Indian or Sri Lankan coastguard of some sort, perhaps they thought the crew were poaching. Then, what looked like a giant firecracker sailed across the front of the ship, and a thin vapour of smoke trailed behind it. It had come from one of the boats, where a man was now pointing what looked like a bazooka at them.

What in God's name? Not even the Burmese navy fired rockets to make their point. Channarong cut the engine. Thank God they had nothing to hide. All the *Prantalay* fleet were sailing entirely legally. He could show them the permits from Djibouti.

Minutes later, armed men barged their way onto the bridge, shouting a lot and pointing guns. They didn't look like normal coastguard, they were in T-shirts, rags and sandals. Must be auxiliaries of some sort. Although how come they looked more African than Indian? The ship was nowhere near Africa yet.

Their commander approached Channarong. He was so skinny that his jacket hung flat off his bony shoulders, like it was on a coat hanger, but he was tall, more than six feet. He towered over Channarong, who was barely five feet.

'GRAAT!'

He pointed to Channarong, then himself, and then out of the bridge's main window. The glass, Channarong noticed, was now frosted by bullet holes.

'GRAAT!'

What was he talking about? The commander gestured at the ship's controls. Channarong clicked. Maybe 'Graat' was a place. The pirate handed him a scrap of paper with some co-ordinates on. Channarong looked it up on the GPS. What he'd heard as 'Graat' turned out to be 'Garacad'. It was nowhere near India or Sri Lanka, though, or even Djibouti. It was on the coast of Somalia, nine days' sail away at least. What on earth did these guys want? Couldn't they just sort whatever problem it was here and now?

Channarong shot the commander a puzzled look. The commander barked 'Garacad' again and thrust his gun in the captain's face. Channarong nodded and set course. The other *Prantalay* vessels, he noticed, were following behind.

Stay calm, Channarong told himself, this was just another tedious brush with the world's maritime policemen. They'd get to Garacad, or whatever it was called, then it would be a few nights in the cells until the company paid whatever bribe these scruffy predators wanted.

The rest of the crew had been herded into a bunkroom. They too had no idea who the gunmen were, but when Kosol, the chief engineer, had seen the dhow approach, he'd recognised the flag it was flying. Blue with a white star – the flag of Somalia.

He'd seen it once before, during a resupply stop at a Somali port a few years ago. It had just been a couple of hours, but he'd never forgotten it. The only port he'd ever been where the captain had given strict orders not to get off the ship. 'This is a dangerous land,' he'd warned. 'A land where kids carry guns. Where religious maniacs chop people's heads off for fun. Go out there and you won't come back.'

Chapter 7

RULES OF ENGAGEMENT

Kampala, Uganda, June 2011

Uganda's Commonwealth Resort Hotel was one of the biggest conference venues in East Africa, a plush retreat where the region's powerbrokers often settled their differences. With five-star restaurants and fine views of Lake Victoria, it was the diplomatic equivalent of a luxury rehab centre, where warring parties could unwind before coming to the negotiating table.

The comfortable surroundings weren't the only reason it was used for peace conferences. Isolated in 90 acres of gardens, it was some distance from Kampala, and easily sealed off from the media. Once groups of delegates were stuck inside, they had little choice but to focus on the task in hand. No flouncing out, no time wasting. That was the idea, anyway. As John Steed and the rest of the assembled diplomats knew all too well, there was never any telling with the politicians of Somalia's Transitional Federal Government.

The TFG, as it was known, had been formed in 2004, as an attempt to give Somalia its first functioning government since the outbreak of civil war in 1991. A mixture of clan leaders, warlords and expatriates, its members were notoriously quarrelsome and corrupt, yet they were still Somalia's best chance in years. Since the civil war, no less than thirteen previous attempts to form a government had failed.

Although the TFG had UN backing, its democratic mandate was limited. Because Somalia was still too dangerous to hold elections in, members of the TFG's parliament weren't selected by popular vote, but by traditional clan leaders. Most seats were reserved for the four major clans, with the rest shared between minor ones. The pragmatic view was that after years of clan warfare, government by bloodline was better than no government at all.

The UN did not want such a state of affairs to go on forever. The conference in Kampala was supposed to be a milestone in a 'roadmap' towards proper democracy. The transitional phase of the government was supposed to end, with its members working out a blueprint for elections and a more even distribution of power. The average Somali would notice little difference, as the country was still too lawless for elections to be held any time soon, but to many already holding office in the TFG, changes to the status quo were unwelcome. It might mean the loss of privileges and patronage. For months, the two main factions in the TFG had been at loggerheads, paralysing the government even more so than normal. The conference, organised by the UN, was supposed to knock heads together, and stop the country drifting back to anarchy.

Scores of diplomats had turned up, along with TFG ministers, MPs and assorted hangers-on. Steed was there in his capacity as military advisor to the UN's envoy to Somalia, a tough Tanzanian diplomat called Dr Augustine Mahiga. The two got on well together, Mahiga appearing to value Steed's advice. In practice, Steed suspected, Mahiga also found it useful to have a British colonel in full military uniform at his side. Diplomacy, after all, was partly showbusiness. Steed's presence reminded the Somalis that behind Mahiga was the power of the wider world, the people who backed the TFG both financially and militarily. The people who provided its life support machine.

As ever, the conference was proving big on talk and short on action. Somali politicians had yet to embrace the soundbite culture, preferring long-winded speeches that went everywhere and nowhere. Away from the waffling and grandstanding, though, such meetings were often stimulating. On the sidelines, Steed would chat and debate with the delegates, asking questions and testing theories, not particularly worrying if he was peddling Britain's line or not. Here, far from Whitehall, there was no need to stay on message too much. You just had to be careful not to lecture. Somalia was a country that taught stern lessons to anyone with grand ideas – be they diplomats like him, aid workers, foreign armies or rulers.

The rot in Somalia had begun in 1991, after the collapse of the regime of Siad Barre, an old-school Cold War strongman. He'd tried to turn it into a Marxist state during the 1970s and 1980s, but the demise of the Soviet Union robbed him of a guarantor, and when his regime crumbled, Somalia's long-suppressed clan leaders saw a chance to reassert their power.

By 1993, the country was reeling from a multi-sided clan war that left hundreds of thousands dying from famine. With pictures of starving African children filling TV screens for the first time since the Ethiopian famine a decade before, the world decided to act, despatching a UN intervention force backed by US marines. Operation 'Restore Hope' then became one of the worst disasters in the history of peacekeeping.

The mission quickly got embroiled in fighting with local militias, culminating in an all-out battle on the streets of Mogadishu when US forces launched an operation to capture two aides to Mohamed Farrah Aidid, a leading warlord. Two US helicopters were downed by rocket-propelled grenades, leading to two days of street fighting with Aidid's followers. The Black Hawk Down episode, as it became known, ended with the corpses of US troops being dragged through the streets of Mogadishu. By the time it was over, nineteen US soldiers were dead and anything up to 1,000 Somalis killed. What had started out as a militarised Live Aid had become a textbook example of the risks of benign intervention. When the Rwandan genocide broke out the following year, America chose not to get involved, watching from a distance as 800,000 people were slaughtered in less than four months. But while post-genocide Rwanda had spent the next decade rebuilding itself, Somalia continued tearing itself apart. Mogadishu became a patchwork of competing warlords, whose foot soldiers raped, robbed and murdered with impunity.

Such was the vacuum that unusual actors stepped into the breach. In 2006, a coalition of war-weary Mogadishu businessmen banded together with local clerics and formed the Islamic Courts Union. The hope was that religion could provide some universal code on which to rebuild civilisation. The clerics were ageing has-beens whose moral authority had long been ignored, but with the businessmen's hired guns behind them, the tough sharia courts they ran were appreciated as a source of law and order. Lashings, canings and amputations were rough justice, but better than no justice at all. As its popularity surged, the ICU took on the warlords themselves, driving them from Mogadishu one by one. By late 2006, the city saw its first days without fighting in a decade and a half.

The peace didn't last. Some of the ICU were hard-line Islamists on UN wanted lists. Much as they professed to have no interest in transnational terrorism, it was a bad time to be setting up what looked to some like a Somali Taliban. President George W. Bush feared the entire thing was a Trojan Horse for al-Qaeda. Wary of another Black Hawk Down debacle, this time America handed the job of intervening to Somalia's neighbour and long-time enemy, Ethiopia.

The Ethiopian forces quickly overwhelmed the ICU in Mogadishu, but far from quelling the threat from extremists, the invasion handed them the initiative. A group called Al-Shabaab – previously just the most hard-line wing of the ICU – was able to portray itself as an army of liberation, fighting the Ethiopians sent to do Washington's dirty work.

By the time Steed took up his job as military attaché in Nairobi in 2008, Al-Shabaab controlled much of southern Somalia and half of Mogadishu. Dancing, drinking or even watching football on TV were outlawed, and harsh penal codes enforced. People accused of stealing could have limbs amputated, while alleged adulterers faced death by stoning. Children took part in Quranic recital contests where the prizes were grenades. The TFG's writ didn't extend much beyond the compound of the presidential villa in Mogadishu, a fortress of concrete blast walls and barbed wire.

In 2009, the Ethiopians were replaced by a Ugandan-led African Union force, deemed more acceptable to mainstream

Somalis. Al-Shabaab fought them for every block of Mogadishu, digging trenches and tunnels that turned the city into an urban Flanders, but by 2011, after losing nearly 1,000 troops, the African Union force was finally getting the upper hand.

Nobody wanted those lives to have been laid down in vain, so when Steed attended the conference in Kampala that year, the pressure was on for the TFG's rival factions to end their deadlock. The origins of the deadlock were mired in the complexities of clan politics, but boiled down to a feud between a faction led by the TFG's president and a faction led by the speaker of the TFG's parliament. The speaker's faction eventually gave some ground, but only on condition that the president sack his close ally, the prime minister. After a few days, agreement was duly reached, and the 'Kampala Accord' signed.

Ironically, the sacked prime minister, Mohamed Abdullahi Mohamed, was one of the few TFG politicians who enjoyed any real popularity among ordinary people. A US-educated Somali who'd previously worked for the New York State transport department, he'd won plaudits for making sure Somalia's civil servants and soldiers got paid their wages on time. The news that he had fallen victim to a backroom deal sparked widespread street protests in Mogadishu, and privately, few of the diplomats who'd helped broker the agreement felt it really was in the people's interests. The Somali ship of state had been kept going by forcing one of its few decent operators to walk the plank.

Two months after the Kampala conference, without warning or explanation, Al-Shabaab announced a 'tactical withdrawal' from Mogadishu, its militiamen deserting their trenches almost overnight. It was nothing to do with the reshuffle in the TFG, but for Steed and others in the Mogadishu diplomatic corps, it was still a rare piece of good news to write up in their cables home. Back in Whitehall, though, it went largely unnoticed. Nobody would be calling Somalia a success story until the piracy – now a much bigger threat to Western interests – was dealt with.

Piracy had featured in Steed's life since boyhood. He'd been brought up by the River Helford in Cornwall, an area steeped in pirate lore. In medieval times, Britain's south-west tip had been a favourite haunt of pirates, offering just what Somalia did now – a vast triangle of remote, lawless coastline, jutting conveniently into major shipping routes.

The Cornish preyed on passing vessels and were preyed upon themselves. Muslim pirates from North Africa's Barbary Coast carried out raiding missions, taking hostages to be kept as slaves or sold back for ransom. In the county records office in Truro, where Steed first went to school, there were accounts of churches raising money to buy the hostages back from the 'barbarous enemies of Jesus Christ'. Back then, nobody in Britain had any qualms about paying ransoms. That only came with Empire, when His Majesty's Government wanted to signal that its colonial foot soldiers were not bargaining chips for the taking.

Sailing around the River Helford on an old fishing boat his parents owned, Steed would often pass Frenchman's Creek, made famous by novelist Daphne Du Maurier in her novel of the same name. It told the tale of a noblewoman's secret liaison with a dashing French pirate, who used the creek as an operating base to terrorise the Cornish coast.

History, Steed knew, romanticised maritime crime. Just look at all the pubs in Cornwall named after pirates and smugglers. Much the same forgiving attitude extended towards Somali pirates. In Nairobi, many aid workers and even some diplomats saw them as maritime Robin Hoods, levelling the score a little against the marauding foreign fishing vessels. They were a symptom of Somalia's problems, not a cause – and a reminder of how the world needed to do more to help.

Steed agreed that more did need to be done. But the scale of the piracy was far beyond anything justified as retribution for the odd bit of poaching. And there was every chance it would get much worse before it got better. Word of the ransom bonanza was attracting new gangs to the pirate coast, including groups of ex-militiamen from the warlord fiefdoms of Mogadishu. A Danish seafarers' handbook, written for sailors currently travelling through the Indian Ocean, listed them by the Somali nickname of '*Will Waal*'. It meant 'Crazy Boys': 'The *Will Waal* are young Somalis who grew up in or around Mogadishu during the civil war. They are dangerous, unstable and unpredictable, and may be deliberately mean and degrading in their treatment of hostages. Do not address them, and avoid any eye contact.'

Unlike some of the original Somali pirate gangs, the Crazy Boys probably wouldn't hesitate to kill or torture captives. The more Crazy Boys flocked to the coast, the more the older players would be sidelined, like ageing Mafia dons forced into retirement. Already, hijackings were getting more violent. In 2011, the crew of the *Merida Marguerite*, a chemical container ship, revealed how they'd faced sadistic punishments from pirates in a bid to drive up the ransom payment. Sailors were hung by their wrists from the masts, had cables wrapped round their testicles, and were locked naked in the ship's deep freeze.

The *Merida Marguerite* case had angered the shipping industry, which already felt that the EU and Nato-led anti-piracy forces were being too soft in their approach. Under the forces' rules of engagement, pirates in their skiffs were often only arrested if they were caught directly in the middle of an act of piracy. Otherwise, they were generally released and told to go on their way. For many in the shipping industry, this was no deterrent at all. One Norwegian shipping magnate, Jacob Stolt-Nielsen, even called for the pirates to be shot on sight, saying history had proved it to be the only way of policing areas as large as oceans.

'Pirates captured in international waters have always been punished by death, often on the spot,' he wrote in a Norwegian newspaper. 'Not arrest them and say, "naughty, naughty, shame on you," and release them again, but sink their boats with all hands.'

His calls were politely ignored by EU and Nato fleet commanders, but other navies weren't quite so squeamish. The Indian navy, in particular, promised robust action when pirates began marauding round their coastal waters. Among those who learned this the hard way were the pirates who had hijacked Captain Channarong and the *Prantalay* fishing fleet.

Chapter 8

MOTHER SHIP

The Prantalay 12, *off the coast of Garacad,*
Somalia, January 2011.
Nine months into captivity

When the *Prantalay 12* first neared their hijackers' requested destination of Garacad, the crew expected a harbour and a town to loom into view. Instead, all they could see were bunches of empty oil drums piled up into improved shacks. Inland was a scattering of brick buildings, home perhaps to more than a few hundred souls, which made Captain Channarong all the more surprised when a skiff brought aboard a translator fluent in Thai.

'Hussein', as he introduced himself, said he had learned Thai while serving time for opium trafficking in a Bangkok jail. He then corrected Channarong of his impression that the *Prantalay* fleet were under arrest for fishing violations.

'We are pirates,' he said. 'Tell your owners that we want $9 million for the release of all three ships.'

It was a fantasy figure. Especially for three ageing fishing vessels from Asia. The pirates believed that because they had nearly 70 hostages on board, a high price was justified. Yet when Channarong had rung the owners on the *Prantalay 12*'s satellite phone, they hadn't seemed too worried. 'Don't panic,' they'd told him. 'Just give us a couple of months to bargain the pirates down a bit.'

Nine months in, the owners hadn't even made a counter-offer, as far as Channarong was aware. He had all but given up on them, and so too, it seemed, had the pirates.

'If your owners will not pay what we want, we will use your ships as mother ships to hunt others,' Hussein, the translator, told him one day. 'Maybe if you help us capture a better ship, we will let you go.'

Channarong had no wish to trade other sailors' freedom for his own, but he couldn't help a sudden sense of hope. From the outset, he'd wondered why the pirates had even bothered taking a bunch of poor fishermen like the *Prantalay* crews. When they'd first neared the Somali coastline, the other hijacked vessels they'd seen were cargo ships twenty times their size. Perhaps if the *Prantalay 12* could help catch another one of these more valuable prizes, they would be allowed to go on their way.

A few days later the *Prantalay 12* was back out on the ocean, this time as hunter rather than hunted. The pirates ordered Channarong and Kosol back to their old jobs in the bridge and the engine room. Soon they were thinking like pirates themselves, scanning the horizon for likely prey, wondering how best to approach without attracting suspicion. When one ship came close and then sped away, going too fast to pursue, Kosol felt a rush of despair. *Even though I am sinning, I have no choice*, he told himself.

Occasionally, a naval vessel would approach, clearly suspicious. If it got too close, the pirates would hoard a few hostages onto deck, guns at their heads. The warship would back off, having done little except convince the hostages that their last moment had come.

By the time they reached the middle of the Indian Ocean, the naval presence had thinned, leaving the *Prantalay 12* free to hunt. Begging the Buddha for forgiveness, Channarong closed in on an ancient Bangladeshi coal carrier. Two pirate skiffs raced towards it, firing a rocket-propelled grenade across its bows, then swarming aboard. Channarong looked on, praying that nobody had been hurt, and that the *Prantalay 12*'s debt was now paid. With any luck, the remaining pirates would now jump ship to the coal carrier, leaving the *Prantalay 12* free to limp to the nearest port.

Instead, they were ordered back on the hunt. They were now nearly 2,000 miles from Somalia, prowling among the Lakshadweep Islands off India's south-west tip.

A chatter of bleeps of varying lengths came through the radio on the *Prantalay 12*'s bridge. The first sound it had made in months. The crew gathered round it, like astronauts picking up an alien broadcast. One of the crewmen recognised it as Morse Code. Dots and dashes, the simplest language on earth. Designed to be audible through the fuzziest radio signals, the most violent storms.

Hardly anyone used Morse any more in these days of satellites and email, but the crewman had learned the basics years ago. He reached into a drawer and grabbed a dusty Morse decoder book, hoping it wasn't an SOS call. If some other vessel was in trouble, the last people they wanted help from was the *Prantalay 12* mother ship.

'THIS IS THE INDIAN NAVY! STOP YOUR SHIP!'

By the time he had pieced the message together, the warship it was coming from was already on the horizon. Unlike others, which usually kept their distance, it was coming straight at them. The pirates went into battle drill. Hostages were posted as human shields on port and starboard. One crewman, Thanakon Kaeokamkong, was put on the ship's bow with a pair of binoculars and told to watch what was going on aboard the warship. His hands were shaking so much he had trouble finding it through the lens. When he did, he saw a huge deck gun, now trained right on them.

'Stop! STOP' Thanakon screamed to the pirates. 'We'll all be killed!'

The pirates ignored him. Let these Indians try to scare them. Thanakon prepared himself to die. As he stared through the binoculars, the naval vessel opened fire. Thanakon felt a deafening blast that seemed to pass right through him. Then came a wall of spray, as if a huge wave had hit. When he opened his eyes, he glanced up and down, expecting to see a gaping hole in the ship's side, but the shell had missed by yards. Just a warning shot.

It was warning enough. The pirates about-turned, heading back to Somalia. The warship followed for a while and then disappeared, satisfied the pirates had got the message.

They hadn't. A month later, the *Prantalay 12*'s sister vessels, the *Prantalay 11* and *Prantalay 14*, were sent off on the hunt to the Lakshadweep Islands. This time, neither came back. The *Prantalay 14* was caught by two Indian warships as it stalked a freighter. The warships fired a warning shot, to which the pirates unwisely responded by returning fire. The warships then shot at the *Prantalay 14*'s fuel tank, setting it ablaze. With smoke engulfing the ship, both pirates and hostages jumped overboard. The warship scooped them out of the water and took them back to shore – the hostages to a hotel, the pirates to jail. A week later, the *Prantalay 11* mistook an Indian coast-guard cutter for a passing merchant ship, and tried to hijack it. After a one-sided gun battle, another 28 pirates were heading to join their comrades in the cells. Once again, confronted with overwhelmingly superior firepower, none of the hijackers had even thought to harm the hostages.

This was a coup for the Indian navy, who were already under pressure at home over the number of Indian sailors in Somali captivity. Unlike their Western counterparts, they were proving that they couldn't be pushed around. Indian newspapers reported the victories in triumphant tones. All that was needed was a bit of nerve, to teach these pirate thugs a lesson.

Yet the capture of the *Prantalay 12*'s two sister vessels also drew attention in the pirate strongholds 2,000 miles away. Up and down the coast, pirate leaders conferred. These aggressive Indian warships could be a threat to the entire pirate business model. Something would have to be done. If the Indians wanted to play rough, so could they.

Chapter 9

Slaughter

The Albedo, *24 June 2011.*
Seven months into captivity

Not long after the Indian navy caught the *Prantalay 12*'s two sister ships, a new translator clambered aboard the *Albedo*. He was the first Somali the crew had seen who wasn't stick-thin. He had a fleshy face, several bellies and what looked like at least two backsides under his robes, giving his body curves. He was closest any of the crew had seen to the female form in a long time.

His name, appropriately enough, was Kilo. Why he'd been brought in to replace Ali Jabeen, the previous translator, wasn't clear, but he seemed keen to make his mark.

'The countdown has begun,' he announced to the crew. 'We will start killing one by one.'

Nobody felt too worried. Deadlines for their execution had come and gone numerous times before. The next morning, Kilo rang the *Albedo*'s owner, Omid Khosrojerdi, 30 times. No reply. In the early afternoon, the guards brought every crew member onto the bridge.

Aman was sitting next to Rajoo Rajbhar, the other young Indian sailor. The pair had become good friends. They'd talk about cricket and life back home, and watch each other's backs. Shy by nature, Rajbhar was finding things harder going than Aman. He tried to avoid direct contact with the pirates, and always looked scared whenever trouble loomed.

'Don't worry, they just want to frighten us again,' Aman whispered to him. 'Some new game of theirs.'

Ali Inke, the pirate commander, cast his one good eye up and down the assembled hostages, like it was a stock take. He muttered in the ear of another guard.

'Rajoo Rajbhar!' the guard called. 'RAJOO RAJBHAR!'

Rajoo got to his feet, looking at the others. Why him? What had he done? The guards tied his hands with ropes and led him onto the deck, out of sight. The sailors exchanged glances. It wasn't unusual for hostages to be singled out for punishment, but usually it was senior men, like the captain or engineers. Pirates were great respecters of rank, especially when it came to making examples. Rajoo was just a youngster.

From somewhere outside, further down the deck, a gunshot rang out. Then two more. Another mock execution, Aman thought. Poor Rajoo. *Hang in there, buddy. Hope your eardrums are okay.*

A few minutes later, Captain Khan was ordered to his feet. The guards took him outside and began walking him down the deck. From a distance, he could see Rajoo lying on his back, his hands still tied. He was motionless, his T-shirt bloodied. They must have kicked the poor lad unconscious. Then, as Khan got nearer, he saw that Rajoo's eyes were wide open. A puddle of blood was also seeping out from under his body. A voice spoke behind him.

'The owner is not listening to us. So we have killed Rajoo.'

Khan was shoved closer. There was a bullet wound right above Rajoo's heart.

'Touch it,' hissed the voice. 'Touch the body.'

'No. NO!'

'Later you will call the company, and tell them what we have done.'

Khan felt tears on his face. He stared at the guards. They looked calm, no different from normal. After all these months of threats, of bluster, of brinkmanship – when it came to the actual act of killing, it was as easy for them as slaughtering a goat.

'We will kill five more soon unless the money is increased,' Kilo said.

Kilo took Khan back to the others. He let Khan break the news to the crew, then cut in.

'We need four of you to come and pick up the body,' he said, matter-of-factly. 'Do you want to dump him in the sea or put him in the deep freeze?'

Aman stared at him. *In the sea or in the deep freeze? Like Rajoo's body was just a bag of trash. Make up your minds, hostages. Can't have bodies cluttering up the deck.*

Four of the crew stood up. Aman stayed behind. He wasn't falling for this. It was just a trick. The pirates must have ordered Rajoo to pretend he was dead. Probably killed a goat and spattered its blood over him, to convince Khan it was real. Half an hour later, the others returned. Their faces said it all.

'No! This has not happened! NO!' Aman felt himself begin to lose control. The guards glowered. *Fuck them. Fuck these bastards!*

'NO! NO!' Aman shouted.

Guns were cocked. The crew gathered around Aman.

'Calm down, Aman. Calm down!'

'They've killed Rajoo! Those bastards have killed my friend!'

'CALM DOWN!! Don't shout, they will make more trouble for you.'

'What does it matter any more? They'll kill us all!'

The deep freeze was a big walk-in cupboard, large enough to hold months of provisions. When Aman went down there the next day and swung its heavy door open, a freezing mist spilled out into the humid corridor. He'd told the rest of the crew that he wanted to say goodbye to Rajoo properly. They could sense, though, that he still couldn't quite believe he was dead. 'Check for yourself,' they'd said.

He scanned the shelves, long emptied of food. There, stashed in a space that once held boxes of frozen noodles, was his friend. One leg straight, the other folded. His face covered by a film of frost. On Rajoo's T-shirt, Aman could see burn marks made by the bullet hole. The fuckers must have shot him at point blank range. Rajoo, of all people, his first and best friend on board. The one he talked cricket with, who reminded him of home.

He draped a white bed sheet over the corpse. Then he shut the door, secured it with a chain and padlock, and hid the key. This would be Rajoo's private mausoleum. For now, anyway. One day, Aman vowed, he'd get Rajoo's body back to his family. If nothing else, it was an incentive to stay alive. Unless, that was, he ended up in the deep freeze alongside him. Aman had now realised why the pirates had chosen Rajoo to kill first. It explained something that a couple of guards had said the week before.

'All our brothers are in the jail in India,' they'd snarled, jabbing angry fingers at him and Rajoo. 'Indian navy are fuckers, not Muslims. We will kill you two Indians first.'

He'd thought it was just more pirate bullshit, now he knew better. Killing Rajoo served two purposes. It was a warning to Khosrojerdi, the *Albedo*'s owner, not to mess about any longer, and it was a warning to India that if they carried on attacking pirate ships, Indian hostages would be executed one by one. By doing so, Ali Inke would reap kudos from every other pirate clan, for showing solidarity with their detained brethren.

The guards seemed to be relishing the prospect of further sacrifice. Every time they saw Aman, they would cuff him, slap him and break out in a chant: *'India, India. You're next.'*

Worried that Aman would react to the taunting, the chief officer, Mujtaba, set him to work in the ship's galley, cooking for both crew and pirates. It was out of the way, and the pirate's resident cook, Abdulessay, was a placid character. 'Stay there and keep your head down,' Mujtaba warned.

The crew had hit a new low. Any hopes that Khosrojerdi would get them out had vanished with Rajoo's execution. Some pondered killing themselves before the pirates did it for them, others argued for fighting back. Now was the time to do it, they said, while they still had strength in their bodies and anger in their hearts.

They couldn't expect success. All any mutineer could hope for was to kill a guard or two before being killed themselves, but it would be suicide with a purpose, a chance to enact some of the revenge fantasies that they whiled so many hours away with. If they were to embrace death, not life, best make it a group hug with their captors. Better than waiting to be slaughtered like goats.

Khan, sensing the despondent mood, decided to act. It was no longer worth dealing with Khosrojerdi. The next time Kilo was aboard, he waited until the usual threats and rants were over, then made a request.

'Can I call my wife?' he asked.

Chapter 10

A Captain's Duty

Karachi, Pakistan, April 2012. Nearly eighteen months into the Albedo *hijacking*

Standing outside Karachi's vast Sultan Masjid mosque with a donation bucket in her hand, Mishal Khan tried not to feel embarrassed. It was a hot, humid afternoon, the temperature past 40°C. The only people out in this heat were hawkers and beggars. Mishal was neither, but judging by the looks she was getting, other members of respectable Karachi society clearly thought otherwise. Like the man who'd just come out of the mosque.

'What are you doing here?' he asked.

'Sir, my father, Jawaid Khan, is the captain of a ship called the *Albedo*. It has been hijacked by Somali pirates. He and his crew have been there for nearly eighteen months, in dreadful conditions. We are trying to raise money for the ransom to free them. Would you be so kind as to donate?'

'Why don't you take your business elsewhere? Go on, go away! You are disturbing people!'

Mishal shook with anger. How could he speak to her like that? Weren't people supposed to feel charitable when they came out of a mosque? A friend pulled her away before she could answer back.

The fundraising wasn't going well. The week before, they'd put a message out via the 'Save the *Albedo*' Facebook campaign page, inviting nearly 3,000 supporters to gather outside the mosque. About 30 had turned up. Most were friends, a few were other *Albedo* hostages' relatives, some of whom weren't far off begging for real.

Standing nearby in a burqa was Sugrah Soomro, whose husband Faqeer was among the other Pakistani captives. Like the rest of the crew's families, she hadn't been paid a rupee in wages since he'd gone missing. She'd taken her two daughters out of school because she could no longer afford the fees. Relatives had offered to help out, but she'd turned them down, knowing they were short of money too. Taking handouts would have cost her what dignity she had left.

Also holding a box was Mishal's mother, Shahnaz. She looked exhausted. For the last few days, the pirates had been ringing her mobile non-stop, demanding to know how the fundraising was going, and reminding her that the deadline for them to start killing hostages again was 15 May. That was just one week away. At times, the calls would come in every twenty minutes, or in the middle of the night. She'd barely slept.

After a few hours, the fundraisers could take no more of the heat. They looked in the boxes. Not everyone had written them off as beggars or fraudsters – a few cabbies and rickshaw drivers had dug in their pockets, but most couldn't part with more than a 50 rupee note, the equivalent of a half a dollar. Even if they'd had 3,000 people out shaking a bucket, it would be nowhere near enough.

Unlike the other *Albedo* wives, Shahnaz was well acquainted with life at sea. When she and Captain Khan had married back in 1980, ship's officers were still allowed to take their wives with them on journeys. She'd spent the first nine months of married life on a ship, and when Khan had got a job with an Iranian shipping line, she'd sailed with him on a supply convoy during the Iran–Iraq war. They'd travelled with lights blacked out, lifeboats half-lowered. An Iraqi missile had hit a vessel just behind them.

War zones aside, the trips to sea were a source of fond family memories. When Khan had taken his first full command of a ship in 1993, his family had sailed with him for a whole year, touring Asia and the Far East. Shahnaz had enjoyed seeing the world, while the couple's two daughters, Mishal and Nareman, had liked the ship's games room and the shore leave visits to zoos and fun parks. Then, gradually, the trips stopped. Shipping agencies, keen as ever to cut costs, no longer wanted to pay the extra bed and board for captains' families.

From then on, Khan's day-to-day presence in his daughters' lives had been largely reduced to phone calls and emails. He typically worked eight months on, two months off. Yet being an absent father hadn't stopped him taking a close interest in their future. Unlike more traditional Pakistani fathers, he didn't just want to marry them off, he wanted them to have a career. 'Do something with your life, be someone,' he told them. 'Don't waste it sitting around.'

They'd taken him at his word. When Khan had set sail on the *Albedo*, Mishal, then 22, had just started a year-long Master's in journalism in London. Nareman, 26, who'd seen her father off from the harbour in Dubai, was a business consultant for the local office of Deloitte. Like their mother, they were smart and worldly. Shahnaz thanked God for this. If she had wallflowers for daughters, they'd never have had the guts to shake a bucket in the streets of Karachi.

It was now eighteen months since the *Albedo* hijacking. When it had first happened, Khosrojerdi, the owner, had promised Shahnaz it would be over in a matter of a few weeks. 'We know people who can help,' he'd told her by phone from Malaysia. 'Don't worry, we'll sort it out.'

Much as she'd wanted to believe him, doubts had soon crept in. After a few phone conversations, he became hard to get hold of. Suspecting that he was evading her, Shahnaz began researching piracy on the internet. If Khosrojerdi thought she was a docile Pakistani housewife who'd believe whatever he told her, she'd prove him wrong.

She was surprised at the amount of information out there. Many pirates were happy to boast about their exploits to journalists, and a website called *Somalia Report* gave a picture of their activities that could have come from *The Wall Street Journal*. It gave a running commentary of the progress of ransom talks for different ships, together with estimates of how much had been paid, with due adjustments for pirates' tendency to exaggerate. Soon Shahnaz knew all the right questions to ask.

'Was the *Albedo* insured?' she asked Khosrojerdi one day.

'Not for this kind of thing, no.'

'Why did you send a boat into this dangerous area without insurance?'

'We were going to renew it on the next journey.'

'So how much ransom have you offered?'

'$300,000.'

'But they are demanding $20 million, aren't they?'

'Do you have $20 million? If you do, then pay the ransom yourself!'

Soon, Shahnaz found she couldn't get through to Khosrojerdi at all. She went to see the director general of ports and shipping in the Pakistani government. He looked apologetic. They'd tried to get hold of Khosrojerdi as well, he said, and had got nowhere. Shahnaz had nodded, as if she'd been expecting to hear him say as much. It was the only way to get an audience with these minister types, by acting composed and business-like. In fact, her life was already a blur of depression and panic attacks, palliated by tranquillisers, sleeping pills and long sessions on the prayer mat.

Occasionally, desperate for news, she rang the pirates herself, using a Somali mobile number that they'd rung her on occasionally to press their demands for money. Sometimes they would answer her call, sometimes they went incommunicado for long periods. At one point, she was unable to get through to them for three months, and convinced herself that her husband had been killed. She wondered if she should hold a funeral, but couldn't bring herself to.

Then, early in July 2011, Khan himself had rung her. It was wonderful to hear his voice, but he didn't waste time with small talk. He told her about the execution of Rajoo, the young Indian crewman. Unless the ransom came soon, he said, further killings would take place. Without thinking, Shahnaz asked him to pass the phone to the pirates.

'Please! I promise you, stop killing people and I will try to raise you some money,' she said. 'You just have to give me time!'

Shahnaz knew she shouldn't have made promises in the heat of the moment. But she'd already been mulling over the idea of raising money herself. During her piracy research, she'd read about the *Suez*, an Egyptian-owned cargo ship hijacked the year before. Several of the crew were Pakistanis from Karachi. The ship's owner could only afford half of the $2 million ransom the pirates wanted, but a public appeal, backed by Karachi's governor, had raised the rest.

Normally, public appeals were a last resort, because it gave pirates the impression that an entire nation was digging into its pockets, and encouraged them to raise their ransom demands even higher. Right now, Shahnaz felt that last resorts were all they had. She went to see Ahmed Chinoy, a well-connected Karachi businessman who'd helped organise the *Suez* appeal. He was reluctant to get involved – the *Suez* appeal was supposed to have been a one-off, not standard practice every time a Pakistani crewman was hijacked. Owners, he pointed out, had to meet their responsibilities. Shahnaz broke down in tears in his office. Unwilling to send a grieving woman away empty-handed, Chinoy agreed to talk to the governor.

Shahnaz rang round the other crew's families to gauge their support for the appeal. If they were going to go public, they'd have to be united. First, though, there was a difficult conversation to be had with Mishal, her younger daughter, who was still in London doing her journalism Master's. Until then, Shahnaz had not told Mishal that her father had been taken hostage. She'd feared it would make it impossible for her to concentrate on her studies. It had been a difficult strategy to take, but she'd agreed it with her husband when he'd managed to call her on the phone once a few months before, via one of the pirate middlemen. Knowing that Mishal was doing well on her course kept his spirits up, he'd said.

As the months had dragged on, it had become hard to maintain the deception. When Mishal had got a distinction in one of her journalism exams, she'd asked why Daddy hadn't rung to congratulate her. Shahnaz had said the ship's communications system was down. Shahnaz didn't want to tell Mishal while she was still in London, picturing her breaking down on her own. She summoned her home to Karachi first, telling her she was feeling lonely. Mishal sensed something was up from the moment she walked in the door.

'What is the matter, Mother, you look like you've aged 100 years?'

After Shahnaz explained, Mishal spent the next three days crying. The shock was one thing, but just as bad was the guilt she felt for enjoying herself in London while the family were suffering. Why had her mother not told her? Shahnaz reminded her of her father's wishes. Knowing his daughter was doing well on her Master's was making him happy, and those journalism skills she was learning could now prove useful.

'You know how to communicate,' Shahnaz said. 'Can you spread awareness about the appeal?'

It was a high-risk strategy. Shahnaz knew that as soon as the case was publicised, it would complicate negotiations with the pirates, who might start asking for more money. Also, how would the media play the story? It wasn't as if Pakistan didn't have enough grim news as it was. The Pakistani Taliban and other terrorist groups were killing thousands of people a year. In Karachi, a city notorious for turf wars between its political factions, kidnappings took place every day.

Then Mishal thought about the young Arab Spring protestors who'd brought down a succession of Middle Eastern dictators that year. She'd studied their tactics on her journalism course. Those protestors knew they couldn't rely on state-censored newspapers and TV. Instead, they'd campaigned via Facebook and Twitter, giving them direct control over their message. Could they do the same?

'Save the Albedo, Save my father's life'

18 September 2011

My father's ship has been hijacked by Somalian pirates. The ship is running out of water, food supply and fuel. Please help us by donating so we can reach the required ransom. You can call on +923318228556 for further details.

Yours, Mishal.

The Facebook page was a simple effort, but within days, pledges of cash trickled in, and so did calls from Pakistani journalists. It wasn't every day you got a story about a Pakistani mother and her daughters taking on Somalia's pirates. Mishal and Nareman, who'd inherited their mother's good looks, found themselves in demand on TV news bulletins and chat shows. No effort was spared in tugging the public's heart-strings, and the Khan family photo album was opened up to newspapers. Ghulam Mujtaba, the wife of the *Albedo*'s chief engineer, went on TV with her four-year-old daughter, who pleaded 'please bring my father home' in a tiny voice. Also filmed was Mujtaba's fifteen-month-old boy, the son he'd not even known was on the way when he'd left for sea. The boy had only ever seen his father in pictures.

Putting their private affairs into the public domain didn't come easily. It was embarrassing to turn one's life into a soap opera. But while the *Albedo* campaign now got plenty of coverage – Pakistani celebrities declared backing for the appeal and Amjad Sabri, a popular singer, put on a benefit gig – the column inches, airtime and Facebook 'likes' didn't translate into much hard cash. Much as the public sympathised with the families, they didn't like the idea of giving cash to pirates.

'This is extortion to which you are becoming an accessory,' wrote one visitor to the appeal's Facebook page. 'Because of ransoms paid in the past, these pirates become bolder and more powerful. The only way to save lives of innocent people is by not paying.'

'That's easy for you say, but not for someone whose father, brother or husband is captured,' countered another.

Six months later, the campaign was still way short of target. Shahnaz had managed to get in touch with Khosrojerdi again, and had reached a joint deal with the pirates to pay $2.4 million to release the ship. The agreement was that Khosrojerdi would pay $1.3 million, and the Pakistanis the remaining $1.1 million. But by 1 May 2012, two weeks ahead of a deadline set by the pirates, the Pakistanis were only a fraction of their way to their target. In an article for Pakistan's

Dawn newspaper that day, Mishal's tone changed from pleading to scolding: 'When it comes to attending a social event, people don't hesitate to be ostentatious and extravagantly spend three to four figure amounts to book a VIP table or purchase designer bags. But when it comes to saving lives, people choose to simply ignore. Where is the humanity?'

On the eve of the deadline, Mishal also went on the TV news, issuing one last plea. 'If we don't get the money, these sailors are going to die,' she said. 'We have just about lost hope.'

It did the trick. Clips of her appearance went viral online. Within hours, TV news announced that Riaz Malik, a Pakistani real estate tycoon and philanthropist, was to pay the rest of the money. Whether he'd seen Mishal on the TV, or been nudged quietly by the Pakistani government – which couldn't be seen to be paying ransoms itself – wasn't clear, but for the first time in eighteen months, the tears on Shahnaz's cheeks were happy ones. *They'd finally raised the money.* Of course, nobody liked having to pay a group of criminals, but how many of their critics had ever had to make these difficult choices for themselves?

As they set to work on the logistics of getting the money to the pirates, a far tougher moral dilemma loomed. It began with what was supposed to be a simple call to Khosrojerdi to work out how to pool their respective payments.

'Send the money to me, and I'll negotiate direct with the pirates,' he said.

That was out of the question. Willing as she was to work with Khosrojerdi, Shahnaz had little trust in him. Certainly not enough to hand him $1.1 million of other people's money. This, after all, was a man who'd skimped on insurance for his crew in the world's most dangerous seas, and who hadn't paid his crew's families any wages since. She couldn't even be sure if he even had the $1.3 million he claimed to have. What if he just took her money for himself?

Khosrojerdi dug his heels in. He already had contacts lined up for the transfer, he insisted. Shahnaz suggested that both sides pay money into an escrow account, but that was ruled out too. The discussions dragged on, going nowhere.

The pirates, sensing the split in the camps, saw an opportunity. They told Shahnaz that for $1.1 million, they would release just the seven Pakistanis. The remaining crew could be ransomed out separately, they said, but that would be for others to worry about, not her.

Shahnaz rejected the offer out of hand. The *Albedo* appeal was on behalf of the whole crew, she told them. Not just her husband and his countrymen. She also feared that as captain, he would refuse to leave the ship unless it was with all those on board. Then, three months later, an anonymous email arrived. A video file was attached, and when Shahnaz opened it, her husband's face stared at her from the screen.

He and the rest of the Pakistani hostages were surrounded by gunmen. They weren't on the ship, but out in the Somali bush somewhere. Their clothes were filthy, their hair matted. Her husband had a long, straggly beard, and was so thin she barely recognised him. He looked close to death. A few days later, the pirates rang Shahnaz again – if she didn't accept their offer, they'd kill him.

She tried not to be frightened. She knew the pirates made these videos as a pressure tactic, but it was her first real glimpse of what her husband was going through. And who knew if this time, the pirates really would kill him?

She began to think the unthinkable. Was a deal to save the Pakistanis not better than no deal at all? They were no nearer on a deal with Khosrojerdi. What was the use of raising all that money, if her husband was executed at the eleventh hour? Or starved to death?

It would be hard on the families of the non-Pakistani hostages, some of whom had tried raising money themselves. None of those appeals elsewhere, though, had had any success. All the cash in the pot had come from Pakistani donors, who now wanted to see their money put to work. As one donor told her: 'If the money was raised here, it should be used for Pakistanis first.'

Eventually, she rang the pirates and agreed to their terms. The next task was persuading her husband. He'd already made it clear that he didn't want to leave his fellow crewmen to their fate. It wasn't in his nature. The family remembered the time years ago when they'd sailed on a ship with him that had come across a vessel that was sinking. Other ships were in the vicinity, and he could have sailed on by. Instead, he'd been first to the rescue.

Shahnaz told him it wasn't about putting himself first, but his family. 'We have been through a lot to get this money,' she said. 'If you don't get out now, who knows what will happen.'

Khan no longer had much fight left in him. These days he felt more like the pirates' slave than a captain of a boat. He eventually agreed. Then Shahnaz phoned the families of the non-Pakistani hostages, glad she didn't have to tell them face to face. There was no such comfort for her husband. When told the deal was on, he insisted on telling his fellow hostages in person.

To make the video of Khan, the pirates had taken him and the other Pakistani hostages off the ship and into the bushland. They'd lived rough, with barely anything to eat or drink. Once the deal was firmed up, they were taken back to the *Albedo* to collect their belongings. Then Khan broke the news to the crew.

'Unfortunately, the Pakistanis have had to strike an independent deal with the pirates due to the pressure being put by the pirates,' he told them. 'This means only the Pakistanis are going home. The owner has not been able to keep his word yet again, otherwise we would have all been going home together.'

His words were met with sullen, resigned stares. The others had sensed that the deal was in the offing, so it came as no great surprise, but it hurt bitterly. It wasn't just the unfairness of it, it was the breaking of the camaraderie, the one thing that had kept them going. Already they felt abandoned by the owner, their governments, and by the foreign navies. Now their own captain and shipmates were leaving them too.

'Captain, you are the father of the ship, please don't leave us,' said Aman. 'There is no help for us anywhere else.'

'I am sorry, but the Pakistani people have collected this money for us. They have gone to great efforts. We have no choice, the pirates put so much pressure.'

'But who will care for us now?'

'There has been no cooperation from your governments or the owner, despite our pleas. Get a negotiator to speak to your respective governments, and hopefully get you freed the way the Pakistanis have done. We will try to do our best for you when we return home.'

Some of the crew were angry. Wasn't a ship's captain supposed to stick with his crew? Others knew that if they'd been in Khan's position, they'd have done the same thing. The captain had had more than his share of punishment from the pirates. He was a wreck as it was. Yes, he had a duty to his crew, but he also had a duty to his family to stay alive.

When it was time to say goodbye, those left behind cried as they hugged the lucky ones. Then the Pakistanis were taken off the ship to begin the journey home.

On 2 August 2012, Khan and his six crewmates flew back into Karachi. Whoever organised the event was clearly not familiar with the practice of 'decompression' time, whereby newly-freed hostages spend their first few days in a quiet, uncrowded setting.

Instead, the former captives arrived to a VIP welcome from the Governor of Sindh, whose office filmed the entire thing. The resulting showreel, dubbed with a soft-rock soundtrack, showed the governor and his entourage strolling purposefully down a corridor in the airport terminal, embracing Khan and his companions like long-lost friends. Only after the photo op were the crew taken to meet their families at the governor's offices, where there were more handshakes, a banquet and an Oscars-style speech by the governor.

Khan, weighing just seven stone and limping with swollen feet, struggled with the attention, and discreetly threw up the rich food that was laid on, but he beamed obligingly. Mishal hugged her father's bony frame, feeling like he was some apparition that had clambered from the grave. 'I feel like I have just got a new Dad all of a sudden,' she told a TV crew at the event.

Yet the new Dad who arrived home that night wasn't the same as the old one. For months afterwards, Khan still lived like he was on the *Albedo*. He couldn't stomach his wife's rich cooking, living almost entirely off potatoes instead. He couldn't sleep in a normal bed, preferring a blanket on the floor, and he struggled with guilt and depression over leaving his comrades behind.

The women of the household told him to seek counselling, just as they had done. But like many men of his age, opening up to a stranger did not appeal. He was even reluctant to talk about his ordeal to his own family. What details he did reveal did not make them eager for more.

Once, he said, the pirates had tied his feet to a rope and dangled him upside down over the side of the ship. They'd lowered him beneath the water until his lungs nearly burst, while firing bullets into the sea around him. He mentioned it in a detached, emotionless way, like it had happened to someone else.

In a cupboard where he stashed what few belongings he brought back, his family also made a strange discovery. A thick stack of dog-eared A4 paper, containing long lists of English words in his handwriting, along with their definitions. It was a dictionary, running to tens of thousands of words.

'What made you write a dictionary, father?' Mishal asked. He'd looked at her hesitantly, as if a little embarrassed that it had been found.

'To pass the time,' he said.

Over the months, Khan's emotional state did not improve. Eventually, despite his promises to his family that he would retire, he took another job at sea.

Chapter 11

SON OF A PIG

The Albedo, *March 2013. Two years
and four months in captivity*

Aman lit a cigarette and lay back on the settee in the *Albedo*'s
lounge. He felt serene, mellow, full of goodwill. Goodwill
to his fellow hostages. Goodwill to the world. By God, yes,
goodwill even to those stupid pirate motherfuckers sat next
to him, guns in their laps and blissed-out grins on their faces.
Grins just like his.

He picked another twig from the pile and chewed the
leaves off, grinding them into more of that green, taste-
less cud. You had to give this khat stuff credit. Who'd have
thought that chewing what looked like a rhododendron bush
could feel so good? And who'd have thought it would make
chatting with a bunch of murderers so nice?

By day, the pirates were their captors and tormentors, by
night, during these dusk-to-dawn khat chewing sessions, they
were mates together of a sort. Not that the conversation was
that great. Mostly, they liked to hear him repeat the Somali
swear words they'd taught him, like he was Long John Silver's
parrot or something.

'*Dufarr*!' he shouted, pointing at the guard sprawled on the settee opposite him. '*Dufarr*! *DUFARR*!'

The guard, a mean-looking fucker who'd given Aman his share of grief in the past, grinned even wider. Green khat juice dribbled down his chin. His comrades lapsed into uncontrollable giggles, rolling around like a bunch of heavily-armed schoolboys.

'*Dufarr*' meant 'son of a pig'. It was their favourite, ahead even of such gems as *hoodaya* (fuck your mother) and *aabahaa was* (fuck your father). It was normally considered a mortal insult, and in less convivial circumstances, could earn a man a bullet in the head, but the pirates never got tired of hearing Aman say it. Even he was laughing now, a crazed snigger. The khat-stoned guffaws grew louder, a collective khat junkie cackle.

The big guard reached over to Aman for a fist bump – the same fist that was sometimes used for punching him. Aman obliged. Times like this were special. When everyone could briefly forget where they were, who they were, the roles they played on this floating hellhole, the hands dealt to them in life.

Time for some music. Aman rummaged through the CDs next to the cheap, Chinese-made stereo. The guards' favourite was Shakira. She'd got a following in pirate circles after releasing *Waka Waka (This Time for Africa)*, the official anthem to the 2010 World Cup in South Africa. Right now, though, Aman put on his own favourite, Jennifer Lopez's *Alive*. A syrupy power ballad, it was written for a film where J.Lo played a waitress fleeing an abusive husband, but to Aman's ears, every word captured his own life on the *Albedo* perfectly.

Time goes slowly now in my life
Fear no more of what I'm not sure
Feeling lucky just to be here tonight
And happy just to be me and be alive
And though life can be strange I can't be afraid
Searching for your soul, the strength to stand alone.

Fantastic. As if J.Lo was stuck here on the *Albedo* with him, getting roughed up by day, high on khat by night. If only. He grazed on another twig, then he lit a cigarette – another bad habit the pirates had got him into. So what? Right now, he didn't care about a thing in the world.

Some of the crew didn't like him hanging around with the pirates like this. Why be mates with those fuckers, they'd ask. Have you forgot what they did to your friend Rajoo? Of course he hadn't, and that was why he was acting the way he was. As the only other Indian on board, Aman knew he was the first in line to be killed the next time Ali Inke wanted to make a point. It was all very well the rest of the crew giving the pirates the cold shoulder – they weren't going to be the ones with a bullet in their chest.

Ever since Rajoo's murder, he'd decided his only chance of survival was to make the pirates his friends rather than his enemies. To work out what made them tick, to make himself useful to them. That way, they'd hopefully decide he was better kept alive than stored in the deep freeze.

Aman's charm offensive had begun in the *Albedo*'s kitchen, where he'd been sent to help the pirate's cook, Abdulessay, after Rajoo's death. He'd soon realised that the quickest way to the pirates' hearts was through their stomachs. Abdulessay was both a lousy chef and a lazy one, and got frequent grief from the guards about the quality of his food. When his young understudy came up with a few ideas, he was all too happy to let him get on with it.

Drawing on skills he'd learned in his mother's kitchen, and ancient jars of spices he found in the *Albedo*'s kitchen cupboards, Aman was soon turning Abdulessay's goat meat gruel into tasty curries and biryanis. Where once the galley had done meals only twice a day, Aman now offered round-the-clock catering, cooking fried fish for hungry, khat-stoned pirates in the small hours. He made constant fresh pots of hot, sugary Somali tea, delivering it wherever it was called for round the ship. He ran a concierge service, washing clothes, delivering cigarettes, fetching water and even cleaning the pirates' guns.

Often, all he got for his trouble was a slap or a kick, and there were times when he felt like serving a kettleful of freshly-boiled tea into a pirate's face. But he ignored their smirking looks, and whatever conclusions the rest of the crew might be drawing. This wasn't toadying, this was survival.

I am their slave, whatever they say, I will follow. If they slap me, I will follow. If they say wash their clothes, clean their guns, I will do it. It will save my life. I have to stay alive for my family. I am their only son.

Abdulessay, the cook, was the first to warm to Aman. He began slipping him extra portions of meat for the crew's meals, and taught him some basic Somali, like 'hello' – *wahadmas-antay* – and 'how are you?' – *wafianti*. Aman coaxed him for more, jotting each word and phrase in a hand-written dictionary. He didn't want to just learn pleasantries, he wanted to be able to talk to the guards properly, and to eavesdrop on their conversations as he poured their tea. If there was a plan to kill him or other members of the crew, he'd know about it first.

As the months passed, he gained fluency, turning titbit banter in his concierge duties into longer conversations. Soon he could tell if the guards were happy or fed up, and what they thought of their commanders. The guards liked the novelty of a foreigner who could speak their language, and the friendlier ones stopped mistreating him altogether. But it was the khat that really made the breakthrough.

When first hijacked, the crew had been mystified by the green shrub that their captors routinely grazed on. Khat is chewed all over the Horn of Africa, its amphetamine buzz filling much the same role as alcohol in the West. It makes users talkative and euphoric, and as with other intoxicants, many users overdo it. The *Albedo* pirates chewed day and night, leaving piles of discarded leaves around them like newly-trimmed privet hedges. As the *Albedo*'s self-appointed concierge, Aman often found himself sweeping up the mess. Then one night, he tried a few leaves himself.

For the first hour, all he'd got was a foul, gritty paste in his mouth, plus a few delighted laughs from the guards. But slowly, he'd felt a pleasant conviviality, and a warm, subtle glow that spread through his limbs. For once, he didn't feel scared or depressed. Instead, he had happy thoughts of home, of the girlfriend waiting for him. *Fuck, this is nice*, he thought.

Before he knew it, he'd been chewing for hours, not caring when he accidentally bit his tongue and felt his mouth fill with blood. He'd woken the next day feeling tired and lazy, his jaws aching, his mouth so raw he found it hard to eat. A few nights later, though, he was chewing again, this time with a few other *Albedo* companions. They'd sat up till dawn, talking about how they'd ended up in this mess, and, for once, laughing about it. At first, they chewed on their own, then with the pirates, Aman gabbling away in Somali.

Soon, the crew was chewing so much of the ship's khat supply that the guards said that they were going to raise the ransom price. It wasn't entirely clear if they were joking, but Aman didn't care. Anything to help him feel happier, and anything, by God *anything*, to help him forget about what those same pirates had done to him a few months ago with those pliers. His fingernails were only just growing back.

Not long after the Pakistani crewmen had left, Aman, Aliabadi and five others were told they were being taken to the mainland. They weren't informed why. A skiff took them to a beach, where a battered SUV drove them through some sand dunes and onto a dirt road. There wasn't much to see, except red, sandy soil, thickets of grey thorn trees, and the odd goat. There was little sign of human life. Occasionally they'd drive past a few tumbledown homes of white breezeblock or mud-thatch. Somalia looked poorer than anywhere in India, Aman noted. It wasn't hard to see why some people were tempted into piracy.

After a 24-hour drive through endless scrubland, they were ordered out of the car and told to sit under a scraggy thorn tree. It was to be their home, if you could call it that, for the next three months. There was no proper shelter from the sun, no mats, not even a blanket. Food was a piece of bread or a potato once a day. Drinking water was from a rain-filled tarpaulin, full of frogs, dead insects and dung. It was a pirate gulag, a place with no escape from discomfort. Even the guards looked unhappy.

Then the torture began. The pirates trussed Aman by his hands and legs and hung him from a tree, asking him why India hadn't paid up when Pakistan already had. They lashed him with a rope until he passed out. They pulled his finger-nails out with pliers, two from the left hand and two from the right. They heated a piece of metal in a fire and branded his arm. At times, they made him call his parents at home in India. His father told him that the village had banded together to raise money for the ransom, but the few thousand dollars they'd mustered was nowhere near enough.

Aliabadi, the Iranian bosun, had it even worse. They tethered him to a car axle, making him lie under the midday sun. They threw him into a spiky thicket, leaving his back full of thorns that his crew mates later had to pull out. They made him lie in a freshly-dug grave and told him they were going to bury him alive. They poured a can of petrol over him and threatened him with lighters, and they kicked him non-stop, knocking out several of his front teeth.

The torture sessions seemed to be a new strategy to get every country with hostages on the *Albedo* to cough up a separate ransom. The pirates figured that if Pakistan could pay, so too could India, Bangladesh, Sri Lanka and Iran. Aliabadi got extra beatings because the pirates had gleaned that he was a cousin of Khosrojerdi, the owner. They were convinced he was secretly telling Khosrojerdi not to pay. Why else, they argued, was the *Albedo* still stuck here after all this time? Even a few of his fellow hostages had their suspicions.

Aliabadi was furious. Some idiot in the crew, he suspected, had told the pirates this bullshit. Yes, it was true that he and Khosrojerdi were related, but they hardly knew each other. It was just a distant family connection that had helped him get the job as bosun. One he now wished he'd never taken. He was as mad with the owner as anyone.

'Do you think I want to die here?' he yelled at the pirates. 'Do you think I don't want to go home?'

After three months, they were taken back to the *Albedo*, and were greeted with hugs from their crewmates. Aman and Aliabadi started spending more time together, swapping stories about their time in the gulag. The two got on well – they were both loners on the ship, with no countrymen to confide in or hide amid. That, Aman reckoned, was the key to surviving here. The more you did it on your own terms, not anyone else's, the better.

In June 2013, the monsoon season came, allowing the crew to take al fresco showers, their first decent wash in months. Then, just as they were enjoying the novelty of smelling clean, a foul odour wafted up from below decks. Part of the ship's hold had filled with water, which had mixed with some unidentified item below decks to produce a noxious whiff. At first they assumed it was all just rainwater from the monsoon, but when the crew tried to pump it out, the hold filled up again. Closer inspection revealed a gaping hole gouged in the side of the hull. Sea water was leaking in.

The crew borrowed a pump from the *Naham 3*, a hijacked Taiwanese trawler. It had been harnessed to the *Albedo*'s stern a few months before because its own anchor had broken. The two captive ships sat about 300 metres apart, tethered to each other by thick towing ropes. Using the pump, the *Albedo* crew kept the flooding under control, but as the monsoon intensified, bringing with it stormy seas, the hold began to fill up.

By early July 2013, waves twenty feet high were crashing into the *Albedo*. One morning, as Aman went about his duties in the galley, the ship lurched violently, sliding plates and cups off the shelves. The floor underneath Aman's feet tilted and a puddle on the floor worked its way from one side of the galley to the other. The entire ship was now listing.

Aman felt a stab of panic. He knew from maritime college that any ship that took in enough water to affect its balance was doomed. If this storm continued, they could sink at any moment, and like many other *Albedo* crewmen, he couldn't swim properly. They were supposed to learn at maritime college, but nobody really took it seriously. It was more important to know about the life vests and lifeboats – which, if you were in the middle of an ocean, offered the only realistic odds of survival anyway. Most of the *Albedo*'s life vests, though, had gone missing during the pirates' looting sprees, and the lifeboats didn't have room enough for both hijackers and crew.

Aliabadi told the pirates of the problems. Best to get off the *Albedo* before it started sinking, he advised. The pirates were as deaf to his warnings as the captain on the *Titanic*: 'No problem, no problem.' Requests for skiffs to take them ashore were refused.

Chapter 12

THE HUMANITARIAN

Nairobi, 1 July 2013

'Hello Mr John, how are you? How is everything?'

The voice on the phone greeted John Steed like an old friend. Awale was one of the main negotiators for the pirate gangs, a man prized for his ability to drive a hard bargain. Like a good football agent, he was much in demand among the top players on the pirate coast, someone who could browbeat the fattest ransom deal from any ship owner. Yet whenever he spoke to Steed, he was always courteous and business-like. As if he'd been a call centre worker in a previous life.

In fact, Steed knew nothing about Awale's past. Like all negotiators, his real identity was a mystery, his name a pseudonym that changed as often as his mobile phone number. Most negotiators weren't even pirates, but teachers or aid workers who spoke some English. Often they were based nowhere near the pirates, doing all their business by phone, and they usually claimed to be acting in a 'humanitarian capacity' rather than for personal gain. Until a ransom was agreed, that was, when they'd demand a fat cut for themselves from the ship owners. They were Mother Teresa one minute, and greedy, amoral bastards the next. Word had it that on one recent hijacking,

Awale had got 10 per cent of the $2.5 million ransom. No wonder he always sounded so jaunty.

Steed tried to be cordial back. If he was going to get any of those poor souls off that *Albedo* ship before it sank, people like Awale were his only chance. Steed spoke slowly and clearly, anxious to be understood over the patchy mobile phone connection.

'Hi Awale, great to hear from you! Listen, you're a well-connected guy, aren't you? Do you know any of the pirates holding that ship the *Albedo*? Can you talk to them? Because if it sinks, everyone is going to die! We need to get them off.'

A patrol aircraft from EU NAVFOR, the EU-led anti-piracy naval mission, had taken photos of the *Albedo* during a flyover. They showed the vessel already leaning heavily into the sea. Steed's contact at EU NAVFOR had emailed the photos to him the day before.

For reasons nobody could quite work out, the *Albedo* hijackers hadn't seen fit to evacuate. Steed presumed they eventually would, but pirates weren't very health-and-safety conscious. There was every chance they'd wait until there were waves lapping round the ship's bridge.

That, though, gave him an opportunity. If he could start a dialogue with the pirates, perhaps he could persuade them to just abandon ship themselves, and then leave the hostages on board for someone to come and rescue them. To do that, though, he had to first figure out a way of getting in touch. The *Albedo* had been incommunicado for as long as anyone could remember. Nobody knew who was holding it hostage, or how to get hold of them, much less whether they'd care to speak to a UN bureaucrat.

When Steed asked a few Somali contacts with connections

on the pirate coast, they'd come back with a blank. The *Albedo* was a basket-case, by all accounts, a rust-bucket that had been stuck there for years. No longer even a subject of interest on the pirate grapevine. Eventually, someone had put John in touch with Awale. A big-shot negotiator like him wouldn't normally have touched a case like the *Albedo* with a barge pole, but he swung enough weight to get the *Albedo* pirates to take his calls.

'So, Mr John, I spoke to the pirate guys of that *Albedo* ship again, like you asked. And I told them, like you said, that you are worried about the ship sinking.'

'Yes, and what did they say?'

'Well, like you know, I have some influence round here. Everybody, they know me.'

'Yes. Quite!'

'They know I get the good deals, so they listen to me.'

Get to the point, man. That was the problem with having to be nice to people like Awale. The more you flattered them, the more self-important they became.

'Yes! So what did they say?'

'These guys, they not listen. They say there is no problem with the ship.'

'But it's sinking! They'll die along with the hostages if they don't get off soon.'

'Yes, yes, Mr John. This I told them. But you know I am just a go-between. Not a pirate. What can I do?'

'Listen, Awale, please go back to them if you can. Remind them that if they are willing to just let the hostages go, we can send a ship to the *Albedo* to pick them up. We won't try to arrest the pirates. We just want to save the hostages. That's better than them drowning, isn't it?

'I tell them that before, Mr John. They ask: "What about the ransom money?"'

'Look, as I said to you already, *there is no ransom money* for this ship. They know that. Otherwise, why would they still be waiting after nearly three years? These hostages have suffered long enough, and now they risk drowning. It's time to let them go. On *humanitarian* grounds!'

He paused, for what he hoped was dramatic effect. Awale often talked about being a humanitarian. It was worth throwing his own words back at him. Besides, as a UN representative, Steed had no money to offer, and no authority to offer any either. He was probably stretching protocol just by talking to characters like Awale in the first place. Still, the only chance was to appeal to the pirates' better nature. If such a thing existed. Awale seemed to doubt it.

'I will try again for you, Mr John, because it is my duty. As you know, all I ever want to do is to help. But I tell you, these people will not let the hostages go without their payment. They have waited a long time too.'

Steed put the phone down. There was sweat on the handset. Talking to Awale always sent his heart racing. You had to choose your words carefully, knowing that everything you said would be relayed to gangs of excitable thugs holding guns to people's heads. And this bunch on the *Albedo* sounded particularly nasty. Rumour had it that they'd executed an Indian sailor in cold blood a while back.

Steed couldn't figure out why the *Albedo*'s owner, one Omid Khosrojerdi of Majestic Enrich Shipping, wasn't doing more to help. He'd tried contacting him, but had got only dead phone lines and emails that bounced back. It wasn't just the *Albedo* who seemed to have been forsaken. The ship it was tied to, the *Naham 3*, which had now been held for nearly a year and a half, had also lost all contact with its owners. So too had a ship called the *Prantalay 12*, further down the coast.

Steed had already seen what years on a hijacked ship could do to people. The previous December, the UN's Hostage Support Programme had repatriated 22 newly-freed crewmen from the *Iceberg 1*, a hijacked cargo ship. Once again, the ship's owners, an Emirati firm, had been uninsured and unable to pay a ransom, leaving the hostages to languish for nearly three years in captivity. As the pirates' frustration had grown, the crew's treatment had got ever worse. They'd eventually been freed after the *Iceberg 1* was attacked by the Puntland Maritime Police Force, a Somali-manned anti-piracy unit supervised by a group of South African mercenaries. Like the Indian navy, the PMPF had gambled correctly that the pirates would back down in the face of superior force.

Two of Steed's UN colleagues had flown into northern Somalia to pick the *Iceberg 1* hostages up. The stories the sailors told were horrific. They'd spent much of the time trussed up in a hot, dark cramped room in the ship's hold, where they'd been whipped constantly and fed a single meal of filthy rice a day. One sailor had lost his eyesight, while for a couple of others, it had all been too much. The ship's third officer had committed suicide by jumping overboard, and another who tried to do the same was fished out of the water and locked away on his own for five months. At one point the pirates, desperate to make a profit from their prize, had even told the crew that they would kill them and harvest their kidneys for sale. Much of the pirates' cruelty towards the crew seemed to be to pressure the owner into paying a ransom. It was reasonable to assume, therefore, that similar horrors would be taking place on board the *Albedo*.

During his phone calls with Steed, Awale had insisted that if the *Albedo* started to sink, the pirates would send skiffs from the mainland. Steed wondered if that would be possible, given the size of the monsoon waves now lashing Hobyo. Every day, his email inbox was getting new EU NAVFOR aerial images, showing the ship getting ever lower in the water. In desperation, he rang EU NAVFOR, using his old colonel's title to get patched through to the chief of staff. He didn't like pulling rank, but it was worth a try. The current chief of staff, he knew, was a fellow Brit. Hopefully, he'd at least get a hearing.

'Hello commander, this is Colonel John Steed. I'm the UN lead on counter-piracy, and I also look after the hostage support programme. Are you aware of this rather urgent situation with the *Albedo*?'

'Yes, sir, we're well aware. Not sure quite what we can do, unfortunately.'

'Listen, your staff are saying it's going to sink any time from now. Is there any way you can get a ship in to rescue them?'

'Not in our mandate, I'm afraid.'

'You realise these guys may drown otherwise?'

'I do, but there are armed pirates on board. We'd be potentially putting the hostages' lives at risk if we came too close.'

Steed tried another tactic, delving into vague knowledge from his days as a yachtsman in Cornwall.

'Commander, isn't there a safety-of-life-at-sea principle here? If people are at risk of drowning, doesn't that consideration come before any others? You can use that to justify going into territorial waters, can't you? And to justify the risk from the pirates.'

'Again, I sympathise, but I repeat, it's beyond our remit. I'm really sorry, but we can't do what you ask.'

'But you surely can't just leave them there like this!'

Steed could feel his voice getting agitated. *Calm down*, he told himself. *This isn't Awale you're talking to.*

'Listen, commander, I realise you have your rules. But the men on board that ship have already been stuck there for nearly three years. They've been through absolute hell. Surely, the safety-of-life-at-sea principle applies?'

'I'm really sorry, no. Believe you me, if there was anything we could do, we'd try.'

Steed knew he was beaten. The commander wasn't being officious, he was just doing his job, and he probably felt just as bad as Steed did.

'Okay. Thanks for hearing me out anyway.'

'We'll be keeping an eye on the situation, sir. If any hostages appear in a lifeboat, we can pick them up.'

By the afternoon of 7 July 2013, the bow of the *Albedo* was so low in the sea that water began flooding over the deck.

Aliabadi rallied the crew. He told them to find all the available life jackets, and forbade them from sleeping below decks. With so much water now flowing into the *Albedo*, things could suddenly reach a tipping point where the ship would begin to sink much more rapidly. It could be all over in minutes. No time to get near the lifeboats. The plan would be to jump overboard, swim to the ropes attaching the *Albedo* to the *Naham 3*, and use them as a lifeline to haul themselves to the *Naham 3*.

'If I give you the warning, you must jump off the ship one by one,' Aliabadi said. 'Once you jump, get away from the ship. If you're near a door or a hatchway, it will create a plug hole as it fills with water. You'll get sucked in.'

The crew stashed the remaining lifejackets in a cupboard, hiding them from the pirates. Those who couldn't find a lifejacket grabbed empty jerry cans, which would work as floats.

As night fell, they heard a scraping, banging sound from the far end of the ship. Some of the *Albedo*'s containers had come loose and were sliding around on the open deck. They were designed to stay fixed in the heaviest storms, but they couldn't cope with tonnes of sea water sluicing around them.

One container detached from the deck altogether and floated away, pitching on the open sea, then another followed suit. Aliabadi decided it was time to abandon ship. If the water around them ended up full of twenty-tonne metal boxes, all smashing into each other, the sailors could get crushed as they tried to haul their way to the *Naham 3*, or the ropes connecting the two ships could get broken. If they were going to go, it had to be now.

The crew headed outside. It was now pitch dark, and waves were streaming across the sloping deck, making it hard to walk without slipping. The wind was screaming so loud they could barely hear each other. At the other end of the ship, the pirates were trying to launch the lifeboat. They no longer seemed to care about the hostages, the cargo they'd guarded for two and a half years. Aliabadi did a head count. There was supposed to be fifteen crew, he could only count fourteen. One of the Bangladeshis was missing. Had he not heard the call to abandon ship? Aliabadi had seen him down-stairs praying earlier – perhaps he was trapped, or just too scared to move.

'Wait here while I look for him,' Aliabadi said. 'If I'm not back in two minutes, go without me.'

Aliabadi went back inside and ran around the corridors, fearing a torrent of water could barrel down on him any moment. When ships sank, it wasn't like in the movies, where the rooms filled with water in a steady trickle. Water could reach the ceiling in seconds.

At the stern, the others lined up to jump. Some had life jackets, others clutched jerry cans roped to their wrists. The non-swimmers stared over the edge. Most wouldn't even choose to jump into the deep end of a swimming pool, now they faced a fifteen-foot drop into heaving night-time ocean water.

Aman watched three of his crewmates plunge in, landing right by the ropes, which were floating on the water. They then began to haul themselves, hand by hand, along the 300 metres to the *Naham 3*, whose hostages had lit the route with the beams of their deck lamps. It was slow going. One lost his grip on his rope and began to drift away. Soon he'd vanished from Aman's view. Then there came a splash from the *Naham 3*. One of their sailors had roped himself to the deck and jumped in. He swam, disappeared, then reappeared holding the missing man.

Aliabadi reappeared on deck. He'd had to give up looking for the Bangladeshi down below.

'Jump!' he shouted at the others. 'Jump now!'

Aman clutched a jerry can, then went to the edge. Wind and spray lashed his face, it felt as crazy as jumping off a cliff. Others already in the water shouted at him from below.

'Jump, Aman! The ship is sinking behind you!'

'I can't do it! I can't swim!'

'JUST JUMP!'

Come on man, Aman told himself. *After all you've been through, you can manage this.* A pair of hands shoved him from behind. He belly-flopped into the sea.

The water was much colder than he expected, jolting the senses like a gut punch. As Aman surfaced, the crewman who'd shoved him in jumped in as well, nearly landing on top of him. A wave broke over them. Aman surfaced again, spitting out seawater. Before he had time to get his breath, another wave buried him again, and again.

Eventually, the waves broke long enough for him to get some air. He got hold of his jerry can and steered his way to one of the ropes connecting the *Albedo* to the *Naham 3*. It was all he could do just to cling on. Every wave forced water down his throat like a high-pressure hose.

God, my life now is in your hands. Please help me.

With every wave that washed over him, he grew weaker. He began to feel faint. He felt like letting go of the rope, there was nothing more he could do.

Goodbye mother. Goodbye father. I tried my best.

A sense of calm settled over him. No point in spending his final few moments thrashing about. The waves closed over him again, and became one vast, churning blackness.

Chapter 13

In Arrears

Nairobi, 3 July 2013

The latest photos from the EU NAVFOR aircraft confirmed Steed's worst fears. One showed the *Albedo*, now totally submerged except for the upper floors of its deck tower. Another showed two luminous orange lifeboats washed up on a beach, lying on their side. There was no sign of footprints in the sand from either. The helicopter pilot had seen bodies floating in the sea. Awale, the negotiator, texted to say that some of the hostages had survived, but that four had drowned.

Still, there was an opportunity here. Thanks to their stupid, greedy decision not to let the hostages go, the pirates were now directly responsible for the deaths of innocent men. Perhaps now they could be pressured into doing the right thing, releasing the rest of the hostages straightaway. This time, he wasn't going to plead through Awale. He was going to do it via a press release, begging for them to show mercy. If private persuasion hadn't worked, maybe public shaming would.

Steed got in touch with the Maritime Piracy Humanitarian Response Programme, a London-based charity set up by the shipping industry to support hijacked sailors and their families. The MPHRP had welfare staff in all the major sea-faring countries, some of whom were in touch with relatives of the *Albedo* crew. If the hijackers wouldn't listen to Steed, perhaps they might listen to a plea from hostages' families.

On 15 July, nine days after the *Albedo*'s sinking, the MPHRP put out a carefully-worded press release.

15 July 2013

Dear Somali Brothers and Sisters

We, the unfortunate families of MV [Maritime Vessel] Albedo, have been separated from our loved ones since November 2010. The owner did not arrange money as demanded by yourself, and we appealed to everyone in this world to pay money towards the release of our people. But no one listened. We have tried our best, but we are very poor people. We even do not have any money to pay for medicines, school fees or to buy food for our children.

Now the vessel has sunk and the owner has no interest to pay money and rescue the crew. Please, at least release the remaining crew on humanitarian grounds, or else they will die in your hands. What will you tell to Allah? You will be punished by Him for taking the life of innocent poor people.

Families of the Albedo Crew.

The press release got no attention internationally. Piracy – once a major story – was now yesterday's news. But it was picked up by Somali news websites. Steed had put his contact details at the end of the press release. He wanted to reach out not just to the pirates, but clan leaders, imams and anyone else who might hold sway with them. Within hours, people started getting in touch. All claimed to have influence with the *Albedo* pirates, most claimed they would need generous fees for 'expenses'. Steed didn't care. The point right now was just to establish himself as the go-to person. It might also get Awale to raise his game, by making him think that Steed had other go-betweens to the pirates. Sure enough, two days later, Awale rang up.

'Hello Mr John, I have some good information for you. I have made contact again with the *Albedo* pirates.'

'Well done. And how are the hostages?'

'Like I said before, some drowned but most are still alive.'

'How do we know that? What if the pirates are lying? What if all the hostages are dead?'

'I know because I have talked to the hostages myself!' Awale replied.

'Really?'

'Yes! I told the pirates that we would need it! For the proof of life! Do you want to speak to the hostages too? I can put you through to them right now!'

He sounded like a call centre worker again.

'I am going to put you on hold for a few minutes. Please wait! Proof of life is coming!'

The first thing that proved to Aman that he was still alive, that it wasn't all just a dream before the afterlife, was the vomiting. Gut-wrenching, salty torrents, spewing everywhere like ocean spray. Litre after litre, it seemed. He could vaguely remember floating somewhere between the *Albedo* and the *Naham 3*, trying to pull his way along that rope. The waves had made it impossible, he'd prepared himself to die. Then it felt like he'd lost consciousness. Perhaps the current had taken him towards the *Naham 3*, or maybe someone had jumped in to rescue him. No matter. If he'd really drowned, his soul would surely be floating up above the *Albedo* now, looking down serenely. Not lying wet and shivering on the deck of the *Naham 3*, in a pool of his own vomit.

He got to his feet, spewing brine again. How could he have swallowed that much water and not drowned? He looked around. The boat's deck was full of people, mostly from the *Naham 3*, it seemed – guys from the Far East. Some were running around, some were at the deck rail staring out to sea. He followed their gaze. In the distance, he could see the *Albedo*, lit up in a yellow glow by the *Naham 3*'s deck lamps. Only the top three floors of its deck tower were now still above the sea.

What about his shipmates? Two of the Sri Lankan boys were recuperating in a corner, a couple more were nearby. And yes, that bedraggled figure over there was Aliabadi, his wet hair swept back over his widow's peak.

'Well done man, you made it!' Aman said, giving him a wet hug.

'I don't know how. I was unconscious when they got me on deck. They said I was shouting all the crew's names when I woke up.'

'How about the others?'

'I've only been able to count eleven. We were fifteen when we jumped off.'

Aman went round the *Naham 3* crew, trying to find someone he had a common language with. Eventually he found a Filipino who spoke some English. It seemed that three of the Sri Lankans on the *Albedo* had never got off the ship at all.

'We're not sure what happened to them, but we know there were some guys still standing on your ship when it went down,' the Filipino said.

Aman cast his mind back to the moment he'd jumped into the sea. Perhaps they'd been too scared. Or perhaps they'd just left it too late, and been sucked back through one of the deck doors as it filled with water.

'What about the guy who came just after me? The guy who pushed me in? Did he survive?'

'What guy? I didn't see anyone else, but we were all busy. Maybe someone else did.'

The Filipino asked around, and people shook their heads. Eventually, another Filipino came forward. He looked troubled. Yes, he'd seen the missing man. He'd watched him making his way along the middle rope. Then one of the *Naham 3* pirates had appeared, carrying an axe. He'd started hacking at all the ropes attaching the ship to the sinking *Albedo*, worried it would drag the *Naham 3* down with it as well. The Filipino had told the pirate to wait, pointing out the sailor still in the water. The pirate had desisted, but then the Filipino had had to rush off to help someone else. When he'd come back later, the ropes had all been cut. The missing sailor, he reckoned, was still in the sea.

Had the pirate cut the rope knowing there was a man still clinging to it? The Filipino couldn't be sure – perhaps the pirate had thought he'd already climbed aboard. Still, these callous fuckers were capable of anything. Either way, cutting the rope had been unnecessary, for the *Albedo* hadn't sunk completely. It was now resting on a sandbank, the upper floors of the deck tower still above the water.

The *Naham 3* crew took the new arrivals inside. The whole ship, Aman noticed, stank of fish. Their hosts looked just like them – pinched, haggard faces; clothes in rags, stained with food, oil and sweat. Judging by how thin they were, the food on the *Naham 3* was barely enough for one crew, never mind two, but their hosts divided up what they had, cooking up noodles for the *Albedo* guests.

The Filipino said that the *Naham 3* crew had been hijacked for fifteen months. Like the *Albedo* crew, it seemed the ransom talks had petered out. Anxious looks crossed their faces when Aman said he'd been hostage for two and a half years, and told of the murder of his friend Rajoo.

A few days later, Ali Inke came on board. He mentioned, matter-of-factly, that eleven pirates had drowned too. They'd clambered into a lifeboat, but hadn't been seen since. Then he got to business. New guards had been arranged to hold the *Albedo* crew on the mainland, he said. They would leave by pirate skiff immediately. Inke was clearly worried about leaving his hostages in another gang's custody.

As they departed, Aman took a last look at the wrecked *Albedo*, sticking up from the waves like a long-abandoned castle. His jail for two and a half years. Now he'd never be able to take his friend Rajoo's body back home. He'd lie buried at sea forever, along with his four drowned crewmates.

He thought about Magdy, the Egyptian electrician who'd mysteriously quit the ship all that time ago in Dubai. What was it he'd had a dream about? That the *Albedo* would end up lying stricken on a sandy beach? *Fuck*! Okay, the Albedo was stuck on a sandbank, not a beach, but it was still spooky. Besides, dreams were supposed to speak in symbols and metaphors, not literals. It was probably just coincidence, of course, but it was hard not to think that Magdy's guardian angel had been looking out for him. And, yes, maybe for Aman too. Hijackings, executions, torture, a sinking – there seemed to be nothing he couldn't survive.

God saved my life out in that storm, not a human. And if he has done it already, he will keep doing it again. If I have survived so far, I can survive anything.

On the mainland, the surviving eleven crew were taken to a village called Camara. New guards arrived, and a new translator. He handed Aman a phone, and told him to say his name down the line and the name of his ship. Then came a voice in reply, British, by the sound of it, like one of those people on the BBC.

'Hello, my name is John Steed. I work for the United Nations. I'm hoping I might be able to help you!'

As Steed waited for Awale to connect him through to the hostages on the *Albedo*, he could hear muffled exchanges in Somali, and the high-pitched hum of one mobile signal interfering with another. Awale was holding the earpiece of one handset against the speaker of a second. If any security services were eavesdropping on his line to Steed, they'd only be able to work out where Awale was speaking from, not where the hostages were. It also allowed Awale to listen in on the call. After he introduced himself, Steed could hear a voice speaking in heavily-accented Indian English.

'Hello, sir. My name is Aman Kumar, from India. I am a sailor on the *Albedo*. We were taken hostage by Somali pirates on 26 November 2010. I was nineteen then. I am nearly 22 now. Please help me.'

The voice spoke in a monotone, addressing nobody in particular. It sounded like something from a seance, a distressed spirit seeking deliverance.

'Er … hello Aman. Good to hear from you. Are you okay?'

'Yes.'

'Are the other hostages okay?'

'Yes. We are okay. But four of us have drowned.'

The line cut. Awale, who'd been listening in, interrupted.

'So you see, Mr John, the proof of life!'

Yes, and proof of death.

'Thank you Awale. So will the pirates now release them as a goodwill gesture? Now that four of them have drowned?'

'I am sorry Mr John, but still they are wanting money.'

'What?'

'Just $1.5 million, that is all.'

'Come on Awale! Four of these men have just drowned! How many more of them must die? You're a man with influence. Please – get these pirates to do the right thing!'

'It is not that simple, Mr John. You must understand that these pirate commanders have run up a lot of expenses looking after these hostages.'

'*Expenses?* What do you mean?'

'They have paid wages for guards for nearly three years. Plus food for the hostages for nearly three years. These things cost money. They borrowed it, so now they are in debt.'

'Debt? How much debt?'

'About $500,000.'

'*Five-hundred-thousand dollars?* Are you joking?'

'Not a bit. Even if they wanted to release the hostages for free, they could not. They need the ransom to pay the debts.'

'Well, like I say, *there is no money* available. And remember, they should not be hijacking people in the first place. It is not the crew's fault if the pirates have spent money looking after them.'

'Mr John, please! The pirates have to pay their debts. Just like in your country, in England. If they do not, they will be in trouble.'

'In trouble? With who?'

'The people they borrowed the money from. The investors, who invested money in this hijacking.'

Investors? What was he talking about? This was Somalia. Not Wall Street.

'Like I say, Awale, *there is no money.*'

'Please, Mr John. See it from the pirates' point of view. The investors have guns too.'

For the next few days, Steed avoided Awale's calls. Even by pirate standards, this was bullshit of the first order. Five-hundred-thousand dollars on food and guards? When the crew were half-starving? Did they think he was that naive?

Yet when he did the maths, it wasn't quite as outlandish as it seemed. If you allowed for, say, twenty guards on board being paid, say, $5 a day each, that was $100 per day alone. Then there were the daily costs of rice, goat meat, cigarettes, water and khat. That could be another $50 daily. Then there was all manner of sundries – phone bills, guns, skiffs, pay-offs, sweeteners, negotiators' fees. Another $50 a day maybe. So maybe at least $200 per day in costs. Since the ship had now been held for roughly 1,000 days, that made about $200,000 in all, plus whatever compensation had been given to the families of the eleven pirates who'd drowned when the *Albedo* had sunk. Maybe another $50,000.

Sure $250,000 was still a long way short of $500,000. But unless they'd had a previous ransom payment, the average pirate gang wouldn't have that kind of cash to hand. So yes, they'd have to borrow it, as Awale said, and in somewhere like Somalia, you couldn't go to the bank and get ordinary high street interest rates. People who lent out $250,000 might well want double their money in return. Plus, Awale had almost certainly inflated the size of the debt a bit, to ensure he could cream a percentage off without telling the pirates.

Who, though, were these feared 'investors', that even the pirates were scared of? Steed asked his Somali contacts, expecting them to laugh at him for falling for such twaddle. Instead, they nodded. Yes, there were Somali clans who'd lend 'start-up' cash for hijacking ventures, the loan being paid back with generous interest if it led to a ransom pay-out. There were even pirate 'stock exchanges' in some pirate coastal towns, where conglomerates of money lenders bought into new ventures. With no courts to turn to, all debts were settled by the law of the gun. After all, no sensible person would lend money to a pirate unless they had a way of getting it back. The *Albedo* hijackers would know that if they defaulted on their loans, some very heavy debt collectors would come looking for them.

The problem was that the longer the *Albedo* crew stayed in captivity, the more debts the pirates were running up, which meant the more they needed a big ransom payment. The ship was stuck in a vicious circle. It was the pirate equivalent of those 'sub-prime' mortgages that had sparked the global recession, where people owed far more than their assets were worth. Persuading the pirates to hand over the *Albedo* hostages for free, Steed realised, was going to be much harder than he thought.

In early August, the MPHRP put out another appeal for the sailors' release. It was timed to coincide with the Muslim festival of Eid al-Fitr, ending the holy month of Ramadan, a time when the faithful were supposed to do good deeds and show mercy. Again, the appeal got nowhere. Instead, Awale rang to say that the ransom demand had been upped to $3.5 million. That made Steed anxious. He'd already stressed that the UN had no money, yet it seemed the pirates thought quite the opposite. Had he simply raised their expectations, by mentioning the UN's name? Did they think he could draw on some bottomless UN fund? Now he could see why some people had warned him not to talk to the pirates in the first place.

Later that month, two FBI men from the US embassy came to see him. They'd heard that an American hostage was being held in the area of Somalia where the *Albedo* crew now were. They wanted Steed to keep an ear out. It was nice to feel that at least someone thought he might be doing something useful. Steed dined with the Americans in the UN's recreation centre. Then, over coffee, the whole world went blank.

Chapter 14
THE LADY PIRATE

The Albedo *crew, Camara, Somalia, August 2013.*
Two years and ten months into captivity

Few sailors held hostage in Somalia had fond memories of the village of Camara. A scattering of ramshackle homes in the middle of a vast, windswept plain, its sole asset was that it was a long way from anywhere. Anyone who tried to escape would find themselves lost in endless sun-scorched scrubland, where they'd likely die of thirst.

Pirates used Camara as their own Alcatraz, yet for the newly-arrived *Albedo* crew, Camara felt more like a pirate Hilton. They had new clothes, fresh water and plenty of food – tinned tuna, pasta, rice, even sugar. In the walled compound that served as their jail, there were mattresses, blankets and razors to shave their long beards. Compared to life on the ship under Ali Inke, it felt like they were being looked after by their own mothers. A feeling reinforced by the fact that the pirate now in charge was a woman.

Arro was an imposing, heavily-set lady, who wore a black burka. A former khat dealer, she'd used her profits to become one of Camara's main pirate financiers. She was as tough as any of her male counterparts, and carried a pistol under her robes. She'd bought into the *Albedo* hijacking late on, and wanted to protect her investment. She brought in new guards, and told them to treat the hostages well. She took a particular shine to Aman because of his fluency in Somali. He reminded her, she told him, of one of her own sons. Yet that didn't stop her seeing the prisoners as just another commodity to be bought and sold. Like the camels on sale in Camara's market, they were valuable livestock that had to be fed properly. But if they couldn't be sold at a profit, they weren't going anywhere.

By now, the pirates were in regular contact with 'Mr John at the UN'. He would ring every week or so, and ask to speak to the crew too, usually either Aman or Aliabadi, the Iranian bosun. He kept stressing he had no money, but the pirates always took his calls, as if flattered to have someone from a big organisation like the UN calling.

Steed and his team at the Hostage Support Programme had devised a strategy. Firstly, they'd try to build a rapport with the pirates, focused on requesting that the hostages were treated well and had access to medical care. If that went well, they'd try again to press for the pirates to free the hostages on humanitarian grounds.

One of Steed's UN colleagues, Leo Hoy-Carrasco, organised for a local Somali medic to visit the hostages. It was just a basic health check, but a good trust-building exercise. The pirates got to nominate the medic, but the UN reserved the right to vet him, just in case he turned out to be a hijacker dressed in a white coat and stethoscope.

Arro brought in a new negotiator. He spent much time drinking tea with Aman, who, with his English and Somali, was now the main spokesman for the crew, as well as retaining his role as camp cook. With the *Albedo* now sunk and its owner uncontactable, the new negotiator seemed to realise it was a lost cause. He told Aman that he'd advised Arro it'd be best to let the crew go.

A few days later, another call came through from the UN. Aman took the phone, hoping for the best. Perhaps Arro had heeded the negotiators' advice. Might this be Mr John, ringing to discuss arrangements for their release? Instead, a different voice was on the line. It was Hoy-Carrasco, Steed's colleague.

'I have bad news, I am afraid,' he said. 'Mr John has had a heart attack.'

It wasn't how Professor Raj Jutley had planned to start his new job in Kenya. He'd flown in from London the night before, and was about to retire for the evening when his mobile phone rang. On the end of the line was a junior colleague from the heart surgery ward at Nairobi's Aga Khan Hospital, his new employers.

'We have a patient with a ruptured aorta who has had a Type A dissection,' the voice at the end of the phone said. 'Can you come in?'

There were two kinds of ruptured aorta, Type A and Type B. Type B was a minor tear in the body's main artery as it led downstream from the heart. It was manageable by slowly reducing a patient's blood pressure. Type A was a major rupture much closer to the heart, requiring major surgery immediately. For every hour that surgery was delayed, the mortality rate grew. It was the difference between a dripping tap and a burst water main.

Jutley already knew that nobody else at the Aga Khan would be able to deal with it. That was why he was there – to start a new centre of excellence for heart surgery. His family had been born here, part of Kenya's East African Asian community. After training in Britain, he wanted to give something back. Still, he could have done without this as his first call out. Type A surgery was notoriously difficult at the best of times, never mind when jetlagged. It involved repairing ultra-thin artery walls, a task rather like stitching together pieces of half-melted cheese. With the best will in the world, the chances were that his very first Type A patient here was going to die under his knife.

He'd done several Type As before at his old hospital back in Nottingham, with better survival rates than expected. Tonight, though, he'd be operating in Kenya, not Britain. Even though the Aga Khan was the best private hospital in Nairobi, he'd have only a fraction of the equipment available back in Britain, limited blood supplies, no fancy tissue glues available and no complex blood products for stemming bleeding. None of the hi-tech monitoring machines for measuring the patient's condition, and a team of new and entirely untested colleagues.

By midnight, as crowds of Steed's friends gathered at the hospital to donate blood, Jutley and his new team scrubbed up. The patient was wheeled in: a Brit in late middle age, balding with grey hair; slightly overweight; high blood pressure, according to his medical records. Some UN type, apparently; he had collapsed at a business lunch, would have died on the spot, had he not been with two FBI men who'd driven him straight to the Aga Khan.

Jutley levered the patient's ribcage apart to get at the aorta. It was pulsating and paper thin. The slightest misplaced touch and it would blow at high pressure. It would all be over before he could even curse. He placed the patient on a heart and lung machine to take over the function of both organs. Then he cut open a femoral artery. He'd use that, rather than the ruptured aorta, as the route to pump blood back into the patient's heart. A bypass, a temporary re-plumbing of the body.

After seven hours of cutting, stitching and clamping, Jutley had repaired the ruptured aorta and replaced it with a Teflon-coated tube. He'd also managed to repair the heart valve, which had been millimetres away from irreparable damage. As dawn broke, he released the clamp holding the tube in place, watching anxiously as the blood began to flow again. It held firm. The patient was wheeled off to intensive care, occasionally moving his head. That was good, a sign he'd probably suffered no brain damage.

Before the operation, Jutley had warned the well-wishers outside that the patient had only a one in five chance of survival. According to his new colleagues, every other patient who'd had a Type A at the Aga Khan had died. When Type A operations were successful, though, the prospects were good. Long-term, the surgery would actually make the patient's heart stronger, as long as he took things easy. Nothing that got the blood pressure up.

Chapter 15

'PROJECT BENEDICT'

Nairobi, September 2013

'Mr John, welcome back! How is everything? We heard what happened and we were so worried about you! Are you better now?'

Awale, the pirate negotiator, greeted Steed like an old friend. Perhaps in Somalia, a brush with death earned you a bit of respect.

'I am okay, thank you, Awale. Getting better slowly! And how are you? Are you still in touch with the pirates holding the *Albedo* crew?'

'Of course! They have been asking after you. They were worried for you too!'

Were they? That probably wasn't a good sign. During his absence, Steed's colleague, Leo Hoy-Carrasco, had taken over the talks. He'd re-iterated very firmly that the UN could not pay ransom money. Perhaps the pirates thought Steed was a softer touch. Still, at least someone was glad to hear he'd returned to work. Many friends and colleagues had thought he was mad, especially if he was going to get involved in hostage negotiations. Some were convinced that that was why he'd had a heart rupture in the first place.

He could see their point. When he'd come out of the hospital, he'd been confined to a wheelchair, so weak he couldn't even raise his arms. His own face in the mirror frightened him. His skin was grey, and he looked older and frailer. Psychologically, too, he felt fragile.

Still, it didn't feel right to sit around moping. Not when he'd been so lucky to avoid dying, and not with those poor bastards from the *Albedo* still captive. He wasn't religious, but it was hard not to feel that he'd been given a second lease of life for a reason. He hadn't said that to anyone, of course – the last thing he needed was people thinking he had a Messiah complex – but the more he'd thought about it, the more he'd become set on getting back to the rescue mission. As it turned out, it had been the perfect motivator to get back on his feet. The rehab had been extremely tough: first a course of acupuncture to get his arms functioning, then long rounds in the gym at the bottom of his apartment block, just to regain basic mobility. Endless sit-ups, weights, crunches, then walking and finally gentle jogging.

At times he'd been in tears of pain, and had only got through it thanks to his trainer, a stern young Kenyan who'd drilled him as unmercifully as his instructors at Sandhurst. Within a month, he'd been back on his feet.

Steed's conversations with Awale took place from the new 'operations room' he'd set up for the Hostage Support Programme. It wasn't as grand as it sounded, it was the spare room in his apartment, where he had a cheap leather armchair, a laptop, and a couple of mobiles. His contract with the UN had expired back in the summer, and as a result of his heart condition, he could no longer pass the medical to be re-employed as a staff member. So he was now running the hostage support programme in a consultant capacity.

This was a polite way of saying he was on his own. The UN was quietly paying him a modest stipend, and allowing him to draw on help from Alan Cole and Leo Hoy-Carrasco, his two UN colleagues, but if his talks to free the *Albedo* hostages went wrong for some reason, he'd be a 'deniable' operation from the UN's point of view. Just some retired old diplomat, who'd meant well but had got in beyond his depth – maybe lost his judgement a bit after that heart attack.

Being distanced from the UN, though, gave him the freedom to mention the one thing that the UN could not – money. It was now clear that the pirates were never going to give up the hostages for free. Pretending otherwise was just prolonging their agony. So, having got past the pleasantries with Awale, Steed cut to business.

'Awale, as you know, I can't pay any kind of ransom. But what if I could find someone who could pay something towards the pirates' expenses? Would that help?'

It was a ransom in all but name, of course. Whatever way one dressed it up, paying pirates' 'expenses' was still paying money to criminals. But if that was what it took to get the *Albedo* crew freed, so be it. And Steed now had a source of cash.

A few days before, he'd been in talks with the Maritime Piracy Humanitarian Response Programme, the sailor's welfare charity that had done the appeal for the *Albedo*. It turned out they already had a small contingency fund ready for just this kind of case. It had been gathered as an 'expenses' payment for the *Iceberg 1*, the other 'forgotten' ship that had been held for three years and then rescued by the Puntland Maritime Police Force. Because the *Iceberg 1* had been freed by force, the expenses money had never been paid to the pirates.

The cash had been raised via a secret whip-round among various big firms in international shipping. The plight of vessels like the *Iceberg 1* were not their responsibility, but as the socially-responsible face of the industry, it was hard just to abandon the crews to their fates. For the *Iceberg 1*, the donors had pledged a total of $200,000 in the event that an 'expenses only' deal could be reached. The charity told Steed that if he could reach a similar agreement for the *Albedo*, the cash was his.

Two-hundred-thousand dollars was far short of the millions the pirates had dreamed of. It might, though, allow them to cut their losses and run. Still, the prospect of talking money with the pirates made Steed nervous. It was one thing playing the high-minded UN type, pleading for a release on humanitarian grounds. Once you started waving cash around, you were playing the pirates at their own game, and that was when things got rough. What if they jacked up their demands and used scare tactics? What if they executed another prisoner? How would his patched-up heart cope with the stress of that?

There were logistical questions too. Assuming he could strike a deal, how did he get the money to the pirates? How did he ensure they kept their word? And how did he get the sailors safely out of a town like Camara, in the heart of pirate turf, without someone else kidnapping them again? It would be hard enough even if he was still at the Foreign Office, with the might of government behind him. Still, if he didn't try to help, who else would? The *Albedo*'s owners had gone to ground, the UN couldn't get officially involved, and nobody was going to send in troops to the rescue. It was him, or nothing.

Awale promised to put Steed's 'expenses' proposal to the pirates. After the phone call ended, Steed got slowly to his feet, shuffled over to the bookshelf, and took down *Pirates: A Worldwide Illustrated History*, a retirement gift from pals in the British embassy's Defence Section. He'd worked with them on getting a legal memorandum so that pirates captured by the Royal Navy could be handed over to Kenyan courts. It had been a very small victory in an otherwise unwinnable war, something his pals had noted in a cartoon they'd stuck in the book's sleeve. It showed a boatload of pirates with their hands raised in mock surrender. A thought bubble read: *'Give up lads, it's John Steed and the Defence Section. They've got a memorandum!'*

He picked a page from the book at random. It was about an obscure pirate called Benedict. Then he went back to his desk, took out the file he'd started on the *Albedo*, and wrote on it 'Project Benedict'. Now that his mission was sailing into murky waters, it somehow felt right to give it a codename. Hopefully, nobody would realise that the mission's leader got his inspiration from pirate picture books.

Camara, Somalia, November 2013.

'Two-hundred-thousand dollars? That's all he can offer? Who does this Mr John think we are? Beggars?'

'It is all we are going to get, my friend. We should take it.'

'Never. What is that Awale playing at? He is supposed to be a decent negotiator! If he shows his face round here, we should kill him.'

'Project Benedict' had not gone down well at the Somali end. Steed had done his best to manage expectations, telling Awale that he'd found an unnamed 'charity' that had agreed to help. He'd declined to say who it was, to stop Awale doing a Google search on them for an assets assessment, but said they'd managed to raise $200,000.

In Camara, the pirates invited the shareholders in the *Albedo* hijacking to discuss the offer. Merchants, elders, creditors and other concerned parties all turned up. It was like a board meeting anywhere in the world, only with khat and guns. Aman was also brought along, as proof of the assets on the balance sheet and as spokesman for the hostages.

The atmosphere was tense. The new guards that Arro had hired, who were led by a junior commander called Miro, were fed up. They'd been looking after the hostages for nearly three months now, and were beginning to fear there was going to be no big pay-out. Miro complained that some of his men hadn't even been paid for the work they'd already done. If they'd known the *Albedo* was a floating junk bond in the first place, they'd never have got involved. They wanted to accept the $200,000. It was a decent cut-and-run offer, the best that could be salvaged from a bankrupt deal.

Like all bankruptcy proceedings, though, the major investors stood to lose most. Arro and several other big players wanted to hold out for more. Tempers grew heated. Sharp words were exchanged between Miro and the guards, dozens of khat-loosened tongues jabbering at once. Several of the guards got up and walked out, cursing. All eyes fell on Miro.

Was he going to let his men mutiny, or bring them into line? Arro made his mind up for him. She got up, pulled her pistol from her burka, and put it at his head.

'We have invested $500,000 in this ship!' she screamed. 'Do what I have paid you to do! The crew is there, do whatever you have to do to get my money back! Torture them, fuck them, I really don't care!'

Miro glowered back. Backing up the authority of Arro's pistol, he knew, was other financial muscle from around town. If he defied them, he'd have to leave Camara.

After the meeting, Arro went to the hostages' compound.

'The offer of $200,000 is not accepted,' she told them. 'And the guards here are going to be replaced, by the ones who guarded you when you were on your ship.'

Aman fell at her feet. It was time to grovel. He stared up at her beseechingly, trying to remind her of her own son again.

'Arro, you have looked after us so well, but are you not a mother yourself? Then you must know how my own mother feels! From where will she find $500,000? Please let us go!'

'Aman, you are a stranger, and I gave you food and khat. For that I don't mind. But I have paid good money on this investment. That is all I care about.'

A few days later, the old *Albedo* guards were back. Aman had managed to get on reasonable terms with some of them, but others were faces he'd never wanted to see again. Like that arrogant interpreter, Ali Jabeen, and that madman Ali Inke, the one who'd shot Rajoo.

Inke wandered in, looked at the hostages without nodding, then pulled the magazine out of his AK-47. He walked over to Aman.

'Here, India boy,' he said. 'Clean my weapon.'

Aman Kumar Sharma in
sailor's uniform.
Aman Kumar Sharma

Aman Kumar Sharma with pirate guard.
Aman Kumar Sharma

John Steed in his days
as military attaché.
John Steed

The *Albedo*.
EUNAVFOR

The *Naham 3*
off the coast of
Somalia.
EUNAVFOR

Naham 3 proof of life
photograph. Each sailor
holds up a paper showing
a security code.
Oceans Beyond Piracy

The *Albedo* after sinking.
EUNAVFOR

The *Albedo* after sinking, with the *Naham 3* nearby.
EUNAVFOR

The $13 million taken out by Richard Neylon in 2013, in the bank vault with copies of *Die Welte*, the *Daily Telegraph* and *Le Monde*.
Richard Neylon

The convoy used by Omar Sheikh Ali to pick up the *Albedo* hostages.

Omar Sheikh Ali

The *Albedo* sailors immediately after being rescued
by Omar Sheikh Ali (in blue baseball cap).

Omar Sheikh Ali

The *Albedo* sailors have a post-release meal at their hotel in Galkayo, Somalia.   *Omar Sheikh Ali*

From Kenya, the freed sailors of the *Albedo* sent a thank-you note to Leslie Edwards.   *John Steed*

Crew of the *Prantalay 12* being flown from Somalia to Kenya. Captain Channarong Navara is second from left.

John Steed

Chapter 16

'CAPTAIN BIRDSEYE'

Nairobi, January 2014

For the first time Steed could remember, Awale sounded less than cheerful.

'Mr John, they shot at me! *They shot at me!* Those stupid bandits! I could have been killed!'

It was all Steed's fault – in Awale's view anyway. After the pirates had rejected the $200,000 offer for the *Albedo* crew, Steed had asked him to try to restart negotiations. He'd wired Awale $200 in travel expenses out of his own pocket, so he could visit Camara himself and speak to them face to face. The personal touch, as it were. Unfortunately, there were limits even to Awale's powers of persuasion. The pirates told him he was a time-waster and a charlatan. All slick talk and nothing else. When he'd tried to reason with them, they'd pulled their guns. Whether they'd really tried to kill him, or simply fired off a few warning shots by way of goodbye, Steed didn't know. He didn't want to know either. He brought the conversation to a close before Awale could demand any danger money.

He slumped back in his office chair. He fought the urge to go the kitchen and pour himself a large glass of wine. That was one part of his doctor's advice he was trying to stick to.

Besides, if he had a drink every time he felt stressed, he'd be permanently drunk.

It was January 2014, midsummer in Kenya. Outside his apartment block, children were playing in the late evening. Normally this was his favourite time of year. Now, though, the changing seasons were a reminder of the glacial pace of 'Project Benedict'. When he'd first got in touch with the *Albedo* pirates the previous July, he'd expected to have the crew out within a matter of weeks.. Now it was past New Year, and he'd still got no further, and that was just 'Project Benedict'. The other two hijacked ships, the *Prantalay 12* and the *Naham 3*, he'd barely had time to look into. He'd assumed, naively, that he could work on freeing all three ships simultaneously. In practice, just working on the *Albedo* case had taken up nearly all his waking hours.

Over the festive period, he'd tried to take time off. It hadn't helped. Every hour spent watching TV or reading a book felt like an extra hour in which the hostages were suffering. The MPHRP, the sailors' welfare charity, had told him that on New Year's Eve, the pirates had called Aman's parents in India and put him on the line. The pirates had been torturing him again, he'd said. They wanted to know if the family had raised any cash. There'd been similar phone calls from Aman the year before, during a previous round of torture sessions, but back then he'd sounded calm, telling his parents to be brave. This time he'd yelled and cursed, asking why the hell they couldn't raise the money. Aman's mother had been taken ill with the stress.

Steed had hoped that as time went on, he would have got extra funding and staff for the 'operations room', and perhaps even a proper office. There no longer seemed much chance of that. The UN high command were already uneasy about a newspaper interview he'd given about his mission to rescue the *Albedo*, in response to growing curiosity from the Nairobi press pack. Some at the UN felt he'd given the impression that the organisation itself was involved in ransom negotiations. Others thought he was trying to hog the limelight, and to underplay the UN's discreet role in supporting him. There was no pleasing some people. Yet he'd agreed to the interview for a reason. By publicising the mission, he was hoping that some wealthy benefactor might come forward with an offer of money. And just before Christmas, one had.

Out of the blue, he'd received an email from one Paul Muller, a German sea captain.* The name sounded vaguely familiar, and Muller mentioned that they'd met at a function a decade ago, when Steed was British military attaché in Dublin – some Anglo-German memorial for seamen killed in the Second World War. It had just been canapé chat, and what Muller actually did for a living, Steed couldn't remember. All he could recall was a big, bear-like man, with a thick white beard, a regular face on the function circuit. People joked that he looked like 'Captain Birdseye', the hearty sea captain who fronted adverts for fish fingers in Britain.

Right now, though, Captain Birdseye had a very serious offer to make. He'd read Steed's newspaper interview about the hostages' plight. He had some contacts in a German seafarers' union in Kiel, the Baltic seaport city where he'd grown up. If Steed still needed money to secure the sailors' freedom, they'd be willing to help out.

Steed had rung Muller expecting to be offered just a few thousand dollars. To his astonishment, Muller had said

---

* Not his real name.

they could go to anything up to $900,000. Steed had almost cried when he'd put the phone down. It was still short of the $1.5 million that the pirates wanted, but a big improvement on his previous offer of $200,000. With a bit of bargaining, that would be enough, surely, to get a deal.

As of yet, he'd told nobody else about Muller's offer, not even Awale. He'd wanted him to gauge the mood in Camara first. With hindsight, though, sending Awale up there without any new money to put on the table had been a mistake. There was now little prospect of Awale ever being trusted there again, and getting a new negotiator – someone *he* could trust, or at least not distrust – wasn't going to be easy. They didn't exactly advertise their services.

As ever, it was one step back for every step forward. Without a reliable go-between to the pirates, it would be unwise to attempt any deal. Then, on 26 January, a text message arrived.

'My name is Ali Jabeen. I am now in charge of negotiations for the Albedo crew. Deal with me only. Not that negotiator Awale. We will not work with him again. He asked for too much money for himself.'

Steed hadn't spoken to Jabeen before, but he knew the name. Awale had mentioned him – the translator who'd come on board the *Albedo* with the original hijacking team. Even Awale seemed to speak of him with a certain wariness. Still, in a way this was good news. At last, he was dealing directly with the pirates, and not some middleman thinking only about his cut. In piracy negotiations, it really was all about the devil you knew.

He went to the kitchen. He was going to have that glass of wine anyway.

Chapter 17

THE GENTLEMAN
AMATEUR

London, December 2013

Buried underneath the office blocks of London's financial Square Mile are a number of high-security private bank vaults. In an age of electronic banking, they are a throwback to the past, containing hundreds of millions of dollars – and any other currency you could need – in ready cash, most of it in $100 bills. It's there, ready to be dished out to banks, casinos, bureaux de change, passing cruise ships, passing oligarchs, and anyone else who needs a few million quick.

In early 2013, one such bank vault near Tower Bridge received a client who took out $13 million in a single visit. Piled up in shrink-wrapped bricks of $100 bills, the lump of cash was as big as a small settee. The size of the withdrawal was not the only remarkable thing. After counting the cash, the client placed copies of that day's *Daily Telegraph*, *Le Monde* and *Die Welte* in front of it and took a photograph on his smartphone, making sure both the date and the headlines were clearly visible. As seen in countless TV kidnap dramas, he was using the newspaper as a date stamp – although in this case, it wasn't held up by a hostage, but wedged between a metre-high pile of money.

The client, Richard Neylon, was a lawyer with Holman Fenwick Willan, a City of London legal firm. They were one of a cluster of maritime law specialists based around Tower Bridge, a legacy from when the Thames was still a proper working river, and Britain the pre-eminent seafaring power. Neylon was one of the firm's crisis-response specialists, and was on call for maritime emergencies 24/7. That could be anything from a ship sinking with all hands through to an oil slick causing an environmental disaster, or so it had been in quieter, easier times. Since 2008, when Somali pirates began hijacking ships in droves, much of his work had been in securing the release of hijacked ships and crews. He would oversee the organising and delivery of the ransom payments, and deal with the many legal and logistical hurdles it threw up.

The $13 million he had withdrawn from the bank vault was a case in point. It was a ransom payment to release a hijacked ship, agreed after months of negotiations. Just as the exchange was about to go ahead, a bureaucratic hold-up at the London end had delayed the payment. The pirates, already on edge, had accused the ship owners of never intending to pay the money in the first place, and of trying to cheat on the deal. To regain their trust, Neylon had to offer proof that the money had been there all along, ready for delivery at the time they had originally promised it. Hence the photo of the *Telegraph* alongside the cash, which he emailed to the pirates later that day.

The hijackers weren't the only people that Neylon had to reassure. Anyone who tried to ship several million dollars through a British airport would get stopped by police or Customs unless they had appropriate legal paperwork on them. Once in transit, there was also a risk that the cash might get stolen, confiscated or swiped by corrupt border officials. It wasn't the kind of thing that the average high-street bank manager knew how to do. So as time went on, Neylon and his colleague James Gosling had become two of the very few 'go-to' operators. Not surprisingly, ship owners about to despatch millions of dollars to Somalia tended to prefer people who'd done the job before, and who could ensure it was all above board.

As lawyers, Neylon and Gosling were the centre point in any case, liaising with the owners, negotiators, insurance companies and crews. Much of the work was nothing to do with actual shipping law. After hijacks were resolved, Neylon would often act as an unofficial sailors' welfare officer, meeting the ships when they limped back into port. He'd arrange hotels, pocket money, doctors and trauma therapists. On one occasion, a ship's captain asked him to dispose of a rocket-propelled grenade that the pirates had left behind.

Both Neylon and Gosling were well aware that paying ransoms was controversial. Critics said it risked simply encouraging the pirates even more, which the lawyers did not dispute. Otherwise, they wouldn't be delivering jackpot-sized ransoms of $10 million. But what was the alternative? In Somalia, there was no proper police force or navy. The odds favoured the villains, not the good guys. It was all very well arguing that ransoms should not be paid on moral grounds, but in the meantime, what was a ship owner supposed to say to the kidnapped sailors and their distraught families? When you took the hostages' dependents into account as well, you were sometimes talking about the welfare of hundreds of people.

By 2013, Neylon and Gosling had handled about 100 piracy cases, securing the freedom of around 1,750 hijacked sailors. Neylon made numerous huge withdrawals from bank vaults around the City, usually in dollars, the pirates' preferred choice of currency. Even with a money counting machine, a big ransom could take most of a morning to count out. The real smell of money, he noticed, was not particularly sweet. Piles of brand-new dollar bills had a distinctive mildewed aroma, said to be from a secret security ink used by the US Federal Reserve. When he left the vault, his hands and clothes would have a fragrance not unlike stale parmesan cheese.

The $10 million Neylon withdrew from the vault was for a ransom for a ship hijacked in 2012. It was one of the biggest hijack payments on record – and also one of the last, for the pirates had become victims of their own greed. Fed up with paying out such vast sums, insurers had finally overcome their reservations about deploying armed guards on ships. From 2012 onwards, most commercial freighters began to resemble floating fortresses. If it came to a gun battle, a skiff of pirates bouncing on the waves were no match for a team of ex-Royal Marines in a decktop machinegun nest. Successful hijacks all but stopped, and as 2013 came to an end, Neylon and Gosling were looking forward to their first uninterrupted Christmas in five years.

Then Gosling got a call from Alan Cole, John Steed's colleague at the UN. Cole, who was a lawyer himself by training, had met Gosling at an anti-piracy law conference. He had a favour to ask. Had Gosling heard about this retired British colonel who was trying to free some hostages stuck in limbo? Something of a gentleman amateur, a bit out of his depth, you might say. Could Gosling and Neylon help?

Cole had known Steed for years. Outside the UN, they often socialised together, and as both a colleague and a friend, Cole was worried that Steed was pushing himself far too hard. As the person who'd scribbled down Steed's last will and testament in the hospital, Cole knew how close he'd been to death. Now, a mere three months later, he saw Steed working flat out on the rescue mission. It was a noble cause, sure, but hardly suited to someone in convalescence. It was all very well for Steed to say that if he didn't help these crews, nobody else would, but he'd be no use to anyone if his heart gave out again.

Cole also wondered how much Steed knew about the legal side of paying ransoms. If he wasn't careful, he'd get himself in trouble with the Kenyan police. Perhaps Gosling and Neylon could at least advise him on how to stay out of jail. The lawyers agreed to help for free. They'd done pro bono work in piracy cases in the past, mostly involving private individuals who couldn't afford the services of negotiators and lawyers. Their firm had clocked up a lot of billable hours from big shipping firms as a result of the piracy crisis, and the pro bono work was a way of giving something back. Besides, like Steed, they'd once been newcomers to the piracy game themselves. Gosling still remembered his first ever hijacking case back in 2005, when a client had rung to say his ship had been captured off the Somali coast. It was the first piracy case that his firm had had since it was founded in the 19th century, and it put him and Neylon on a steep learning curve. For a start, was it even legal to pay ransoms?

That was one question they could answer for themselves. Their research took them into arcane areas of the law, starting with the Ransom Act of 1782. That prohibited the payment of ransoms for 'ships or vessels captured from His Majesty's subjects'. But that had long been repealed. As things stood, it was legal to pay ransoms, as long as the money was going to criminal groups rather than terrorists.

Having satisfied themselves that neither they nor their clients' cash would end up under lock and key, the lawyers had to work out how to get the money transferred to Somalia. The professional negotiator they had hired to reach the deal with the pirates had never done a ransom delivery there, nor had anyone else that he knew of.

Eventually, the negotiator found an ex-SAS man who was willing to act as a courier. For £1,000 per day, he agreed to take the money in a backpack into Somalia from Kenya and hand it to a pirate intermediary. How exactly he did it, Gosling was never told, but after a three-day trek through the Somali bush, the cash was delivered, and the hostages released.

Since that first hijacking in 2005 – settled for a sum barely into six figures – Neylon and Gosling had mastered most of the legalities and logistics, but the process of actually negotiating with the pirates, and arguing over how much money to pay, was a different skill set entirely. For help there, Steed would need somebody else.

The lawyers approached Leslie Edwards, a professional negotiator who'd worked for them on previous piracy cases. An ex-army officer, Edwards had twenty years of experience as a kidnap response consultant, dealing with militias and warlords, gangsters and terrorists all over the world. He now ran his own firm, Compass Risk Management. Like most people in his line of work, Edwards was calm, pragmatic and good under pressure. He also had a sense of humour, and unlike many ex-army officers, wasn't a stickler for procedure. That, the lawyers figured, might just make him willing to babysit someone like Steed. Other negotiators they knew of wouldn't go near him.

It was clear to the lawyers that the 'gentleman amateur' was indeed out of his depth. He'd already told the pirates, apparently, that he now had $900,000 to offer. That was a mistake. The pirates would simply assume that if he could get that much, he could find the same amount again. A smart operator never revealed how much they really had. It wasn't a great starting point, and Edwards could easily have made his excuses, but he too had had a lot of business out of the piracy crisis, and was keen to give something back. He agreed to take a backseat role advising Steed on the dos and don'ts of negotiation.

First, he advised Steed to draw up a contract to be signed by both sides, promising to stick to any deal. It was a tactic he often used himself. While it might seem unlikely that pirates would respect a written agreement, it flattered their self-image as 'businessmen with guns'. Treating them like they were clients in a London shipping boardroom brought out their better nature, even if they couldn't be taken to court if they broke their word. Crucially, it also let Edwards nail down the precise amount to be paid, and how any exchange would be done – details the pirates sometimes tried to haggle over at the last moment. Edwards would type a contract up and email it to a pirate negotiator's mobile. He always made sure they signed a clause confirming themselves as 'men of honour', whose word could be trusted. They weren't, of course, but if they'd signed a piece of paper saying otherwise, they'd be less inclined to mess about. Hopefully.

Chapter 18

A LEAD-LINED SUITCASE

The Albedo *crew, Camara, Somalia, February 2014.*
Three years and three months into captivity

One morning, the *Albedo* crew noticed that the pirates were in a better mood than normal. Even Ali Inke seemed cheerful, a lopsided smile creasing his face in novel directions. The guards were waving a piece of paper and cheering, even though many of them couldn't read. Ali Jabeen, the interpreter, thrust the paper in front of Aman, along with a pen.

From Mr John Steed

This is to confirm my verbal agreement with the pirates of the Albedo *of Tuesday 12 February 2014.*

Please accept the compliments of the families of the MV Albedo *and my thanks to the investors and Mr Ali Jabeen.*

The seafarers' charities agree to pay the pirates $900,000 compensation for the release of the crew, under the following conditions.

1. This is the one and only payment the charities will make.

2. Each crew member must be able to call his family and confirm that he is in good health.

3. The pirates are men of honour. After the money is delivered, they must deliver the crew within four hours or so.

4. The charities will begin preparations for the delivery of the money from today, but please understand that it will take some time to prepare the funds.

5. Both pirates and hostages must sign this agreement.

If you agree to these terms, please sign and return.

Aman scribbled his signature at the bottom. Jabeen explained that this was to make the crew feel included as well. This had been at Mr John's insistence, he added, as if worried that Aman might think he had developed a caring side. Aman didn't really care if Jabeen cared. The point was, they might *finally be going home.* He wondered if his parents had been told yet.

Aman's parents hadn't yet been told of the deal. Nor, unfortunately, had the lawyers or Edwards. It had been some time since they'd heard from Steed at all. They'd expected him to tell them if he was closing to striking a deal, as there was all manner of paperwork to be done in advance. It wasn't just a matter of handing the cash over, there were legal frameworks to be drawn up, indemnities organised and letters of introduction to be prepared. Arrangements would also have to be made to turn Muller's $900,000 offer into cash and transfer it to Nairobi, no simple task. Steed had now agreed a handover date of 21 March, only a month away.

The lawyers and Edwards were taken by surprise when they were finally told, and not best pleased. It left a great deal of admin to be done in relatively little time. But postponing wouldn't go down well with the pirates. If everyone worked quickly, it could be done. Their first priority was the money. Edwards contacted Muller to help supervise the logistics of transferring his ransom cash. Muller's money was coming from two sources – a German seafaring union, and a German shipping conglomerate. Muller said the donors didn't want to be identified, but to comply with British money laundering regulations, the lawyers would need to know the exact sources of the cash. They also needed to get it to London to count and photograph it.

Muller, who was still living in Dublin, told Edwards that the money was currently in safekeeping in the city's German embassy, having been couriered from Germany in diplomatic bags. When Edwards offered to help him transfer it to London, he refused.

'I'm sorry, but the German Seafarers' Union only want the money to be handled by me,' he said.

Edwards pointed out that the clock was now ticking, and even once the money had arrived, there was the much more complicated task of getting it to Nairobi. Muller still refused. Edwards began to suspect that the idea of playing the knight in shining armour had gone to his head. Steed had warned Edwards that Muller was rather egotistical, forever name-dropping, boasting about contacts in the German secret service and so on. Still, Edwards dared not upset him. He didn't want the chief donor pulling out in a huff.

'Listen, Mr Muller, I do actually need to see the money, just so we can at least check it's all there,' Edwards said. 'Why don't I fly over to Dublin and then we can visit the embassy together?'

'No need to do that, I can get the money to London myself no problem.'

'Are you sure? Moving that kind of money across borders isn't that easy, you know. It could end up getting confiscated.'

'Okay, in that case, I'll drive it up myself from Dublin across the border to Northern Ireland. Then I'll fly it from there. There are no proper Customs checks on the flights to London.'

'I wouldn't do that either. They will still screen your bags at the airport.'

'Fine, I'll get the money put in a lead-lined suitcase. That'll stop the airport X-ray machines seeing it.'

A lead-lined suitcase? Muller had clearly been watching too many B-movies. Only an idiot would think that that would fool modern-day airport security. Plus, a lead-lined suitcase big enough to carry $900,000 would probably be far too heavy to carry by hand. Then, suddenly, it hit him. Why was Muller being so cagey about where the money had come from? Why wouldn't he let anyone near it? And why this cloak-and-dagger briefcase plan? A plan which only a fantasist would come up with? Might that be what Muller was? A fantasist? A Walter Mitty? It would explain quite a lot. All the evasiveness, all the prevaricating, and all the bullshit talk of friends in high places.

Edwards knew colleagues who'd run into these kinds of people. They were drawn like moths to the world of kidnap negotiations, because of its air of mystique, and the opportunities it allowed for posing as international men of mystery. Edwards rang Steed.

'I hate to say this, but I'm worried about this guy Muller. I fear he may be a fantasist or a fraudster or some sort.'

'Eh? How do you mean?'

'Well, every time I've phoned him, he's been evasive about where he's getting the money from, and how he's going to get it to us. Then today, he's come up with this idea of bringing the money in a lead-lined suitcase. Total fantasy stuff.

'Er ... are you sure?

'Well, we've been asking him to give us the cash for weeks now, and every time, he's given different excuses. And now this suitcase bullshit. I might be wrong, but I think something is up.'

'Oh my God, please, no ...'

'Look, we can't take his word for any of this any more. He gave you the name of that German Seafarer's Union that's donating the money, didn't he? Did you check him out with them at some point?

'Er, no. No, I didn't. Never even crossed my mind.'

'Ah. Well, it's easy for me to say this with hindsight, but that would have been a good idea. Always verify the sources of the cash.'

'Shit, I just took him at face value. When he was cagey about who the donors were, I thought it was just because they wanted things kept quiet. It didn't occur to me to ask too many questions. I guess I was just desperate to find anyone who could help.'

'Well, check with them, but I'd assume the worst. If this guy was genuine, we'd have the money by now.'

'What are we going to tell the pirates? They'll go mad, won't they?

'Look, I don't like saying this, but yes, this is pretty serious. One of the key rules is never to offer money you don't have. This could start them killing the hostages again.'

Edwards' hunch about Muller proved correct. The German Seafarers Union confirmed they had made no such pledges to him. Muller, meanwhile, stopped returning calls. There was no money. There was no secret benefactor. Indeed, there was probably no such person as 'Captain' Muller at all.

Belatedly, Steed began trying to find who he really was. He wasn't just a Walter Mitty, he was a prolific conman. Steed got in touch with a German journalist that he knew. It turned out that Muller had been doing the rounds of Germany's TV channels, offering to sell them an exclusive on his remarkable mercy mission to save the *Albedo* – all about the brave German sea captain and his British colonel pal who were raising money for Somalia's forgotten hostages. He'd even claimed that he would pilot the plane that would do the ransom drop.

One TV channel, which had covered Somali piracy cases before, had thought it all sounded rather too good to be true, but another had fallen for it. They'd recorded an interview with Muller on the bridge of a ship in Kiel docks, clad in a captain's uniform. It wasn't clear where he'd got the uniform from, or whose ship he was on, but he certainly talked a fine game. Staring purposefully out to sea, he spoke eloquently about the need to save the *Albedo* crew before it was too late.

He made good TV. Clearly, TV channels in search of scoops were just as easily fooled as amateur hostage negotiators in search of donors. One German journalist told Steed that Muller had been dropping his name into his spiel, describing him as 'a high-ranking British military contact'. They'd met in Ireland at the height of The Troubles, apparently, when Muller was working on a sensitive counter-espionage mission.

'Why did none of these people he approached in Germany ever call me to check any of this?' Steed asked the journalist.

'He said you were very busy working on the case and couldn't be disturbed. But he had a document with your name on. A kind of contract that you had written up with the pirates, agreeing to pay them $900,000.'

How had Muller got hold of the contract? Then he remembered – he'd sent it to Muller himself, to prove to would-be donors that the whole thing was genuine. That would explain a lot. Muller was presumably waving the contract around to get money out of people, money he no doubt intended to keep. Using the name of Colonel John Steed (rtd), ex-military attaché to Her Majesty's Government, to make it all look respectable.

Steed's humiliation was complete. To their credit, the TV crew who had filmed Muller had eventually got suspicious and pulled the interview from broadcast. Steed, on the other hand, had never suspected a thing. He'd fallen for it completely. Muller's bluff seadog persona now seemed almost like a deliberate piss-take, as if to test how gullible he could be. Captain bloody Birdseye indeed.

The only consolation was that Steed was by no means Muller's only victim. Indeed, it seemed he'd been deceived by an absolute master of the game. Another German reporter got in touch, who was making a documentary exposing all Muller's different cons over the years. He seemed fond of casting himself as a man of action, working in the shadows to expose injustice, and his exploits seemed endless: he'd been a mercenary during the Angolan civil war, where he'd come across Russian-backed units using banned weapons; he'd discovered a factory in Germany that was selling illegal arms to Iran; he had inside information on a scandal involving a senior German politician and he was an agent for German intelligence, with high-level contacts in the CIA, and MI6.

German police would later issue an arrest warrant for Muller on suspicion of multiple counts of fraud. No action could be taken over his involvement with Steed, as it couldn't be proved that he'd made any money through it. The German police seemed to be playing a somewhat belated game of catch-up. An informal 'wanted' notice was already hung on the wall of a pub Muller frequented in Ireland. Someone he'd scammed had printed out a picture of him with the words 'Wanted – dead or alive. €5,500.' Steed would have happily obliged on either count. How could anyone be so callous as to exploit the plight of the *Albedo* sailors for their own ends?

'I swear I will kill Muller if I ever see him,' he told Edwards. 'Words cannot describe how fucking angry I am. He's put the crew's lives at risk. It's despicable.'

Steed also wondered how he was going to explain it to the UN. To his mind, the main reason he'd been taken in by the scam was because he'd met Muller before during his days in Ireland. Most people at embassy functions in Dublin weren't criminals or fraudsters. Just his luck to bump into Germany's most prolific conman over the canapés. Neither that excuse nor any other, though, would wash with the UN's high command. The way they'd see it, someone closely associated with the UN had agreed to pay a bunch of pirates $900,000 that he didn't even have. Pirates with a track record of killing hostages when things didn't go their way. This was why people had warned him not to get involved in negotiations in the first place.

Steed decided that he'd had enough. It had been six of the most exhausting, stressful months of his life, yet all he'd done was give false hopes to the very people he was trying to help, and put their lives at even greater risk. As well as making himself look like a naive, meddlesome fool. He was best out of it. He'd try to find someone else to take over. It was clearly a job for a professional – maybe Edwards would do it?

Edwards refused. Giving occasional advice to Steed was one thing, taking the lead was another. The *Albedo* case was now more of a mess than ever. Getting involved would carry serious reputational risk. There was a dark joke in his profession, about what could happen if a job went badly wrong. While the hostages could get fucked only once, the joke went, your reputation was fucked forever. Edwards prided himself on having never messed up a case in his entire career. He didn't want to start now.

'I understand,' said Steed, when Edwards told him. 'I'll find someone else, don't worry.'

But Edwards did worry. He doubted Steed would find another negotiator to help – anyone who agreed was probably best avoided. The industry had its share of hucksters, people no better qualified to run a kidnap negotiation than

Captain Muller was to run a ship. If Steed got as desperate to find a negotiator as he'd been to find a donor, he might just pick such a person.

Edwards always kept an emotional distance from his work. Families often thought the world of him after he'd secured their loved ones' lives, but since it usually involved paying large amounts of cash to criminals, he'd never regarded himself as any kind of saint. He was a professional, doing a job, for which he was well paid. He was not a do-gooder. Willing as he was to do some pro bono work, his charitable instincts had a limit. Getting more closely involved with the *Albedo* case right now, with no money to negotiate with and a bunch of very pissed off pirates, was madness. But could he really leave Steed on his own? It was obvious that if Steed couldn't find anyone to take over, he'd just carry on with the mission himself. He was obsessed with it. To his credit, if he hadn't been, he'd never have got this far. And yet there was no way, *no way on earth*, that Steed was match-fit to handle kidnap negotiations on his own.

It was all very well to argue that the stress was mental rather than physical, but in Edwards' experience, it could be both. He'd once suffered chest pains himself while on a very difficult job, and had thought he was having a heart attack. A GP had later told him he was fine, and explained that pro-longed, acute anxiety could produce stress hormones with physical symptoms. He'd never had it again, yet it showed, surely, that this kind of work was, quite literally, not for the faint-hearted. A few days' later, Edwards rang Steed back.

'Okay, I've changed my mind,' he said. 'I'll work with you. We'll sort this out together.'

'Eh? Are you sure? What's made you change your mind?'

'I'm not quite sure. But believe me, I'm not doing it out of the kindness of my heart.'

'No?'

'Not my style. Somewhere deep down, there might be a humanitarian imperative, but no, that's not it. It's for the same reason as you – if I don't do it, then nobody else bloody will, will they? But there's one thing I need you to do first.'

'Yes, of course. What?'

'You need to break it to the pirates that we've got no money. The sooner we tell them, the better. Just be honest. Tell them you got ripped off.'

'Sure. But is it best that I do it, rather than you? I'm worried about making a mess of things again. Won't you be better at it?'

'If I'm going to be taking over from here, I don't want that to be the first thing I have to tell them.'

Besides, he felt like adding. *This is your mess. You can sort this bit out yourself.*

⚓

On 24 April 2014, Steed broke the news of Muller's deception to the pirates. They called Steed a liar, vowed never to speak to him again, and gave a few of the crew a beating. But there were no executions, no serious torture, and within a few days, the mood seemed back to its sullen norm.

'I thought they'd be angrier,' Steed told Edwards.

'So did I. Then again, pirates tend to be more forgiving on problems like fraud or robbery. That's stuff they can relate to. It's when you tell them that the ransom money has got delayed because of banking regulations in Europe that they tend to get angry. They have less experience of that kind of thing, so they think you're lying.'

'Really?'

'Yes. If you'd told them the cash had been confiscated by Customs at Heathrow, they'd probably be doing their nut.'

Chapter 19

'Not in My Children's Children's Lifetime'

Lincolnshire, March 2014

Few of Leslie Edwards' neighbours really knew what he did for a living. If anyone ever asked, his stock answer was that he worked in insurance, 'sorting out insurance problems around the world'. It was dull enough to make most people change the subject.

Discretion was paramount in his line of work. At home in Stamford, a Lincolnshire market town 90 minutes from London, he could pass himself off as just another commuter enjoying the country lifestyle. In his spare time he rowed with a boat club and went pheasant shooting, occasionally breaking off to take an urgent 'business call'. On long-running hostage cases, where you might hear nothing for months, there was no telling when the kidnappers would suddenly ring up – it was always best to answer. Hostage takers didn't always leave a number to call back on.

Edwards was part of a small fraternity of professional 'response consultants' retained by major insurance companies worldwide. He kept a passport on him at all times, ready to head anywhere at short notice. In his travel bag he kept several pairs of dark blue trousers and light blue shirts, to be worn in the same combination each day. The fewer decisions to be made on a job, the better.

There were probably no more than 50 people like Edwards worldwide. Most were retained by major insurers, who did not advertise the fact. Firms who paid for kidnap and ransom insurance cover weren't supposed to even tell their employees that they had it. The fear was that if an employee knew that they were insured for $10 million of ransom cover, they'd blurt this out the moment a kidnapper stuck a gun in their face. That would make it difficult for a negotiator like Edwards to bargain them down.

One of the walls in Edwards' office in Stamford was covered with newspaper clippings of his past cases, usually showing newly-released hostages grinning for the cameras. None made mention of Edwards himself, or the means by which he'd secured his clients' release.

Despite its low profile, the kidnap and ransom industry was booming. Until the 1990s, kidnapping hadn't been something the average Western traveller had to worry about, unless they did business in the likes of civil-war era Lebanon. All that changed with the collapse of the Soviet Union, which opened up vast new areas of the world to get into trouble in. Suddenly, insurance firms started getting calls from British and American businessmen who'd come unstuck in Moscow or Chechnya. In Latin America, revolutionary groups that had lost their Soviet paymasters needed new sources of funding – some turned to cocaine smuggling, others to kidnapping. By the mid-1990s, a passing knowledge of Spanish was all but essential for anyone in Edwards' trade.

While the negotiators tried to keep their work quiet, their exploits soon attracted the attention of Hollywood. *Proof of Life*, released in 2000, starred Russell Crowe as an ex-SAS man sent to negotiate the release of an oil executive in Colombia. Based on the true-life kidnapping of an American business-man, it was the public's first real glimpse into the ransom negotiation business. The film was a hit, though not for its accuracy. Every now and then, Edwards still found himself explaining to clients that he wasn't a real-life Russell Crowe. No, he wasn't ex-SAS, and, no, if all else failed, he wouldn't be grabbing an assault rifle and charging to the rescue himself, as Crowe did at the end of the film.

Instead, the qualities that Edwards prided himself on were more like those that made a good poker player: calm-ness under pressure, patience and a belief in making his own luck. While some of his colleagues did have Special Forces backgrounds, that was more to impress clients than anything else. Edwards himself had had a more conventional military career, reaching the rank of major in the Princess of Wales Royal Regiment and serving in Northern Ireland. When a colleague first recruited him to Saladin, a security firm that opened a kidnap response wing in the mid-90s, it had been mainly for his ability to speak Spanish.

He'd done a two-week training course at Saladin's offices in London, not expecting that someone with no experience would ever be brought in other than as a back-up man. Then, as he was celebrating his wife's birthday one May afternoon, he got a call at home in Lincolnshire. Could he get to Venezuela straightaway? He was on the plane that night.

The case involved a wealthy landowner's teenage daughter, abducted by a criminal gang. The kidnappers wanted several million dollars, a hopelessly unrealistic sum. Edwards planted an advert in a local newspaper saying the family were selling off their farm machinery, hoping the gang would infer that they were short of cash. The case had eventually been settled for $460,000, and the girl released unharmed. It wouldn't quite have made a script for *Proof of Life*, but Edwards was still on a high when he got back to Stamford seven weeks later. He'd found his vocation – a fascinating, exciting job, with a sense of achievement that Cold War soldiering never offered.

From then on, he'd taken nearly every case that came his way. It had sometimes been tough on his wife and children, especially when he'd abandoned family holidays to deploy at short notice, but the pay was good, and the work ever more plentiful.

He moved from Saladin to work for Clayton Consultants, a US kidnap response firm. Its founder, Thomas Clayton, had been the real-life negotiator in the case that *Proof of Life* was based on. His firm was now the in-house contractor for AIG, one of the world's biggest insurance companies. Working for them confirmed Edwards' reputation as a reliable operator. It also brought much more challenging assignments. The 9/11 attacks and the Iraq War led to a spike in abductions in the Middle East, where kidnap gangs made their point not with severed ears or fingers, but with severed heads.

One of Edwards' early cases was in Iraq in 2004, when Sunni Muslim insurgents were kidnapping foreigners to fund their fight against the US presence. One gang attacked a car carrying Turkish construction workers as they drove near Saddam Hussein's hometown of Tikrit, raking the Turks' vehicle with automatic gunfire to make them stop. Two days later, the kidnappers beheaded one of their two prisoners. By the time the hostages' employers engaged Edwards' services the following week, the gang had released footage of the killing on the internet. For the life of Abdurrahman Yildirim, the surviving hostage, they were demanding something that wasn't in Edwards' gift – the withdrawal of all foreign workers from Iraq.

'This guy is going to die,' Edwards thought as he touched down in Istanbul.

Edwards went to see Yildirim's mother, wondering how it would feel to have a case end in failure. She cut a sorry figure – a widow with five other children, for whom Yildirim was the main breadwinner. It gave Edwards an idea. If he felt sorry for her, the kidnappers might too. Two days later, pictures of her appeared in various Arab newspapers, begging the kidnappers to show mercy, and asking them to make contact. Every word of her heartfelt plea had been carefully scripted by Edwards, but it did the trick. The kidnappers got in touch, and straightaway he managed to turn the conversation to money. With the prospect of a ransom payment dangled in front of them, the kidnappers quickly forgot their political demands. They asked for $100,000, which Edwards negotiated down to $60,000, couriering the cash to Baghdad in a car driven by Yildirim's colleagues.

The kidnappers took Yildirim to their safe house in Baghdad, where he woke up the next morning to find his guards gone. He fled, unable to believe his luck. In the cuttings about the case on Edwards' wall in his office, Turkish newspapers speculated that his kidnappers had a flash of conscience and let him go. As ever, Edwards' role wasn't mentioned, yet it was one of his proudest cases – proof that if the right buttons were pressed, kidnappers who demanded blood could be persuaded to accept payment in cash. True, there was little doubt that the gang were terrorists rather than just criminals, and that made the ethical side of it even murkier than normal, but in the chaos of post-war Iraq, nobody asked too many questions.

What *was* important, in Edwards' view, was that a man who would otherwise almost certainly have died was still alive. Those who queried the morals of it hadn't sat in a room with Yildirim's mother.

Compared to dealing with terrorists in the Middle East, Edwards found Somali pirates fairly biddable characters. They didn't chop captives' heads off as an opening gambit, they didn't complicate matters by making political demands, and once a deal was reached, that was usually that. No tricks, no holding back one or two hostages in the hope of squeezing extra cash. It wasn't a question of clan honour, just shrewd business sense. They'd grasped that the way to get Western shipping firms to pay ransoms in the first place was to stick to their side of the bargain. If the firms could be confident that paying the ransom would yield the desired result, it became the path of least resistance.

Politicians sometimes criticised the shipping firms for being too ready to pay up. Yet in terms of shipping economics, paying a ransom was nearly always cheaper than trying to hold out. Any large vessel typically cost around $50,000 per day alone in terms of running costs, fuel, staff wages and so on. So a hijacker only had to hold onto a ship for around twenty days before the costs to the owner hit the $1 million mark, and that was before one even took into account things like penalties for late delivery of goods. The meter, in effect, was running from the moment the crew got taken. It was in everyone's interests – especially the owner's – to reach a deal quickly.

So effective was the pirates' business model that between 2010 and 2012, they were estimated to have extorted nearly $500 million in ransoms. Their success attracted interest from economists as well as law enforcement. The *Financial Times* and *Forbes Magazine* had fun with analysis pieces on how pirate economics worked. In 2010, students at Harvard Business School voted Somali piracy as their business model of the year. The 'businessmen with guns' image was even endorsed by a few ex-hostages. They'd recall chats over tea with their captors, who'd offer polite apologies for detaining them. *Nothing personal, you understand, just business. We Somalis are very poor – not even a government. This is our only way. Who knows, maybe one day we can be friends … Hey, do you have an email address?*

By the time Edwards came to work with Steed, he'd resolved a dozen Somali hijackings and one land-based kidnapping. He spent a lot of time reading about Somalia and studying the culture. Most kidnappers were by nature volatile, unpredictable people, but you could improve your odds against them by studying their psychology and personality. The more you knew, the easier it was to judge when to push and when to give.

This was especially true of Somali pirates. They were products of a shattered society, where trust was gone, and compassion was often seen as weakness. Understanding their mindset was hard for a Westerner. Prior to the piracy epidemic, Edwards had spent time working in Somalia, acting as a security consultant to foreign aid agencies, but there was always more to learn. In his office were books on Somali history and society. His favourite was Gerald Hanley's 1971 classic *Warriors: Life and Death Among the Somalis*.

Hanley had been stationed in Somalia as a British army officer during the Second World War. He'd been in command of a remote desert outpost, tasked with stopping inter-clan warfare. The mission was a thankless one, but it gave him insights into Somalia's tough warrior culture. It was a world of tribesmen who survived wounds that would kill most other men, where the idea of death before dishonour wasn't just an army motto. *Warriors* fell out of print, but was re-published in 2004, spurred by demand from a new generation of foreigners who were grappling with Somalia's problems, this time diplomats and aid workers. It mattered little that *Warriors* was based on the insights of a colonial foot soldier. In a country where life often seemed to have got worse rather than better, much of what Hanley had to say still seemed depressingly pertinent.

After five years of dealing with pirates, Edwards too had compiled his own field handbook to the Somali mindset, including a compilation of all the ruses pirates would use to drive a bargain. So far, he had 37, ranging from running a Google search on an owner's background to see how much they were worth, through to threatening to sell hostages to Al-Shabaab. The handbook also had a section called 'Somali self-image and national characteristics', which was pinned above his office desk as an aide memoire:

- *Brilliant improvisers, entrepreneurs, and oral communicators.*
- *A politicians' skill in seizing the advantage. Will exploit any weakness displayed by the opposition.*
- *Generosity in receiving guests. The stranger often encounters conflicting attitudes in his hosts.*
- *A generally egalitarian society – amongst men of the same clan. Chiefs and elders do not have the same degree of influence as in other parts of Africa.*
- *Secretive of their culture – only willing to share details on their own terms. Suspicious of outsiders' attempts to use language.*
- *Suspicion is the default mode and defence mechanism, in the context of harsh competition for survival and scarce resources.*
- *Independence of mind. Displays or threats of superior force earn only temporary respect.*
- *But also pragmatic e.g. in terms of religious observation and getting a deal done.*

If Edwards' assessment of the *Albedo* pirates was right, they weren't the smartest operators on the coast. Savvier outfits would have taken a lesser deal by now, rather than run up huge debts in the hope of a jackpot that clearly wasn't there. Sadly, being dumb didn't make them any easier to deal with. Fools rarely listened to reason.

He also had a very weak hand to play with. Without the $900,000 from Muller, the 'charity' was back to the $200,000 raised during the MPHRP's original whip-round. Edwards always liked to put serious money on the table straightaway – it calmed the other side down, and usually ensured the hostages got better treatment. Two-hundred-thousand dollars, though, didn't count as serious money. Not these days. Especially not when they'd been expecting $900,000.

⚓

Edwards' first phone call to Ali Jabeen went much as expected.

'Two-hundred-thousand dollars? This is bullshit! Are you no different from Mr John, Mr Leslie? Do you want the crew to start getting hurt again?

'I am sorry, but $200,000 is all the charity has. And if you hurt the crew, you will get nothing at all.'

'Bullshit! First Mr John insults us, and now you. Anyway, the ransom has gone up. Now we need $3 million.'

'Three-million dollars? I am sorry, that is not going to happen. Not in my lifetime. Not in my children's lifetime. Not in my children's children's lifetime.'

It was an expression he often used at times like this. Somalis, with their clans, were big on genealogy. It conveyed what he hoped was a sense of emphasis. Only on this occasion, he wasn't bluffing – there really was no more money.

Over the next few weeks, all Edwards got was abuse and threats. Nothing he hadn't heard many times before. Nonetheless, he worried. This bunch, after all, weren't just dumb. They were violent. And to his well-tuned ear, they sounded very wound up. If you looked at it from their point of view, the *Albedo* hijacking had been a disaster. First they'd had the owner vanish, then the Muller debacle. Now it was back to cheapskate money and to pleas to show mercy again.

If his own psychological assessment of this lot was accurate, they'd have nothing to lose by killing another hostage. Or this time, maybe more than one. It was the logical next step. Edwards didn't want anyone to die on his watch. If nothing else, it wouldn't be good for the reputation of Compass Risk Management.

'We need more money,' he told Steed. 'Otherwise this isn't going to happen.'

Back in London, Neylon and Gosling launched a new fundraising drive. They'd helped raise much of the MPHRP's original $200,000, tapping up wealthy contacts in the shipping and insurance world. Many held the two lawyers in high regard because of their help when their ships had been hijacked. Now, though, Neylon and Gosling sensed a degree of donor fatigue. It wasn't surprising – piracy had been financially disastrous for the shipping industry. They'd paid out nearly half a billion dollars in cash ransoms alone, and lost multiple billions more in damaged ships, delayed cargoes, compensation pay-outs to crews and extra security precautions. It wasn't a good time to be asking.

Neylon and Gosling phrased their pitch carefully. Rather than asking for help in paying a ransom, they'd ask for help in 'saving some people's lives'. Even then, a tentative 'yes' from one CEO would often be followed by a firm 'no' upon further thought. The legal compliance department would have issues; a board member would worry about the firm's reputation. Many firms already had some charity that they supported; giving that money to pirates instead was a hard sell.

Neylon and Gosling tried people outside the shipping industry as well, as did Steed. It was tempting to think that there was some billionaire philanthropist somewhere, a Sir Richard Branson or George Soros, willing to write a cheque for a few million – anything to help a crusading ex-colonel and his team on their mercy mission. Again, it didn't work. If people inside shipping were wary of getting involved, people outside were even more so. Cold-calling involved a lot of explaining, about why the ships had got stuck, why the owners couldn't help, why ransoms weren't actually illegal, and so on. To the outsider, it probably looked like some Muller-style scam. Occasionally, there was an extra pledge of $5,000 or $10,000, but no game-changing 'big money' offers came in. Well-run firms simply didn't have spare millions kicking around, the cash was usually tied up in assets or investments. Passing the begging bowl around was also time-consuming. Each approach had to be individually tailored and thought out. There were only so many hours that Neylon, Gosling and Steed could spare.

Edwards was beginning to despair. Then, one afternoon at his office in Stamford, he got a call from an unfamiliar Somali number. He didn't recognise the voice at the other end as one of the pirates, and he waited until it introduced itself as Shahriar Aliabadi, the *Albedo*'s Iranian bosun.

Edwards switched his mobile onto loudspeaker and grabbed his tape recorder. He braced himself for unpleasantness. When pirates put crew members on the phone first, it was often so that whoever they were calling could hear them being tortured. This time, though, there was none of the usual background hubbub. No pirates shouting or laughing, no stereo blaring.

'It's okay, I'm alone,' said Aliabadi in a low voice. 'I'm on a phone that Ali Jabeen gave me. Listen carefully, Mr Leslie. I don't have much time.'

Edwards grabbed a notepad. Why had Jabeen given the hostages a mobile phone? As he scribbled down what Aliabadi told him, he began to smile. He'd already got Jabeen down as a treacherous, untrustworthy rogue, but *bloody hell*. Not this treacherous. Something new for his book of pirate ruses.

Chapter 20

MEN OF HONOUR

The Albedo, *late April 2014. Three years
and five months in captivity*

Aman didn't find Ali Jabeen the most relaxing of khat companions. Chewing with the rank-and-file pirates, you could listen to Shakira, sing, smoke, and exchange token good-natured abuse. Chewing with Jabeen, you had to keep your wits about you. He wasn't just a foot soldier, he was an evil, sadistic fucker, who enjoyed torturing people. An evening with Jabeen was like supping – or chewing – with the Devil himself. For that very reason, though, Aman never turned down the chance. Jabeen was the only one who knew what was going on in pirate high command, and he opened up on khat, especially if no other pirates were around.

One night as they chewed together, Jabeen had gone on one of his usual rants about the state of the ransom talks. He cursed Mr Leslie, then Mr John, but he also began cursing the other pirates. There'd been a falling out, he said. The pirates had divided into two factions: a smaller group of himself plus a few others, and a much bigger faction making up the rest.

As the negotiator, Jabeen was under pressure from the pirates to get more money. The bigger faction were beginning to question his competence. He was trying his best, but that Mr Leslie was proving to be a real hard-ass, worse than Mr John. He hadn't budged one bit from his $200,000 opener. Jabeen was tired of it all, he wanted out of the whole thing, but he didn't want to miss out on his share of the cash. Not after all this time.

Aman listened politely. The khat buzz gave him a crazy idea. There was no point in him pleading again to be released for free. Jabeen, the merciless bastard, would never go for that. But if he couldn't appeal to Jabeen's sense of compassion, perhaps he could appeal to his sense of greed. *Shit, dare he say it?* The khat spoke up for him.

'Why don't you just take the $200,000 for yourself?' Aman asked.

'What do you mean?'

'Take it for yourself, all of it. Cut the others out of the deal. Just help us escape first.'

'What are you talking about? I can't do that.'

'Yes you can. Forget about the others. What have they done for you? Do a secret deal with Mr Leslie for the money – just you and him. Then help us escape somehow.'

Jabeen stared at Aman. His mouth was half-open, full of khat mush. Then he slapped him hard in the face, and walked off, muttering angrily. *Cheeky little Indian runt. Thought that because he spoke Somali, he could tell a man to betray his brothers.*

Aman watched Jabeen stomp off, his face still stinging from the slap. He wasn't worried. If Jabeen had really been offended, he'd still be getting beaten right now. He hadn't gone off in a huff, he'd gone off to think it over. Sure enough, a few nights later, Jabeen came back to chew again. He had a plan. If the $200,000 could be given to him in secret, he and a few other pirates from his own faction would arrange for the hostages to 'escape' from the compound one night. The 'escape' would have to look authentic, because if the other faction ever found out, Jabeen would be a marked man, and so would anyone else in his family, for generations to come. Jabeen thrust a mobile into Aman's hand.

'Keep this phone hidden,' he said. 'Talk the plan over with the crew, then call Mr Leslie. He will need to hear about it from you. He won't believe me alone.'

For the next few nights, the crew mulled it over. Putting their faith in Jabeen was a big risk, given how he'd treated them before, and could he really be relied upon to mastermind a workable escape plan? First, he'd have to spring them from the compound undetected. Then he'd have to smuggle them through miles of turf controlled by other armed groups, to some spot where they could be safely picked up by Mr Leslie's people. That would be a hazardous enough task even with the help of the entire gang. Doing it on the sly, with just Jabeen and a few others, would be much harder. Still, what did they have to lose? Their lives, of course, but were those lives worth living any more? Like this?

'My view is that we've got to escape, or we die,' said Aliabadi.

When Aliabadi spoke these days, it was with a slight lisp. Since that torture session in the bush, when he'd had several teeth kicked out, others had rotted and come out too. It was a reminder of how even the strongest of the sailors were gradually falling apart. Beatings, illness, bites, stomach upsets, diarrhoea and who knew what else. Muhammad Bisthamy, the Sri Lankan second engineer, had just turned 60, and had bronchitis. Another year in captivity could finish him off.

The escape had to be a group decision, Aliabadi insisted. The one thing the crew had going for them was that they looked out for each other. One for all, all for one. They all remembered how painful the split had been when the Pakistanis had left. They couldn't afford that this time. If they were going to escape, it had to be all of them. Anyone who stayed behind might well be killed by the pirates, but nobody should be forced. If any man had doubts, now was the time to speak up. There'd be no room for second thoughts on the night. They voted on it. All hands went in favour.

Edwards told Aliabadi to forget all about it. No responsible negotiator ever encouraged hostages to try escaping. Not even Russell Crowe in *Proof of Life*. Not unless a client's life was in absolutely imminent danger. But what else could they do? The more he pondered it, the more it seemed like the only option. It was outlandish, for sure – not just organising an escape, but cutting a faction of kidnappers out of a deal. He'd be tearing up every page of the negotiator's rule book. Sometimes, though, there was a window of opportunity in hostage cases, where you had to take your chance, however unpromising it seemed.

Edwards had never forgotten a case he'd worked on for an Egyptian telecoms firm who'd had some staff kidnapped in Iraq. He'd gone straight to Cairo from another job, ready for a flying start, only to find that no one in the firm was willing to make tough decisions. It was as if they'd rather do nothing at all than take a chance and get it wrong. Two months in, the kidnappers cut off communication, and the hostages were never heard from again. All because people had been scared to take risks. Was he being too risk-averse himself here? Was this the window of opportunity? Edwards discussed it with Steed.

'It's a gamble, but perhaps there's no alternative,' Edwards said. 'Look at these hostages – they've been shot, drowned, beaten endlessly and held for more than three years. No cavalry is coming in, and it's very clear that we're not going to get much beyond $200,000 in donations. When things are this bad, I think we're entitled to take extra risks.'

Edwards usually made his own calls on operational matters. The rule of thumb was that whoever was talking direct to the kidnappers was best qualified to judge the mood. It made for clearer lines of responsibility, and usually better judgement calls. This, though, wasn't a decision he wanted sole ownership of. The plan was too radical, the stakes too high. If it failed, it would put Steed in even worse odour with the UN. He ran it past the lawyers too.

'Not an option I'd normally support, as a home team strategy,' he told Gosling. 'But frankly, the circumstances are exceptional.'

Gosling agreed, but the donors would have to be consulted. It was their money, and there was no guarantee that Jabeen wouldn't just disappear off with it. Even suggesting such a plan to the donors might look like they were getting desperate. Boardrooms weren't used to signing off deals where one bunch of kidnappers ripped off another. To his astonishment, not a single objection came back. One donor, a wealthy speculator in the insurance market, took it in his stride.

'I like taking risks,' he told Gosling. 'It's what I do for a living.'

Chapter 21

BANDIT COUNTRY

The Albedo *crew, Camara, Somalia, May 2014.*
Three years and six months in captivity

Straightaway, a weakness in the plan was evident: as the only person who knew the terrain outside the compound well, only Jabeen was in a position to work out the details of the escape plan. He talked it over with Aman and Aliabadi, who consulted with Steed and Edwards, but in practice, everyone would have to go along with whatever Jabeen came up with, and for all his cunning, scheming ways, he was a novice as an escape artist.

Every night, all eleven hostages were locked in a shack, one side of which overlooked an alleyway. The shack was watched by half a dozen guards, one of whom was an accomplice of Jabeen's, in on the plan. He said the rest of the guards only kept a cursory eye on the hostages, and usually slept on the job, but that they never left their posts.

The hostages had one thing in their favour. As the camp cook, Aman prepared meals for both guards and crew. What if he could drug the guards' food, Jabeen suggested? The guards spent the night shift sleeping anyway, this would just ensure that none of them woke up. A few days later, Jabeen slipped

Aman several packets of strong sedatives, enough to knock out at least a dozen grown men. Meanwhile, the hostages worked on a way to sneak out of the shack.

High up in their room was a foot-wide window that overlooked the alley. It seemed too small for anyone to climb through, but if the frame could be removed, the space would grow a little. The hostages loosened the frame a little each night, always making sure it could be put back in place. One evening, they did a test, removing it entirely and hoisting up the largest sailor, a Sri Lankan, to see if he could get through. It was a tight fit, but he could squeeze through as far as his waist. With a firm push on the night, he'd manage. For once, they felt glad of all the years on the pirate plan diet.

Back in Nairobi, Steed began putting together an extraction plan. Jabeen had said that once hostages were out of the compound, they were to walk to a nearby mosque, where he and an accomplice would be waiting for them with cars. From there they would head to a handover point near the village of Ba'adweyn, an hour's drive from the nearest city, Galkayo. Ba'adweyn was as close to civilisation as Jabeen was willing to go. Steed would have to arrange for someone to pick the hostages up from there and then drive them to Galkayo. The route was still through bandit country. They'd need an armed escort.

This was where Steed would have to pull some favours. Somalia, for all its lawlessness, wasn't a place where foreigners could just stroll in and go about their business, not even for a hostage mercy mission. Permit letters would have to be sought from the relevant power brokers in Galkayo, and all manner of players would have to be brought on side: the regional president, the police chief, the head of intelligence, the boss of the local airstrip. All it took was one of them to object – which they occasionally did, either in hope of a payoff, or just to throw their weight around – and everything could grind to a halt.

Steed went through his contacts book. All those endless meetings over the years in diplomatic contact groups, UN steering committees, working parties and protocol visits did have one benefit. It meant he'd met nearly every regional apparatchik and politician in Somalia at some point. Even so, there was only one person that he knew well enough in Galkayo to approach. Omar Sheik Ali was the local counter-piracy representative, who'd sat in with him on countless regional strategy forums over the years. While the two couldn't exactly claim success in defeating piracy, they'd at least become friends.

Omar was well aware of the plight of the *Albedo* hostages, who'd been languishing on his patch for years now – it was a stain on the reputation of the area. He agreed to be the go-between who'd pick up the hostages from Ba'adweyn. This was no small favour, given how dangerous the territory around Ba'adweyn was. It was a haunt not just of pirates, but Al-Shabaab, various militias, and all manner of other freelance rogues. To get the prisoners out safely, he'd need to put on a show of force – at least fifteen armed guards, plus a couple of pick-up trucks armed with heavy machine guns.

Even the flight to pick the hostages up from Galkayo would be a headache. The UN was willing to send in a humanitarian flight to Galkayo's small airstrip, but to ensure the airstrip itself would be secure, Steed would have to hire yet another 30 armed men to patrol the perimeter and buildings. Even then, no amount of hired muscle would guarantee safety.

The month before, two of Steed's UN colleagues, a Briton and a Frenchman, had been shot dead at Galkayo airport terminal by a man dressed as a policeman. The reason for the killing was still unclear. All one could be certain of was that in somewhere like Galkayo, even the men in uniform couldn't be entirely trusted.

As well as planes and gunmen, a secure hotel would have to be arranged for the hostages in Galkayo, plus doctors for medical check-ups, emergency travel documents, spare clothes, meals and travel documents. Every possible contingency and cock-up had to be factored in. At times, Steed felt like he was back on the battle plan exercises he'd done in the army, only here, his assets weren't British troops under his direct command, but a few crews of Somali gunmen in a town 1,500 miles way, plus Ali Jabeen – pirate, torturer and turncoat, a man so treacherous he'd even rip off his fellow hijackers. What if the sleeping pills weren't strong enough? What if the guards woke up halfway through the escape? What if the hostages got spotted by a villager as they fled? What if Jabeen just took the money and ran? It made *The Great Escape* look simple.

The evening of 10 May was agreed as escape night. There'd be no moon, which would make Camara's alleyways all the darker. In London, the lawyers made arrangements to wire the $200,000 to Jabeen, through a route they kept secret. Edwards drafted another contract for Jabeen and his co-conspirators to sign. To the lawyers' amusement, it still described the pirates as 'men of honour', even though they were planning to rip off their fellow pirates. In several centuries of maritime contract law, there'd probably been nothing like it.

On the morning of 10 May, the UN flight was put on standby. In Galkayo, Steed's friend Omar scrambled his armed escort and headed out to the rendezvous point near Ba'adweyn. The plan was for Aliabadi or Aman to call that night, as soon as they were out of the compound and in Jabeen's car. In Nairobi, London and Lincolnshire, Steed, the lawyers and Edwards waited for Aman to ring. But the call did not come until the following morning.

'Where are you, what's going on?' Edwards asked.

'We are still at the compound,' Aman said.

'What happened? Did you manage to drug the guards?'

'We put the pills in their food, but they were chewing khat all night. It kept them awake.'

Edwards put his head in his hands. Another entry for his Somali fieldcraft manual. If drugging pirates, make sure there was no khat around.

The following night Aman tried drugging the pirates again, this time with more pills. They did fall asleep, but not until halfway through the night, when there was only two hours of darkness left. It wasn't long enough to give them time to get away.

Steed called off Omar's rescue team, who were already uneasy at hanging around near Ba'adweyn for so long. The plan wasn't going to work, no point pretending otherwise. He tried ringing Jabeen to ask what else they could try, but got no reply. Now that the $200,000 was safely in Jabeen's pocket, they'd probably never hear from him again. Indeed, who was to say that he'd been serious about the escape in the first place? What if those pills had just been just paracetamol? Had they made the wrong call? Had they been too desperate to do something rather than nothing? With hindsight, Steed began to worry that the whole thing looked like madness. For once, expert opinion seemed to be on his side, if the verdict of his more experienced mentor was anything to go by.

'It looks like we are a bit fucked here, John,' Edwards told him.

They'd done their best, Edwards insisted. A gamble in difficult circumstances. There'd always been the possibility that Jabeen was planning to rip them off, nothing they could do about that. Yes, they'd lost the money, but at least the hostages were still alive. Steed didn't have Edwards' sense of professional detachment. Nor was he looking forward to explaining things to the UN. Being ripped off by a conman was one thing, but being ripped off by a pirate? He could hardly say he hadn't seen that one coming.

There was one last card to play. Edwards still had a copy of the contract bearing Jabeen's signature. It might be useless in a court of law, but it wouldn't be something that Jabeen would want the other pirate faction to see. If Edwards were to threaten to show it to them, might that encourage Jabeen to come up with another escape plan? Jabeen still wasn't answering his phone, but a week later, Edwards got through to one of his accomplices.

'Tell Jabeen that as he knows, we are all men of honour here, but he hasn't kept his side of the bargain. Ask him, what will happen if this was to get out? No other negotiators like me will be able to treat him as a man of honour again, and neither will any of his fellow pirates!'

The tone was more-in-sorrow-than-in-anger, but the hint of menace was there. The accomplice insisted to Edwards that Jabeen was still onside. He was just lying low, because the pirates already suspected something was up. Word had reached them of the mysterious armed convoy that had turned up near Ba'adweyn a couple of weeks ago.

A fortnight passed. Edwards began to wonder how much longer he could afford to work on the case. Unlike Steed, he wasn't on any UN stipend. Besides, when you reached the point of trying to blackmail pirates, it probably was time to admit defeat. Steed, meanwhile, was wondering if he could find any new donors. He doubted it. Then, at 4am on 5 June, Steed's phone rang. It was Aman. He sounded out of breath.

'Please, Mr John, you need to help us,' he said. 'We are lost.'

'What do you mean, you're lost? Where are you?'

'Out in the bush somewhere. We drugged the guards again and got out through a window. But Jabeen isn't here. We don't know where we are.'

Jabeen had turned out to be a more resourceful escape artist than expected. First, he'd got his accomplice to smuggle Aman more sleeping pills. Then, in a stroke of initiative that would never have occurred to the home team, he'd tracked down the pirates' khat dealer and bribed him to sell his stock elsewhere. The only problem was that he hadn't bothered to tell Steed or Edwards that the escape plan was back on.

As before, Aman had stirred the pills into the guards' evening meal. This time, it worked perfectly. By midnight, the guards were snoring heavily. By 3am, though, there was still no call from Jabeen to say he was ready with the car. Time was running short. One of the guards had already woken up, and was chatting drowsily to Jabeen's accomplice.

At 3.25am, Jabeen rang Aman's secret phone. 'Okay, come out quickly,' he said. 'The driver is waiting.'

'It's too late! One of the guards is awake again now!'

Jabeen showed yet more initiative.

'Don't worry. My friend is going to distract him by showing him porn movies on his mobile phone. You will be fine, just be very quiet.'

The crew readied themselves, pulling on their darkest clothes. A practised drill, honed during thousands of hours of idleness, went into place. Aliabadi, the Iranian bosun, took charge, giving out directions using sign language. Even talking in whispers, eleven grown men made too much noise, and most were so nervous they could barely speak anyway. This was as big a gamble as jumping off the *Albedo* during that storm.

The pre-loosened window frame was removed. A crewman knelt down in front of it so the others could use his back as a step. Largest first, the big Sri Lankan squeezed his way through, trying to land softly outside. He crouched still for a minute. All clear. One of the Bangladeshis followed, then the rest.

The air was cool after the sweatbox of the shack. As a village with limited electricity, Camara by night was pitch black. Jabeen had said the car would be waiting in the bush about half a mile away. He'd given Aman the route a few days before, using landmarks that Aman knew from shopping trips to Camara's market, where the pirates took him sometimes to buy cooking supplies. But everything looked different by night. Aman squinted in the gloom, trying to remember Jabeen's instructions: *Past the tree near the shack. Then round the house where the fat lady lives. Up to the left, past the shop. Then past that tamarind tree, like the one in Mum and Dad's garden. Look for the mobile phone tower out in the bush.*

The group walked in single file – their first steps as free men in more than three and a half years. They were painful ones too. The pirates had taken their footwear from them when they'd first brought them to the mainland, knowing it would make it harder to escape. The hostages were used to walking barefoot round the compound, but roaming outside in the dark was another matter. Every so often, a crewman stifled a yelp as a foot or toe hit something sharp.

They crept from alley to alley, silhouetted block to silhouetted block, ducking into the shadows where possible. When they halted for breath or to work out the way, they huddled down together, hoping they looked like a bunch of sheep or goats. Crouched on their knees, they could hear their own heartbeats, all the louder for the silence. At each corner, they checked the stretch ahead. In Camara, people went to bed expecting trouble. Houses often had night watchmen who slept outside, sometimes dogs too. One glimpse, one bark, and it would all be over. The agreement was that if even one of them got caught, the rest would give up too. No leaving anyone behind.

Aman was up in front. Where the hell was the mobile phone tower Jabeen talked about? Then he spotted it, a jerry-built citadel sprouting over some wind-blasted thorn trees. An ancient Land Cruiser was parked there. A door opened, a figure beckoned to them to come forward. Aman couldn't make out the face in the gloom, but it wasn't Jabeen.

'Who are you?' Aman hissed in Somali.

'I am Ali Jabeen's friend. I am here to drive you.'

'But where is Jabeen?'

'He said Camara is not safe for him, so he sent me. Get in the car, quick.'

'He is supposed to be here!'

'I have no idea about any of that. All I was told is to bring this car here.'

Fucking Jabeen. He was probably safely in Mogadishu now, or wherever it was he lived, spending his $200,000 on khat and girls. Leaving them with this stranger, and only one vehicle for eleven men.

They squeezed in front and back, on each other's laps, sitting half-perched out of the windows. They lurched off, looking like the overloaded Somali bush taxis Aman had seen on his trips round Camara. The driver picked his way along a track, his lights switched off. Occasionally they had to jump out when the overloaded jalopy ground to a halt on a bump.

Aman kept ringing Jabeen, to no reply. Out here in the bush, there was barely even phone reception. The driver, he noticed, kept stopping and changing direction. *This does not look good*, Aman thought. Half an hour later, after miles of crawling through rutted, sand-baked tracks, the driver halted again.

'This is as far as I go. It is not safe for me to go further.'

The crew looked around. They'd been expecting a convoy, headlamps aglow. All they could see was more bush.

'Follow that track for 100 metres,' said the driver. 'They are waiting for you down there.'

'What track? There isn't one.'

The driver handed them a flashlight.

'Down there. Government people are waiting for you. If you don't see them, just keep walking.'

The hostages conferred. This was not what had been agreed. But as ever, what choice did they have? They set off. Every step they took, they got more suspicious. Was this some kind of trap? A way of luring them out in the middle of nowhere, so they could all be recaptured by some new gang of pirates hired by Jabeen? Or killed? They trudged on, no longer trying to be quiet. The 100 metres became 500 metres, the track led on into the dark. Aman tried Jabeen's phone one last time. A sleepy voice finally answered.

'Jabeen, you motherfucker, where are you? We are out here in the bush while you are sleeping and comfortable! Where are the people to pick us up?'

'Are they not there?'

'Nobody is here! We are in the middle of nowhere!'

'Didn't you call Mr John to arrange the pick-up?'

'What? That was your job!'

'You didn't call them as well?'

'We thought you had! What do we do now?'

'I don't know. I have done my bit! Just keep walking in the direction you are walking in. You will find Ba'adweyn.'

Jabeen hung up. Aman and Aliabadi tried not to panic. It was true, they'd been so focused on the escape, neither had thought to ring Mr John or Mr Leslie. But that wasn't their fault. Jabeen had promised everything would be arranged. They carried on. The soles of their feet were now raw and bleeding. Earlier on, when the adrenalin was still surging, they could have run across broken glass and not cared. Now every step was agony. Bisthamy, the elderly second engineer with bronchitis, began to lag behind. He hadn't walked this far in three years.

'I can't go much further,' he gasped.

The crew took turns to give him a piggyback. Nobody was getting left behind. They scanned the inky horizon constantly, hoping to see pinpricks of light that might be a convoy signalling to them. The air felt fresher, as if they might be near the sea. After another couple of miles, they took cover in some bushes. Dawn was breaking. If a pirate hunting party wasn't out for them already, it would be soon.

The phone was almost out of battery. There'd been no reception for the last hour. Aman found a spot of high ground, where a single bar of signal appeared on the screen. He dialled Mr John's number in Nairobi.

Steed listened to Aman's voice on the phone, trying not to panic himself. *Why hadn't Jabeen warned him the escape was back on?* Now the hostages were stuck out in the bush, unable to walk another yard, with no food or water. If they didn't get caught by the pirates, they'd die of thirst in a couple of days. Some hunter would find their bones in years to come. Steed rang Edwards. He'd just had a distress call from Aman too. He was now pacing up and down in his dressing gown in his kitchen in Lincolnshire.

'Can you see if Omar in Galkayo can try to pick them up?' Edwards asked. 'Can he get there ahead of the pirates?'

'I'll try him, but I doubt it. He can't just organise a convoy on the spot, and we don't even know where the hostages are. I asked Aman, and he cut out before he could tell me.'

'If Aman rings back, ask him for as much detail as you can. I'll do the same if he calls me.'

Steed dialled Aman's mobile non-stop. Half an hour later, Aman picked up.

'Aman, can you describe to me where you are? I'll try to get someone to pick you up. Can you describe any landmarks?'

Aman did his best – maybe half an hour's drive from Camara … near a track that bent round a hill … no houses in sight anywhere … perhaps near the sea? What else … yes, there was a mobile phone mast. Probably why he could get a reception. Steed rang Omar in Galkayo, expecting to be politely told to get lost. He'd already gone beyond the call of duty by hanging around in the bush for two days the last time.

'Yes. Mr John?' a sleepy voice asked.

'Omar, we have a problem. The good news is that the hostages have escaped. The bad news is that we didn't know about it. They are out in the bush, somewhere between Camara and Galkayo. Maybe near Ba'adweyn. Is there any way you can go and pick them up?'

'What, right now?'

'Yes. I am sorry. It needs to be as quick as possible.'

'I don't know, Mr John. It's a very dangerous area. I can't go alone.'

'No, of course not. Can you get an escort with some Toyotas and armed guards? I am so sorry, I know this is such short notice, but the hostages will die if we don't get to them. I can pay whatever extra money you need, I don't care how much.'

'Do you know the hostages' location?'

Steed read out the scrawled entries in his notebook. To his amazement, Omar seemed to vaguely recognise Aman's description of where the phone mast might be.

'I'll see what I can do, Mr John. Let me call you back.'

An hour later, Omar rang to say he and his men were on their way. He sounded as calm as a cabbie being asked to do a slightly-out-of-the-way pick-up. Quite how he'd managed to scramble fifteen armed men, two armed trucks and a convoy of pick-ups in the middle of the night, Steed had no idea. Maybe that was what living in a war zone taught you.

It was nearly 5am. Out of the window in Steed's spare room, sunrise was peeping over the Nairobi skyline. His only hope now was that it would take the pirates even longer to find the hostages than it would Omar. If they could be found at all. Steed rang Aman's phone again, but got no reply. His battery was probably long gone. He tried to go back to bed, but couldn't sleep. He spent the next few hours drinking tea and making phone calls. Edwards was doing the same in his lounge in Lincolnshire. Two men close to retirement, both wondering if this might be what people remembered them for. There were no more texts or calls. Steed wondered if the next update he'd hear would be on the news headlines: '*Pirates massacre escaped hostages*', '*Al-Shabaab militants claim capture of escaped hostages*'.

Christ, what had they done organising this escape caper? Had they lost all sense of perspective? What were the hostages' families going to say? Edwards was worried too. When word of this got out, as it surely would, it would not look good among his peers. His was a small world, and a competitive one too. He could see rivals using this fiasco as a sales pitch: '*Les Edwards? Yeah, used to be a good operator. But did you hear about that business in Somalia? Not for us to comment, of course, but …*' He night never work again.

Mid-morning came, then lunchtime. Then, just before 4pm, after ten of the longest hours of his life, Steed's phone bleeped with a text from Omar: 'CONFIRMED THAT WE HAVE THE HOSTAGES. ALL ARE SAFE AND WELL.'

Chapter 22

HOMECOMING

The Albedo *crew, somewhere in the bush
near Camara, Somalia, May 2014.
Three years and six months in captivity*

Sometime around dawn, as the first sunlight pricked through the thorn bushes, Aman's phone gave a mournful warning bleep. It was running out of charge. Then it burst into life, a tiny luminescent square in the semi-gloom. A local number. A voice, Somali, claiming to be with a rescue party.

'We think we are close, can you see our headlights?'

'No, nothing. We have been looking out.'

'Can you describe where you are?'

'Like I said before, near a mobile phone mast.'

'There are many mobile phone masts here. We are close to one, but we can't see you.'

Aman had an idea. Guns had held them three years in this place, now, maybe, guns could help them get out.

'Have you got weapons?' he asked. 'If so, fire a few shots in the air. We will see if we can hear you.'

In this sparse, rocky terrain, a burst from a Kalashnikov might carry several miles. The crew fell silent, listening, but heard nothing. Still nothing. Then it came, two bursts

– somewhere east. Then again. Aman climbed up a rocky knoll and shone the flashlight. Another burst followed, as if in reply. The hostages set off towards the sound, trying to keep a straight line. The gunfire came again, this time louder. Then, no more than a mile away, headlights pinpricked through the bush. As they drew near, they could see figures standing around, holding guns.

To check it was the right men, Aman rang the mobile again. One of them rummaged into a pocket for his phone. The gunmen approached.

'Follow us,' they said. 'Move as fast as you can.'

They moved off in silence. Something seemed odd to Aman. There was no welcome, no smiles, but still they followed. Ten minutes later they came to a beach. A dozen more Somalis stood in front of them. They had pick-ups, more guns, and lots of questions. Where had the hostages come from? Had money changed hands for their release? The tone wasn't friendly.

'Who is in charge here?' Aman asked back. 'Can we talk to him?'

'Never mind that. Stay where you are and wait.'

The crew were ordered into the cars and told not to talk. Aman looked around, anxious that they weren't split up. The Somalis were on the phone, arguing with someone. Aman tried to ring Mr John, but before he could raise the handset to his ear, a Somali slapped him in the face.

Fuck. Who were these people? Some bunch of bounty hunters, hired to drag back them back to Camara? Two hours passed, another convoy arrived. Ten pick-ups this time, one with an anti-aircraft gun welded to the back. More gunmen leapt out, taking positions on the beach. The hostages braced themselves. This was probably the rest of the pirates – Kilo, Ali Inke and all the others, mad at being ripped off.

A man with glasses and a baseball cap appeared. He argued with the group of Somalis who had found them, then strode over to the crew. His baseball cap had a UN logo on it, but round here, that meant nothing. Lots of Somalis wore cast-off leisurewear advertising the likes of the World Food Programme, Chelsea FC, or Coca Cola.

'Don't worry, you are safe now, I am from the government,' he beamed. He passed out sandwiches from a bag.

'What is going on?' Aman asked.

'I am sorry, there was a problem with these men. They are not my staff, they are local people that we asked to help find you. When they found you, they wanted extra money, but everything is okay now. We are taking you to Galkayo.'

Was Baseball Cap for real? Certainly, his sandwiches were fantastic. Proper fresh bread. But friendly faces meant nothing round here. Arro, that lady pirate, had spoken kind words and fed them well, only to hold onto them. Until they were out of this place, on a plane back home, nothing was sure.

The convoy took them to Galkayo. The town seemed huge. Concrete roads, traffic jams, crowds, four-storey buildings. They pulled up outside what looked like a squat office block. The crew assumed it was a police station or prison. Then, on the roof they spied a broken neon sign: 'Five Star Hotel'. It didn't look like the five-star hotels Aman had seen in Dubai, but inside the lobby, the air conditioning was deliciously cool. If this was going to be their next place of incarceration, so be it. Someone handed out room keys and cellophane-wrapped packs of trousers and shirts.

'Relax, go upstairs and take a shower,' said Baseball Cap. 'Dinner will be in half an hour.'

They came back down to a banquet. Chicken, spaghetti, salad, the flavours exploding on the palate. Bottled water and fizzy drinks, cigarettes, whole packs of them. Baseball Cap sat at the table, still all smiles. Throughout dinner, a procession of officials came in. Several had their photos taken with the hostages. Aman began to wonder if they really might be free. If so, half of Galkayo seemed to want to take the credit.

Baseball Cap's mobile rang. He passed it Aman. 'Mr John for you,' he said. *God, it must be all real!*

'Hello Aman!' said Steed. 'You're in safe hands now. We're flying into Galkayo tomorrow to pick you up. Go to bed and get some rest.'

That proved impossible. The crew had been awake for 24 hours, but nobody could sleep. The beds were too soft, the excitement too great, and it felt odd being in rooms without dozens of snoring companions. Aman stayed up chatting all night with one of the Bangladeshis. Even now, they still weren't sure it was all over – after all, Mr John had made promises before that hadn't worked out. So had many others.

From the window of the plane, Steed looked down at Somalia through a blur of propeller blades. The vast coastline peeled past, a strip of butterscotch desert meeting the emerald of the Indian Ocean. Thank God for UNHAS, the UN's humanitarian air service. They'd set aside a 25-seater plane the night before. There were private Kenyan pilots who'd have done the job too, but they'd have charged a fortune. He and his UN colleague, Leo Hoy-Carrasco, had left at dawn from Wilson Airport, a back-up to Nairobi's main international hub. It was a favourite for anyone dropping off or picking up hostages, as there were fewer prying eyes.

On his tray table, he ploughed through a mass of emergency travel paperwork for the crew, filling in forms and cutting out passport photos. Kenyan immigration officials weren't impressed by people who turned up undocumented, even if they'd just spent three years as hostages.

The plan was to spend no more than two hours in Galkayo. There'd be a brief, tightly-choreographed round of glad-handing with local VIPs, after which they'd leave before anything went wrong. In his security assessment for the UN flight, Steed had game-planned for everything from arrest on arrival to an armed assault on the airport. Word would have already travelled round Galkayo about the pick-up. Because it had the blessing of the local power brokers, their rivals might be tempted to spoil the party, so too might the disgruntled pirate investors, who'd presumably realised by now that they'd been ripped off. It still all felt too good to be true. Even yesterday, there'd been a stand-off with the clansmen whom Omar had roped in as an extra search party. They'd refused to hand the hostages over until a finder's bonus was paid. Steed had had to dash to a Somali money wire agency in Nairobi and send over several thousand dollars.

Galkayo airport finally loomed below them, a neat grey square on the red-brown scrub. Touching down, Steed could see the armed guards he'd hired, positioned round the perimeter. Hopefully they wouldn't demand bonuses too. Steed and Hoy-Carrasco disembarked, looking round anxiously as various officials gathered. They'd asked for the hostages to be brought to the airport in advance, which might be expecting a bit much, but no, there they were on the other side of the runway. Another group of foreign faces, staring back at them with equal curiosity.

As Steed walked over, he wondered what to say. It was the one thing that had been impossible to prepare in advance. For all that these men had dominated his every thought for the last year, he still didn't really know them. The only ones he'd had much contact with were Aman and Aliabadi, the two English speakers. Even then, there'd never been time for small talk on the phone – not when you had to spend half the call just checking if everyone was still alive.

He could see the two of them now, dressed in the crisp new shirts and plaited trousers that Omar had bought for them. Both three years older and several stone thinner than the passport mugshots he'd used for their travel documents. They were grinning and waving. Seeing Steed getting off the plane was the sign they'd been looking for. *This was actually happening.*

There were hugs all round, and Steed felt tears in his eyes. Never mind the British stiff upper lip, he thought. This wasn't Stanley-meets-Livingstone, it had been far bloody harder than that. If he wanted to cry, he would do. He kept his words brief.

'Finally!' he said. 'I feel like we're all family together.'

They had barely exchanged a few words before some dignitaries appeared for a photo op, then some more. Then Galkayo's vice-president arrived, official photographer in tow. The hostages lined up, smiling shyly like a group of cultural exchange students. Steed stood at the back, grinning like a man who'd been chewing khat all night. *They'd saved these people. They'd finally done it.*

The glad-handing would have gone on all day, had the pilot not announced, at Steed's prior suggestion, that they now had to fly back to meet their landing slot at Nairobi. They clambered into the plane. Even as it taxied along the runway, Aman was still fretting that some man with a gun would appear and take them away again, but then the plane jerked into the air. *Fuck this place*, he thought to himself, staring down at the disappearing landscape. *Now I will finally go home.*

On the flight, cheers broke out as Steed announced that they'd crossed the Kenyan border.

'Welcome to Kenya, goodbye Somalia,' he told the sailors. 'Now you're free.'

He resisted the urge to dance down the aisle. While Aman and Aliabadi were happy to talk, the rest of the hostages were mostly quiet. Several looked like they still didn't realise they were free. They sat toying with their water bottles, not even speaking to each other. Some trauma therapist could probably write a thesis on this lot. Already, he'd noticed how they stuck together, doing everything as a group. In the VIP hubbub at the airstrip, they'd looked nervous if one got separated from the rest. Working as a pack had got them through captivity, now it was ingrained. During their stay overnight at the Five Star Hotel, several had felt uncomfortable sleeping in rooms on their own. In coming days, they'd be going their separate ways, flying home to different corners of the globe, but it would be good to break them in gently.

'We've booked six rooms at a hotel in Nairobi for you,' Hoy-Carrasco told them. 'They are all doubles so you can share, but if you want to put more beds in a room, to have five beds in one and say two in another, that's fine. If you want to have your own room too, we'll fix it. You decide your own lives from now.'

The plane stopped first at Wajir Airport, just across the Kenyan border, where all incoming Somali air traffic had to undergo security screening. The hostages gathered round a TV in one of the lounges, screening a Kenyan soap opera.

'Are you fans of that show?' Steed asked.

The hostages shook their heads. It was just the first TV screen they'd seen in years.

By late afternoon, they were back at Wilson Airport, where another VIP reception party was waiting. This time it was diplomats from the hostages' home countries of Iran, India, Sri Lanka and Bangladesh. Using their diplomatic passports, they'd got themselves airside. As they chatted to the sailors in their own languages, Steed saw one diplomat ushering two hostages towards the fast-track diplomatic channel.

'Sorry, where are you going?' he asked the diplomat.

'Where are we going? Why, I am taking the hostages back to the embassy.'

'Actually, that isn't the plan. We don't want them split up right now.'

'Well as of now, I am responsible for my countrymen. Don't worry, we can take care of them.'

'I don't think you understand. These men have been together for nearly four years, through all sorts of trauma. It won't be good for their mental health to split them up right now. They need a few days to readjust first. We've already booked a hotel for them where they can stay together.'

'And may I ask who you are, sir?'

Steed could guess the diplomat's game. He probably had orders to whisk the hostages away, before they could bad-mouth their own governments to any waiting news teams outside the airport. The other diplomats were likely planning the same, judging by the anxious looks he was getting. Tough luck. If they were that concerned about bad headlines, they should have done more to help in the first place. It had been hard getting some of them to even assist with the travel documents. If they wanted to pull rank, so could he – when it came to putting on an air of overbearing, presumptuous authority, nobody could do it like a British-army-officer-turned-UN-bureaucrat.

'My apologies, I assumed you already knew who I was. Colonel John Steed, ex-military attaché to Her Majesty's Embassy, Nairobi. Now with the UN Hostage Release Programme. Senior Liaison Officer to the UN Joint Contact Group on Counter Piracy. These men are my responsibility for now. Splitting them up is out of the question. If you don't mind, we'll be getting along now. We have a lot of formalities at the airport to complete.'

He nodded to the hostages and they fell in alongside him. Right now, he was the only person they trusted. The diplomats let them pass. They were probably still trying to work out all the titles he'd reeled off.

For the next three days, Steed and Hoy-Carrasco did their best to help the hostages 'decompress'. Allowing captives who'd been away for so long to go straight home to family life could backfire. Their partners and children might barely recognise them, for a start, and no matter how warm the welcome as they walked back through the door, there'd be problems to deal with too.

Wives might have got used to living without their husbands, or started new relationships. Relatives might have stepped in to help, changing the household power dynamics. There could be bitterness over their decision to go to sea in the first place, and, of course, agonising over whether to go back again. For someone who'd spent the last three years having to ask permission just to use the toilet, that kind of decision could be difficult. All the more reason to give the hostages a few days to adjust a little, to think things over, and to spend some quality farewell time with their other 'family'.

Steed called in a favour from Dr Raj Jutley, his old heart surgeon, to check the hostages' physical health. They were in surprisingly good condition. Jutley had expected to see evidence of cachexia, a muscle-wasting condition brought on by malnutrition, but he found nothing, just a single case of a fungal nail infection. The UN medical packages that the hostages had been sent had allowed them to look after themselves.

Mentally, it was a different picture. Jutley spoke both Hindi and Urdu, which got some of the quieter hostages to open up. They described ordeals that brought him out in goosepimples, in a detached, matter-of-fact fashion. They ticked off different months and years in captivity like they were days. 'They seem hollowed out emotionally,' he told Steed.

The hostages continued to act like a herd of sheep, always doing things together, always glancing round nervously. Jutley noticed that they also did exactly what they were told, without question. It made them easy patients, but hardly fit yet for the outside world. Still, he was impressed by Aman's command of Somali, without which the deal with Jabeen would probably never have been hatched. That was Indians for you – great with languages, good at assimilating into other cultures. Men from other parts of the world might not have been so adaptable.

To help get the hostages used to crowds again, Steed took them shopping in Nairobi. The lawyers in London had sent £100 spending money for each crewman. It was always nice, the lawyers said, for ex-hostages to arrive home with gifts for their children and some cash with which to enjoy some treats with their partner. Wandering round a shopping mall, Aman bantered with some Indian shopkeepers. He marvelled at how small mobile phones had got.

After four days, preparations began for the journey home. As a final excursion, Steed and Hoy-Carrasco took the hostages on a safari at the Nairobi National Park, just outside the city. It was by special request from the crew – the treat they'd promised themselves when they'd first set sail from Dubai to Mombasa nearly four years ago. The safari wasn't one of Kenya's best, but was right on the edge of Nairobi, and could be done in a day. It had become a popular destination for decompressing hostages from Somalia.

They drove around in a four wheel-drive, savannah on one side, Nairobi's skyscrapers on the other. Aman watched the antelopes and zebras, their eyes scanning the horizon for predators. There were dangers in this jungle, for sure, but at least the animals could move around as they pleased. More freedom than he'd had during the last three years.

On the last night before they began flying home, the hostages said their goodbyes to each other. There were hugs and thanks, apologies for arguments and times of weakness, promises to meet again. Steed gave a few final words of advice.

'Don't let this spoil your life,' he said. 'Just get on with it. You're going home now, but we're always going to be brothers.'

There was one final photo op to do. On the day they'd been freed, Leslie Edwards had celebrated quietly with a bottle of champagne at home in Lincolnshire. He'd toasted the hostages for their bravery, Steed and the lawyers for their perseverance, and the donors for showing faith. He'd also drunk to his reputation still being intact. What had felt like the worst moment of his career was now his proudest. On the morning the hostages left Nairobi, Edwards received an emailed photograph. It showed the hostages holding up six pieces of A4 paper. Each piece had a word written on it in blue felt tip. It spelt out 'Thank You, Leslie, Crew MV *Albedo*'.

Edwards pressed his computer's 'print' button. One for the office wall.

On 12 June 2014, some 1,294 days after the *Albedo*'s hijacking, Aman flew back into Mumbai airport. A frail and elderly-looking woman was waiting. Her skin was wrinkled, her hair white, her eyes had dark, heavy bags. His mother. Aman hugged her for fifteen minutes, then did the same to his father and sister. They arrived back in Kardial late the following

evening, where thousands lined the streets to greet him home. Banners proclaimed him as the village son who'd been twice born. The first time on his birthday on 11 November 1991. The second time on his homecoming from sea.

After prayers at a Hindu shrine, there was drinking, dancing, a DJ and firecrackers. Aman and his father, Kewal, were presented with thick garlands of 500-rupee notes. Watching his son being feted, Kewal felt a surge of pride. He was made of much tougher stuff than he'd realised. Would have been good army material, probably.

Aman got drunker and happier by the hour. His feet still hurt from the cuts inflicted when they'd escaped barefoot through the Somali bush, but he joined in the dancing anyway. The party went on, and at 9am the next day, he collapsed into bed. He'd told his story a hundred times over that night, but when he woke up, there was a crowd of villagers outside the house, eager to hear more, and people from the village nearby. The rumour mill was already in overdrive. Was it true the pirates had given the crew prostitutes? Had he really dined off fresh mutton every day?

He learned a few stories from his family too. The darkest moment, his parents said, had been when he'd rung them that previous New Year, cursing them for not raising any ransom cash. His mother, Pushpal, had collapsed with stress. It hadn't sounded like her son on the phone any more.

She'd gone downhill from then on, as if she'd lost the will to live. His father hadn't known what to do. Only a pep talk from an official with the sailors' welfare charity, the MPHRP, had given her the will to carry on. Chirag Bahri, the head of the charity's office in Delhi, had spent eight months hijacked himself, and had come home to find his own mother had died during his captivity. When he'd heard about Pushpal's difficulties, he'd flown up from Delhi to visit her.

'I don't want Aman to come back and find that his mother isn't here for him either,' he'd told her. 'If you can't be strong for yourself, be strong for Aman. Live for him.'

The celebrations in Kardial lasted three days. By the end, Aman wanted to be on his own. There was much to think about – what should he do with the rest of his life? Sweet as it was to be home, there was nothing to keep him in Kardial. Shortly after his release, he'd had a call from his old girlfriend. The one he'd thought about in dark moments on the ship. As soon as he'd heard her voice, he'd known what she was about to say.

'Aman, I got married to someone else.'

'You did?'

'I am sorry, after all this time, I just didn't know if you were coming home or not. My family arranged another boy for me. If I'd known when you were coming back, I could have fought their wishes. But the way it was, I couldn't.'

It hurt, and she sounded like she expected him to be angry. But he couldn't be. God had already been good to him. If he tried to get her back now, he'd mess up not his own life, but hers. And the life of that boy she'd married.

'What has happened has happened,' he said. 'Live your new life and stay with your husband. Just don't forget the good times we had.'

When he told his family, his father asked why he hadn't mentioned it while he'd been hostage. He could have fixed it, he said. Aman told him not to worry. He wouldn't have wanted it anyway. From now on, he alone wanted to be in charge of his life. Nobody else. Not kidnappers, not useless ship owners, not even family. Besides, there were other girls out there. Some of whom, he dared say, might like a merchant sailor with a few stories to tell. A change, if nothing else, from dating all those bloody engineers.

Chapter 23

OCEAN SWELL

Bangkok, June 2013. Three years and two months since the Prantalay 12 *hijacking*

The funeral, if that was what it had been, was a simple one. Only one mourner, and no deceased. After not hearing from him for a year, Sheli Navara had decided there was no longer any point in pretending that her husband, Channarong Navara, captain of the hijacked *Prantalay 12*, was still alive.

They'd talked a few times in the early days, when the pirates had got the hostages to ring home direct to demand the ransom. It had been awful, listening to his voice, hearing the armed men around him. Sometimes the pirates had beaten him up just beforehand, but most of the time he'd sounded calm, strong, telling her he was praying every day. Pray for us too from Thailand, he'd said.

Then the phone calls had stopped. No word from the ship's owners either. A year to the day from Channarong's last phone call, she'd gone to a local Buddhist temple, sobbed her story out to a sympathetic monk, and asked him to perform a funeral ritual. In the absence of a body, she'd written Channarong's name on a piece of paper. The monk had blessed it and then burned it with incense. A lifetime of happiness together, cremated in a few seconds. Still, better than leaving his soul in limbo. Then she'd wandered home, a widow by her own declaration.

The Prantalay 12, *July 2011. One year and three months into captivity.*

In July 2011, the pirates holding the *Prantalay 12* quarrelled with some pirates holding a Bangladeshi vessel nearby. There were too many hijacked ships corralled in the same bay, and not enough anchorage space to go round. A gunfight erupted, the belligerents taking pot shots at each other from the decks of their ships. The distance was too great, and the marksmanship too poor, for any serious risk, but a guard on the *Prantalay 12* copped a minor wound, which couldn't go unavenged. The *Prantalay 12* pirates decided to ram the Bangladeshi vessel and sink it. No amount of warnings from the hostages could deter them. Honour was at stake, and khat had been chewed.

When the *Prantalay 12* rammed the Bangladeshi ship, the attackers came off worse. The *Prantalay 12*'s bow crumpled and split, letting in water. The pirates moved it to another bay, only to hit a reef. Realising it would soon sink, they grounded it on a beach, evacuating the crew. The hostages spent the night camped out in the dunes while the battle raged on, rounds kicking up the sand around them. The next morning they awoke to find trails of blood across the sand, left by a guard who'd been shot. The pirates marched them off into the bush, looking for somewhere to hold them.

Guarding hostages on land was harder than at sea. On a ship, the ocean acted as a prison wall, keeping the hostages in and other pirates out. On the land, there were limited places where eighteen foreign prisoners could be held securely and discreetly. They required at least the same number of men to guard and feed them. Maintaining a camp that big was no small task of quarter mastering, and even in the remotest bush, there was always some local clan whose silence had to be bought.

For the first few weeks, the gang moved the crew from one patch of bush to another, moving on before any local landlord came to claim their due, but such a large caravan was unviable long-term. They needed to find a way to reduce their burden. Hussein, the interpreter for the pirates, suggested they get rid of the fourteen Burmese hostages. He'd met a few Burmese during his time behind bars in Bangkok, when he'd been in jail for opium trafficking. He knew that Burmese who'd left their homeland illegally were considered non-persons by the Burmese authorities, be they in a jail cell in Thailand or hostage in Somalia. With the four Thais, there was at least a chance that their government would pay up. With the Burmese, not a hope. It was better just to let them go.

In November 2011, the pirates dumped the Burmese near a village close to the city of Garowe and told the locals to drive them into town. The hostages ended up in a run-down hotel, still clad in their work shirts bearing the Prantalay company logo. Steed's UN colleague Alan Cole, who happened to be in town and was alerted to their presence, went to the hotel to help them. Cole informed the Thai embassy in

Nairobi, but when checks revealed that the Burman had been in Thailand illegally, the Thai diplomats lost interest. That the hostages had been working for a Thai company, and resident in Thailand for years, counted for nothing. Instead the UN flew them back to Burma. By then the Burmese government was too busy grappling with political reform to care about punishing a bunch of illegal migrants. One of them, Hassan Pan Aung, even felt free to give an account to a local newspaper: 'We were lucky to be from a shit-poor country like our Burma,' he declared.

The pirates' decision to release the Burmese hostages wasn't just pragmatic, they hoped to portray themselves as humanitarians, reasonable actors with whom a deal could be struck. Not like those crazies on the *Albedo*, torturing for the fun of it. Yet the *Prantalay 12* pirates already had ample blood on their hands. Earlier on in the hijacking, when the crew were still on the ship, they had put them on a starvation diet that had had dreadful consequences. First, they limited the crew's meals to a portion of noodles or rice per day. Then, they gave them smelly drinking water that tasted brackish. Sometimes the hostages would get no food or drink for 24 hours. They lost weight rapidly, and several also noticed a jaundiced, yellowy tinge to their faces, which they put down to a lack of fruit and vegetables.

At first, they thought it might be scurvy, the sailor's age-old nemesis. Caused by lack of vitamin C, scurvy had once claimed more sailors' lives than any other hazard at sea, rotting the skin, teeth and eventually the organs. But the jaundiced sailors started to have other symptoms too. Where once they would daydream for hours about food, now they didn't feel hungry at all. One sufferer, Than, seemed to be actually putting on weight. His calves were no longer like sticks, his ribcage was less prominent than before. When he looked in the mirror, the pus-coloured features that stared back now seemed puffy. When he went to the bathroom, he found himself constipated. It even got difficult to pass water.

Over the following days, the swelling increased. The wrinkles on his fingers disappeared, leaving them bulging like sausages; the gaps between his toes vanished; his calves thickened. He tried taking paracetamol, the only medicine on board, but it made no difference. His body began to look as if it had been inflated. When he pressed his fingers into his arm or leg, the skin remained indented, like modelling clay. There was no pain, yet he felt tired and breathless, as if the swelling was squeezing his lungs from inside. Eventually he could barely move from his bed.

'What is happening to me?' he wailed to the others.

A week after his symptoms had begun, Than began struggling to breathe. His pulse raced, yet his lips had a bluish tinge. One night, delirious and confused, his breaths grew shallower and shallower. Then, in the small hours, they stopped altogether.

The crew put Than's body in the deep freeze used to store the *Prantalay 12*'s fish catches. As they said Buddhist prayers, they wondered how many others might end up in there too. Five other men were now bed-ridden, and several more had symptoms. What the hell was it? Some kind of infection? Something they'd eaten? And why was it only affecting some of the crew and not others?

Had the crew been able to see a doctor, they would have learned that their symptoms were those of beriberi, an illness caused by lack of thiamine, or vitamin B1. A normal pirate-plan diet of goat meat, pasta, tuna and brown rice would have given the sailors all the thiamine they needed, but on their meagre rations, it wasn't enough. Normally, beriberi can be treatable within hours through vitamin supplements, or within weeks through a change of diet. Left unchecked, it can be lethal. In trying ever harder to pump blood through swollen limbs, the sufferer's exhausted heart will eventually fail.

By the time Than died, there were nine other yellowing faces on board the *Prantalay 12*. The next to die was another Burman, twenty-year-old Saw. He was a particular favourite of Captain Channarong's, a strong young man and a good worker. Before they were hijacked, when Channarong had finished a long shift on deck, Saw would massage his aching legs for him. It was something the young traditionally did for their elders back in Thailand, and it reminded Channarong of home.

Like many of the younger sailors, Saw referred to Channarong as 'Dad'. The captain took it as a compliment, proof that he'd treated his crew well, not like some of those brutal skippers on the seafood slavers. Yet now Dad felt like he was losing his own sons.

In the small hours one night, a sailor woke Channarong up. 'Saw is asking for Dad to come and see him,' he said. Saw was in bed, propped up by pillows. If he lay flat, he couldn't breathe. His face stared upwards, cheekbones that had once been painfully prominent now covered by a podgy mask. He could barely move. His eyelids were swollen and heavy, like a toad's and he only opened them briefly.

'Dad, I can't take it any more,' he rasped.

Channarong scooped him up from his bed, resting Saw in his arms. He held him close, whispering gently.

'Don't worry, it's going to be okay. We are going home soon, and when we do …'.

Before he could finish the sentence, Channarong felt Saw's head slump slightly. He felt for a heartbeat. Nothing. He cupped his hand over his nose. Nothing. Only the warm wetness of his own tears dripping off his cheeks.

Fuck, I have taken my crew members here to Somalia to die. These boys have suffered so much already, and now this. There was one last thing he could do for Saw, a dignified burial. Not lying forever in the freezer room along with Than. It was already running low on power. Channarong approached Hussein, the translator. The coast was just a few miles away. Could they take the bodies over there, so they could be interred with a brief Buddhist ceremony? It would only take a morning.

'Throw him overboard,' Hussein said.

'What?'

'Throw him overboard.'

'Please, no. We are human beings like you. Don't be cruel. Let us bury them on the land.'

'It is not possible. Somalia is a Muslim country. You are Buddhists. You would need permission from our government.'

'Please, it is not our fault that we are stuck here, dying. You attacked us, not the other way around.'

'Put him in the sea, and that other one who died.'

Channarong was wary of arguing too much. Already he was missing a couple of teeth for answering back to one of Hussain's comrades, a thug called Mahad. Saw's body would have to go over the side. Call it a burial at sea.

Hussein let the crew gather on the deck for a ceremony. The crew fashioned a shroud from some bedsheets and some of Saw's clothes. They brought his corpse on deck, lit some incense, and heaved him over the side. Channarong made a prayer to Mae Phra Ko Ka, the Thai sea goddess: *Goddess, my crew member has died. I cannot keep him in the boat at this time, please take care of him. If I ever reach home again, I will make merit for him at the temple.*

They disposed of Than's corpse the same way. Afterwards, Channarong sought solace in worship. Each night, he would burn incense and pray to the Buddha for three hours. The pirates told him to stop, worried he'd lost his mind.

'Your captain is going crazy,' they warned Kosol, the engineer. 'It is not good to pray that much.'

Kosol ignored them. He too was praying a lot. What else could you do, when you'd just heaved your dead crewmates off the ship like garbage? And who knew who would be next? There seemed no way of telling who would get the illness. They all slept in the same fetid quarters, ate the same lousy food and drank the same stinking water. Maybe it was down to fate. *We are born with a certain amount of merit and a certain amount of sin. This is how it works out.*

Then, slowly, Kosol began to feel it too. At first, he thought he was just gaining weight, the pirates having belatedly improved their food ration. But no: his legs were getting fatter, and the veins at the back of his hand were no longer visible. His skin felt hot and sensitive to the touch, like a blister. He could still piss, but it was getting difficult. His urine had a ruby hue.

He tried not to panic. Not all the other yellow faces on board were at death's door. Some hadn't developed the breathing difficulties. He prodded and poked at his arms and legs, morbidly fascinated by the way he could leave handprints in his own skin. The swelling increased. He struggled to get his clothes on and off. His breathing became laboured. He went to bed each night wondering if he'd ever wake up again. If his time had come, hopefully God would take him in his sleep. Whenever he woke, the same thought always came into his head. *Shit, I didn't die.*

One day, anxious for time alone, he went down to the engine room. It was hot and sweaty, and a hard climb down several flights of stairs, but it was his private fiefdom. The pirates didn't like it down there, nor did the other crew. He paced slowly up and down, feeling at home among the machinery. A complex mechanical puzzle that he, the humble farm boy, had mastered.

An hour later, he hauled himself back up the stairs, expecting his lungs to burst with the effort. Instead, the pressure on his chest seemed less. Strange. He'd thought the engine room's hot, oily air would make things even worse. He lay on his mattress, breathing fine. Two hours later, the wheezing was back. It set him thinking. Could the exercise have helped? The next day he returned to the engine room, pacing round once more. Once again, his breathing improved for a while. He told the others. They'd long suspected that the problem was something to with their digestive system seizing up, they just weren't sure how. Perhaps the exercise was helping with that. Someone remembered their mother saying that walking helped loosen the bowels.

Kosol spent two hours walking up and down the engine room the next day, and the next. It was exhausting, but it helped, and it was better than sitting around waiting to die. Soon it became an obsession. The two hours became three, then four. Other yellow faces joined in. Soon Kosol was pacing for six hours a day, clambering up and down the stairs as well, before collapsing in an oily, exhausted mess on his bed.

After a month, the swelling subsided. Kosol could fit into his old clothes again. The jaundiced tint in his skin faded. It was hard to be certain if it was down to the keep-fit therapy. Maybe it was because the food had improved too, but whatever it was, it didn't work for everyone. In the month that it took for Kosol to get better, he buried four more of his crewmates at sea.

The Prantalay 12 *camp. Somewhere in the Somali bush, late 2014. Three years on from the beriberi deaths, four years into captivity*

The checkers board was always an improvised affair, sketched onto the flattest piece of rock anyone could find. First, they'd get a piece of charcoal from the campfire, dipping it in water to make a sooty ink. Then they'd draw an eight-by-eight grid as neatly as they could, shading in the black squares. Instead of counters, they'd use twigs or pebbles. Of course, the endless games got boring. Kosol vowed that if he ever got home, he'd never play checkers again. But it wasn't about having fun. It was about stopping the mind turning to mush, a workout for the brain. It had been hard enough keeping sane on the ship, where they'd had a TV and a DVD player. Out here in the bush, where they had been since the autumn of 2011, there was nothing. For the last three years, they had lived like nomads, never staying put more than a week, mostly camping rough.

Sometimes they'd doss under thorn trees, draping sheets to make tents. Other times they'd camp in dried-up river channels. Once, during a flash flood, they'd found themselves up to their chests in water. The guards had been scared to move them because of other armed groups on the prowl – they were fugitives as well as prisoners.

Occasionally, the crewmates would chat, but they'd run out of subjects to talk about years ago, and conversation felt like an effort. It was easy, therefore, to spend the hours staring listlessly into space. Which, surely, was where the path to madness began. Your mind frayed to pieces, like poor old Ton Wiyasing over there.

Ton was one of the three other hostages in the camp, but in his head, he was already somewhere else far away. While the others played checkers, he spent all day walking round in endless circles. He talked to himself, in a language no one else could understand. Not, though, because of a mind left idle too long, or a spirit that had given up. It was the price he'd paid for trying to escape.

Ton had talked about making a break for it ever since they'd left the ship. After so long cooped up at sea, the mere fact of being on dry land seemed to him like an opportunity, as if the chance to charge off blindly into the bush, with no idea where to run to, was one he'd be crazy to pass up. He'd cited three things in support of his plan. First, as long as the crew were camped in remote bush, the pirates no longer felt the need to keep them under close guard; they were allowed to wander out of sight, to use the bathroom and fetch water. Second, Ton spoke a little English; enough, he reckoned, to ask for help should he reach a friendly village. Third, he was desperate.

'I can't stand it any more,' he told the others. 'I'd rather risk trying it and die out in the bush than die here.'

The others pointed out the flaws in his plan. There were no friendly villages, as far as they knew. Indeed, there might be no villages at all. The bush stretched around them, as unbreaking as the sea in the middle of the Indian Ocean. Ton would get lost, then starve. And what if the pirates caught him? They might all get a beating, not just him. The guards were in a foul mood anyway, stuck out here in the bush without khat. A while back, one guard had shot another in the leg for stealing a cigarette off him.

'Don't even think about running,' Kosol told Ton. 'You think you'll meet some friendly local? At best all you'll find is more pirates. Maybe even worse than these ones.'

They thought that had settled it. Then, late one afternoon, Ton had gone to collect water from a nearby ditch, and he hadn't come back. The pirates despatched a hunting party. An hour had passed, then two. As darkness fell, Kosol and the others began to wonder if Ton had got away with it. The thought of him dying out there was awful. Almost as bad, though, was the thought that he'd escaped, and that they could have done the same.

A few hours later, the pirates returned, dragging Ton with them. His face was already bloody and bruised, his clothes ripped. The pirates dumped him in the middle of the camp.

They summoned the other three hostages. The hunt, they laughed, had been simple. The quarry had run quite a distance, holing up in a dense thicket as night fell, but all they'd had to do was follow his footprints. They stood out easily in the soft red desert soil. No need for the legendary skills of the Somali bush tracker. A fool could have found him.

A pirate belted Ton in the face with a pistol. Then again, and again. By the time the pistol-whipping ended, Ton was unconscious, his face a red mush, like a half-eaten watermelon. One of his eyeballs looked like it was hanging out. Hussain, the interpreter, threw the others a first aid kit.

'Help your friend,' he said. 'This will happen to you too if you try to do what he did.'

Ton hadn't been the same since. While his face eventually healed up, his mind didn't. He seemed stuck in a world of his own. Ask him one thing, and he'd talk about another, as if unable to comprehend. He no longer even understood brute force. When told by the guards to sit, he'd walk. When told to piss in one spot, he'd piss in another. When told to sleep, he'd carry on circling round the camp, sometimes going all night. No amount of beatings could stop him.

Eventually, bored of roughing him up, the pirates took to tying him to a tree for long periods. Just like a dog, thought Kosol.

Chapter 24

DELIVERY PROBLEMS

From: Leslie Edwards
To: John Steed
Date: 17 November 2014

Situation appreciation, Prantalay 12, hijacked 18 April 2010

Situation: Four Thai crewmen held ashore by Somali pirates. All alive as of 5 November 2014, as per proof of life call. One hostage is clearly mentally unhinged. While still on the ship, six others died from unspecified illness, probably beriberi.

Observation: We should make it clear to pirates that it will be difficult to pay them anything if there are any more casualties. We can say the charity is already sensitive about paying pirates anything at all, given that they allowed six crew to die. We can also use hostage's mental condition against pirates.

Situation: Large medical packs sent in by the Hostage Support Programme were also used by pirates and local community, creating much goodwill. Food and medicine now in short supply for hostages AND pirates.

Observation: Pirates should be ready for a deal. We should avoid resupply, which would just sustain them.

Location: Crew now moved from bush locations to inside Camara village (wild and lawless).

Funds: Lawyers hold $500,000.

Whenever he began a case, Leslie Edwards would write what he called a 'situation appreciation'. If you couldn't boil your strategy down to some key points, all that time spent sizing up the kidnappers would be in vain. Like any battle plan, it didn't always survive contact with the enemy, and sometimes had to be re-written, but it was more an intellectual exercise, a way of making sense of what was always a chaotic, incomplete picture. Get it right, and you had some rules to fall back on when something went wrong, as they usually did.

After taking so many gambles on the *Albedo* case, Edwards could have ended any further involvement in Steed's mission. If nothing else, it had taken up a lot of his free time. But their triumph with the *Albedo*, against all the odds, had made it hard to walk away from the challenge. He'd now agreed to help with the *Prantalay 12* and, depending on how that went, the *Naham 3* too. Besides, it felt like he had a reasonable hand to play for the *Prantalay 12*. There was moral leverage to be exercised over the deaths of the six sailors, and Ton's lurch into insanity. The deliveries of medical packs had gone down well with the 'community', the polite term for the shopkeepers, khat dealers and clan chiefs who were sheltering the pirates. Plus, this time, they finally had half-decent money to offer.

This was thanks entirely to their success with the *Albedo*, which had proved all their critics wrong. Steed was now almost a minor celebrity in Nairobi, the acclaim all the greater because everyone had assumed his mission was doomed. More importantly, would-be donors now took him seriously. Within weeks of the *Albedo*'s release, he'd written up a PowerPoint presentation about 'Operation Benedict' and flown to Thailand to try to raise money for the *Prantalay 12* ransom. This time he hadn't had to cold-call. The Thai government had backed his visit, and he'd delivered his spiel to high-level audiences of fishing officials and bigwigs. A few weeks later, on the strict condition that the source be kept confidential, a donor had sent $500,000 to the lawyers' bank account. The pirates were still wanting $2 million – well down on their $9 million original demand – but it would be enough for Edwards to start negotiating.

One postscript to the *Albedo* rescue wasn't mentioned in the PowerPoint presentation. One morning not long after the *Albedo*'s release, a Somali contact rang Steed to say Jabeen was dead. Gunned down in Mogadishu, apparently. It was presumed to be the work of the other pirate faction that Jabeen had ripped off.

His death left Steed with mixed feelings. Jabeen had briefly been the team's partner in a conspiracy. On their side, in one sense. They'd always known that he could have just walked away with the ransom cash, leaving the hostages stuck where they were. Instead, he'd kept his side of the bargain. Steed was reminded of something Jabeen had written on the 'contract' that Edwards had drawn up. All he'd been required to do was sign his name, but he'd also scrawled a phrase in boyish handwriting: 'We signed this agreement, and we'll do it as it is, thank you.'

Steed had wondered exactly what he'd meant at the time. With hindsight, perhaps it was Jabeen trying to show good faith. Who knew, perhaps he had a good side? Perhaps in Mogadishu, he'd used his share of the ransom cash to support a wife and family? Then he thought back to when the *Albedo* hostages had arrived in Nairobi. They'd given detailed accounts for the first time of the tortures inflicted upon them. Until then, he'd had no idea of just how bad it had been. Much of it had taken place under Jabeen's watch. It had been hard to listen to those stories knowing that he'd got away with all the ransom cash.

Fate had clearly caught up with Jabeen. Steed wasn't happy at his death. But he wasn't sad either.

Edwards started the bidding for the four Thai hostages at $240,000. He told the pirates that it equated to $1,000 per month in 'expenses' for each hostage. It was, he argued, a generous offer, given that the hostages had spent much of their time living rough. The pirates protested that another gang had just got $3 million for releasing one single American hostage.

'The US is a wealthy country, not poor like Thailand,' Edwards replied. 'Also, in that American case, nobody died.'

By November 2014, they settled at $400,000 and a contract was signed. The lawyers told Edwards it wouldn't be possible to wire the money direct to Somalia, as they'd done in the *Albedo* case. The regulations had been tightened, amid fears that Somali money wire agencies could be used to transfer cash to Al-Shabaab. The cash would have to be flown in by a bagman instead.

Edwards' heart sank. He'd used bagmen for Somali runs before. Many of them were "Kenya Cowboys", men with British or South African connections who'd been in the armed forces and now ran private security companies in Nairobi. The pilots among them enjoyed a swashbuckling reputation. Anyone flying a private plane into Somalia loaded with cash had to know how to look after themselves. There wasn't just the prospect of breaking down in the middle of hostile turf, at Somali landing strips, there were always nosy police and Customs agents to worry about.

In 2011, three British bagmen had been jailed for between ten and fifteen years apiece after $2 million was found in their plane at Mogadishu airport. They were quickly pardoned, although the cash was 'confiscated' and never seen again. It was no surprise, therefore, that bagmen charged a hefty premium for their services. A typical ransom run into Somalia could cost anything up to $200,000. If a pilot had to make a landing, rather than just dropping the cash by parachute, it would be more. To make matters worse, a few big security companies had now cornered the market. Some now quoted $500,000 as their standard fee, well aware that clients like Edwards couldn't exactly go to DHL instead.

That wasn't a problem when he was retained by a big insurance company. For the *Prantalay 12*, though, they'd only have $100,000 left of the Thai donors' money after paying out the ransom. Nowhere near enough for a standard bagman's going fee. Luckily, Steed knew an independent operator who agreed to do it for only $40,000, a third of his normal fee.

Frank Harding* was the classic grizzled bush pilot. He'd spent years flying in the British armed forces before ending up in Kenya, where he was a trusted operator. He'd done numerous ransom deliveries in the past, plus various other missions for embassies that he wasn't allowed to talk about.

In early January of 2015, Edwards flew out to stay with Steed at his flat in Nairobi. The exchange date was set for the following week. He was keen to supervise the final details. He couldn't fault Steed's commitment to the task, or his contacts in Somalia, but if something went wrong this time, he didn't want to be dealing with it from his lounge in Lincolnshire. He also still worried about Steed's heart giving out on him at any minute.

The plan was for Harding to fly the cash to an airstrip in Somalia, where he'd hand the cash to Steed's local contact, Ahmed*. Ahmed was a colleague of Omar Sheikh, the man who'd picked up the *Albedo* hostages. Harding would hand Ahmed a black British Army-style rucksack, the sort that Steed and Edwards had both used at Sandhurst. The rucksacks had a sealable compartment at the bottom – designed for storing dirty laundry, but ideal for concealing cash. Four $100,000 bricks fitted in very neatly. On top would be clothes, water bottles and other odds and ends, packed in tight to deter less diligent Customs officials. Harding would ask Ahmed for a secret code number to ensure he was handing the bag over to

---

* Not his real name.

the right person. Ahmed would then head off with an armed escort to Ba'adweyn – the same rendezvous point as with the *Albedo* hostages – to exchange the cash for the hostages.

One morning in late January, Steed and Edwards sat in the operations room of Steed's flat. Ahmed had received the cash from Harding and was now en route to Ba'adweyn. Steed and Edwards settled in for a long, anxious wait. In the contract, Edwards had tried to lay down timings for everything, knowing that things would inevitably slip. Pirates were always late, even when turning up to collect their booty. Still, at least this time everything was pre-arranged. They didn't have a dozen hostages lost in the bush.

The plan began to fray in the usual fashion. The pirates squabbled with their own negotiator, then they fussed over where to meet. Over the next 24 hours, half a dozen different locations were discussed and rejected. Eventually, Edwards decided enough was enough.

'Just get on with it,' he barked down the phone.

Steed was listening in. It was fascinating to see a professional negotiator at work. Edwards always seemed in control, knowing when to cajole and when to be aggressive. From the way he kept rolling his eyes at Steed, he got the impression that this was entirely routine. Finally, later that day, the handover was back on. Then, as Edwards took another call, his calm expression vanished. He listened quietly for a minute, then put the phone down.

'You're not going to believe this,' he said. 'Some of the ransom money seems to be missing.'

'What?'

'That was Ahmed. They've just met up with the pirates for the handover. He and the lead pirate counted the money up inside the car together, but $100,000 is missing. The pirates are saying it's no deal.'

'Eh? How can $100,000 be missing? They must have counted it wrong.'

'Not possible. It was in those $100,000 bricks, remember? There were four of them in the bottom of the rucksack, but when they opened it, there was only three.'

'You are fucking joking! Where has it gone then?'

'I don't know, I just lost the line to Ahmed. He's probably getting lynched by the pirates.'

'Shit! What do we do?'

'Get them to look for it. Maybe he's dropped it in the car somewhere. I fucking hope so. This is serious, John. This is *not good*.'

Edwards rang Ahmed back.

'Ahmed, there were definitely four bricks in the rucksack. I packed it myself. Can you check the car? What? Right, well listen, take a deep breath, calm yourself down, and then check the car again. Then check the rucksack again. Then check the area around the car as well. Maybe you mistook it for something else in the dark. Call me back when you're done.'

Ahmed rang back. The missing brick was nowhere to be seen. The pirates had already driven off. By some miracle, they'd left the rest of the cash with Ahmed, rather than taking it with them as a down payment, the balance to be paid with interest, and by some equal miracle, nobody had been shot. Edwards told Ahmed to get back to Galkayo before the pirates changed their mind.

But what had happened to the money? Edwards had counted it and loaded it into the rucksack himself. He'd got Steed to witness him doing it. Then they'd handed it to Harding, who'd handed it direct to Ahmed. No one else had touched it in between, and Ahmed had been told only to open it in the pirates' presence. He hadn't even been told how much was in there.

'Could any of the pirates have stolen it while Ahmed wasn't looking?' Steed asked.

'He doesn't think so. He says he was alone in the car with the pirate leader when they opened the bag, just like I told him to be. Plus, the cash was in four big bricks. It would be hard for someone to swipe one from him without him noticing.'

'Er, I hate to ask this, but could Ahmed have stolen it himself?'

'Seems unlikely. You've met him, and so have I. I wouldn't have trusted him with the cash if I hadn't liked the look of him. And Omar vouches for him too. Plus, he sounded genuinely spooked when I was on the phone to him. Thought the pirates were going to kill him.'

'Could he have faked the meeting with the pirates?'

'No. Remember, I had the pirate negotiator on the phone just beforehand. He was there too. They certainly all met up.'

'Could they have cooked it up between them? The pirates and Ahmed, I mean? To fake a theft so they can ask for more?'

'No, if they were going to do that, they'd have taken the lot. Not just $100,000. What about your man Harding? Could it have gone under his watch?'

'Seems impossible. Frank's a professional, he does this for a living.'

They stared at each other, exhausted. They'd hardly slept in the last 36 hours, things might seem clearer after a night's rest. Thankfully, the cash was insured for loss in transit – at a heavy premium of 5 per cent – so they'd be able to claim it back. But that wasn't really the point. Weeks of planning the handover had been wasted, plus $40,000 on a pilots' fee, and somewhere out there in the bush, a bunch of hostages who'd been told they were finally going home were now going nowhere.

Once again, they'd made promises that they couldn't keep. Just like with the Muller debacle, and once again, they were going to have to apologise to a bunch of pirates for wasting their time. In his email to the lawyers that night, Edwards offered his resignation. His operation, his responsibility. The home team had to make sure they got the basics right, like turning up with the right amount of money.

The insurers re-imbursed the missing money anyway, but Edwards compiled a report for them into the circumstances of the missing cash. He felt a sense of professional duty to give them as full an account of what had happened as possible. It wasn't pleasant to put colleagues under suspicion, but everyone who'd been near it would need to give statements. Edwards took the view that if the cash had been stolen, whoever had done it would have to have both motive and opportunity. As the last person to have the cash, Ahmed had the opportunity, and sadly, like anyone in a place as poor as Somalia, he surely had motive.

Edwards spoke to him via a video link to Galkayo. He asked him to demonstrate what he'd done with the bag, and how he'd dealt with the pirates. Nothing Ahmed said gave rise to suspicion. He'd just started a steady job working for an international NGO. For many Somalis, that was a dream ticket, as good as they could hope to get. Would he jeopardise it all, Edwards wondered, by stealing cash? Plus, he was vouched for by Omar. Omar, the man who sent in scrupulous receipts for every expense he'd run up while running missions on their behalf.

That left Harding. He was vouched for by Steed, and his past credentials were impeccable. Yet the lack of hard evidence made Edwards begin to question the actions of everyone involved in the operation. On the day of the drop off, after flying back to Nairobi, Harding had sent over photographs of the rucksack being handed over to the Somalis. Edwards had made nothing of it at the time, but with his mind in overdrive, might it have been a little overzealous? Could even Harding be in the frame?

Harding protested his innocence. After taking the bag from Steed's house, he said, he had not opened it until handing it over to Ahmed. The only time he didn't have his eye on it was during the overnight stop he had had to make en route, at a heavily-guarded Kenyan airport near the Somali border. He had spent the night at the airport hotel, leaving the bag in the plane in a secure area patrolled by guards. It was much safer, he reasoned, to leave the bag there than take it with him to the hotel, and then have it searched by airport security upon his return. The bag was concealed out of sight at the back of the plane, which had enhanced security locks on its doors. Besides, nobody at the airport knew the cash was even there. When he did go back the following morning, there was no sign of the plane's locks being tampered with.

He was, he insisted, as baffled as anyone else as to what had happened to the money. He said, though, that the final handover to the pirates had not taken place until two days later, which left plenty of time for something to have gone wrong. Other people could have been in Ahmed's company in that time, he argued, and while they might not have known there was money in the bag, they could have made an educated guess. When he'd handed the money over to Ahmed, for example, there'd been a few other people at the airstrip. Any one of them might have wondered why a foreigner in a private plane was landing there, and reasoned that something important was being handed over. Either that, he reckoned, or somebody had simply mislaid one of the cash bricks in the dark in the run-up to the handover. A single $100,000 brick wasn't that big. Either way, he said, how could he be held responsible for money that had left his care two days before?

He added that he had done numerous previous ransom drops, and for far bigger sums. Why would he risk his personal and professional reputation, for what amounted to a relatively small amount of money? He, of all people, also knew the risks of trying to rip kidnappers off. 'I know better than most that one does not short-change these people,' he told Edwards. 'My conscience is clear.'

Edwards was still not convinced. He felt Harding was being too quick to blame the Somalis, insinuating that they could not be trusted. If that was the case, Edwards thought, why hadn't he said so beforehand, during all the weeks of preparation for the handover? His thoughts stemmed from the approach that no one was above suspicion, but they proved absolutely nothing, of course. They were just a reaction to the circumstances – and they were thoughts that Steed did not share.

'I've known Frank for years, he's a real gentleman,' he told Edwards. 'I just can't believe he would do something like that – he's done lots of these jobs before with no problem.'

Steed felt mortified. Once again, it felt like his character judgement had come under question, just as it had with Muller. Plus, whoever the culprit was, it seemed that once again, all their hard graft had been undone by a malign hand. Or had it? Part of him suspected that nobody had stolen it at all, not even the pirates. The mundane explanations, in his experience, were always the most likely. He was inclined to go with Harding's theory that in all the excitement of the hand-over, someone had probably mislaid the cash in the dark. Some passing herdsman had probably picked it up the next day.

Steed feared that Edwards was being a little blinkered. He too had a stake in this, as the person who'd supervised the handover. Sure, Edwards had offered up his resignation – which the lawyers had duly refused, but might he be seeking a scapegoat?

In the end, Edwards brought in a third party to investigate – a fellow negotiator, who'd previously served as a detective superintendent in the British police, was paid to speak to all those involved and compile a report. Edwards voiced a wide range of suspicions and theories to him, but asked him to keep an open mind.

The report, which was also sent to the insurers, did not identify anyone conclusively, but it did conclude that on the balance of probability, the cash had gone when Harding was in charge of it. Edwards wrote to Harding: '*This is not a finding of guilt, but the review found that there was "reasonable suspicion" that the loss was your responsibility.'* He gave Harding a choice. Either the matter could be taken to the Kenyan police, or Harding could return his fee for the operation. If he did so, it would not be interpreted as any admission of liability. Harding duly returned the fee.

Steed always remained unconvinced. Paying back the fee could have been the action of a guilty man, but it could equally have been the action of an innocent one, keen to avoid entanglements with the Kenyan police. Even if they'd put him in the clear, the mere fact that they'd investigated him over missing money could be the end of his career as a bagman. Harding's wife had also just passed away. He had enough to deal with as it was.

Steed wished he'd never got Harding involved in the first place. A man he'd long regarded as a friend was now bitterly hurt at what he saw as a slur on his reputation. Throughout the mission, he'd worried about getting other people into trouble, be it the hostages, his UN colleagues, or even the late Ali Jabeen. He'd never imagined it would be someone like Harding.

Before the investigation was even completed, Edwards organised a second exchange. This time he flew into Galkayo with the cash himself, and handed it to Ahmed personally. The next day, the four Thais were picked up by Ahmed and his armed escort, and given a phone to ring their families. Captain Channarong was already in tears by the time he called his wife. When she heard his voice, the first thing she asked was if he was being tortured again.

'No,' he'd sobbed. 'I'm crying because I'm free.'

This time, everything went to plan. Back at the Five Star Hotel in Galkayo, Omar Sheikh had even arranged for suits and ties for the men to change into. On the photos that Steed received back in Nairobi, they looked like a slightly baffled Thai business delegation, who'd somehow ended up spending three years in the Somali desert.

The four Thais from the *Prantalay 12* arrived home to a blaze of publicity, all the more frenzied because hardly anyone had known they were in captivity. When the Burmese contingent on the *Prantalay 12* had been released three years earlier, it had been widely presumed that nobody else remained behind. The only people who knew otherwise were the ship owners, the government and the hostages' families, who were asked to keep things quiet. Thai television now made up for lost time, with a four-part special on the sailors' ordeal. Wherever Captain Channarong went out, people stopped to shake his hand. *How did you survive four years of that, grandfather?* Thailand's prime minister, who rang Channarong personally, told him that he himself wouldn't have lasted three days.

Yet while the sailors became celebrities, their families remained paupers. During their time in captivity, the *Prantalay 12's* owners had tried to pay monthly maintenance money, but according to the sailors' families, it never amounted to much. What money had been handed over had sometimes ended up in the hands of relatives who'd fritter it away. Channarong's wife had had to take a low-paid job in a squid factory, and was living in a tiny room near the harbour.

The couple's grandchildren, whose school fees Channarong had previously paid for, had dropped out of class.

The sailors' claims that they had been neglected were disputed by the *Prantalay 12*'s owners, Union Frozen Products. One of those involved in the firm's response to the hijacking was Songsang Patavanich, the director of PT Interfishery, a subsidiary that ran the *Prantalay* fleet on Union Frozen Product's behalf. He insisted that from the outset, they had done their 'utmost' to help, trying to negotiate a ransom and also supporting the hostages' families, who had been paid a monthly stipend.

The negotiations had not gone well. Until the hijacking, Patavanich had thought that pirates only existed in movies, and at first neither he nor anyone else in the firm had had any idea how to respond.

As they pondered what to do, a business partner in Djibouti who had organised the *Prantalay* fleet's fishing licences there offered to put them in touch with a Somali clan leader he knew, who could help in dealing with the pirates.

It had ended, Songsang said, in disaster. After much argument, a $1.4 million ransom had been agreed, the firm sending the cash through Dubai to a contact of the partner. The contact had then disappeared in Somalia en route to the exchange, never to be heard of again. It was presumed that he had been robbed and murdered, rather than doing a runner with the cash, although nobody could really be sure. But it cleaned all the cash from the firm, which was only insured against the total loss of its vessels.

In all, Songsang said, the hijacking had cost them around £3 million, including the loss of the *Prantalay 12* itself. When the *Prantalay 12*'s two sister ships had been rescued by the Indian navy, Patavanich had also spent several months in India dealing with legal formalities to get the crews freed too. They had also paid for flights home for the fourteen Burmese sailors who had been released early. He denied that they were illegal migrants, insisting the company only used registered workers.

Throughout the hijacking, he said, the firm had liaised with the Thai government, although they had refused to get closely involved with the negotiations. At times, the pirates had also split the hostages up into three different groups held by different commanders, who sometimes made different demands. That had left it hard to know who was holding who at times, delaying the negotiations substantially. It had also made communication far harder, making it difficult to keep the families in the loop as to what was happening. Contact had been especially difficult when the four Thais had been held on their own, as the pirates had constantly moved them from place to place.

The company tried to make amends. One day, the firm's president invited Channarong to their offices, where a group of executives were waiting, all smiles. They offered him $5,000, plus a deep freezer filled with a year's supply of frozen Prantalay seafood products. A photographer was on hand to record the happy event. To Channarong, it just looked like a PR stunt. The freezer even had the firm's logo on it. Five years of his life, for a fridge freezer and a few thousand bucks? He'd rather have nothing at all. He walked out of the meeting.

The others decided they couldn't afford to be so principled. Kosol took the money, grimaced his way through the photo op, and got the deep freezer lugged up to his house in the forest near the Cambodian border. He soon had to disconnect it because it overloaded his electricity supply.

For Ton Wiyasing, there never really was a homecoming. When he arrived back in Bangkok, his face still bore the scars of the pistol-whipping he'd got for trying to escape. He stood with a glazed expression on his face as reporters tried to ask him questions. Then he returned to his family home in the forest. His mother had hoped his trip to sea would earn him enough to make him an eligible bachelor. Now, she was stuck with a son who could no longer even work. He spent his days in the house, talking to himself and watching TV. Whenever he saw guns being fired in a movie, he hid behind the sofa.

Chapter 25

RAT CURRY

*The crew of the Naham 3. Somewhere in
the Somali bush, August 2016. Four years
and five months in captivity*

The camera lens slowly panned over the sailors' faces. None looked up to meet its gaze. They were sitting cross-legged in rows, on a patch of ground surrounded by thorn trees. Behind them were several masked pirate gunmen, brandishing AK-47s, a belt-fed machine gun, and a grenade launcher. The effect, clearly, was intended to terrify. The crew of the *Naham 3*, though, barely registered their presence, as if long past caring whether they lived or died. Towards the end of the video, a Taiwanese sailor, Shen Jui-chang, stood up to deliver a long rant to the camera. He was bare-chested, and looked in his 60s. Malnutrition had reduced the middle-aged spread around his torso to flaps of shrivelled skin, as if he'd had liposuction.

'There is no water, there is no food, and every one of us has some kind of illness!' he screamed at the camera. 'The pirates have told us that our boss will not pay for our freedom. I am old, but what about these young people here? Two of them have already passed away because there is not enough medicine here. Does the world want to leave them all here to die?'

Leslie Edwards had watched dozens of hostage videos like these. They were designed to shock the viewer as much as possible, although they usually involved a degree of theatre. The captives would often be roughed up beforehand, so they looked distraught as they addressed the camera. If they didn't sound scared enough, the kidnappers would sometimes get them to do another 'take', like demanding Hollywood directors.

These days, Edwards felt no emotion when he watched them. Once you'd had to watch some of the jihadist videos, in which prisoners were executed, everything else paled by comparison anyway. If the hostages were alive, that was all that mattered – torture, threats, mistreatment, they all just became part of the bargaining process.

Still, the *Naham 3* video was a reminder of what a difficult group of kidnappers he was now dealing with. For a start, it wasn't even a proper 'proof of life video'. He'd been asking for that for more than a year now, without success. The pirates, venal as they were, reckoned that he only wanted the video to sell it to a TV station. For some reason, they figured that footage of a group of poor Asian hostages that no one was even willing to pay a ransom for would be worth thousands of dollars to a TV channel.

With that in mind, they'd invited a Somali TV reporter in to film the hostage video. It had then been broadcast on a Somali cable channel. Whether money had changed hands wasn't clear, although it wasn't a very professional job. The camera wobbled all over the place, panning randomly over the hunched, ragged figures sitting amid the thorn bushes.

It was hard to tell how many of the 26 hostages were even present. Either the cameraman hadn't been allowed to do his job properly, or was some local amateur, chosen because the pirates trusted them.

It had taken days just to work out who was who in the video. On Edwards' office wall was a series of printed video grabs, each with a Post-it Note identifying the different hostages. The Hong Kong branch of Neylon and Gosling's law firm had helped, matching the snatched, grainy images on the video with pictures of the sailors' passport photos. A few hadn't been identified yet, and had question marks scrawled on the Post-its. All looked gaunt and undernourished.

One of the men, a Chinese sailor who seemed to be in his 30s, stared into the screen with a glazed look. He also seemed to have difficulty moving one leg, as if it was paralysed. The guess was that he'd suffered some kind of a stroke.

By now, Edwards was exhausted. After the release of the *Prantalay 12* in February 2015, he'd moved straight onto the *Naham 3* case. Once again, he was doing it because if he didn't, nobody else would. Retrospectively, he'd been paid a small stipend for his work on the first two ships by donors to the ransom fund, but it had barely covered his expenses, let alone the time he'd had to put into the case. He was beginning to question his charitable instincts. The pirates holding the *Naham 3* were the hardest he'd ever dealt with. Not because they were wily and cunning, but because they didn't know how the game worked. They were amateurs from the sticks, bumpkins, latecomers to the piracy game, with no idea of what the going rates were.

From the outset, they'd wanted $20 million, twice the biggest pay-out on record. Edwards had spent hours talking to their negotiators, patiently explaining why that wasn't going to happen, but a year on, they were still nowhere near a deal. They were acting like they'd hijacked a brand-new Saudi oil tanker, staffed by 30 Westerners. Not another clapped-out junk, full of poor Asian seamen that nobody seemed to care about.

The *Naham 3* was owned by a Taiwanese firm, its 26 crew a mix of Chinese, Filipino, Indonesian, Taiwanese, Cambodian and Vietnamese. For most of their four years as hostages, they'd had barely any communication with the outside world. What little information did come out was via a Filipino hostage, Arnel Balbero, who acted as the liaison between the pirates and hostages because he spoke English.

Balbero was from a farming village called Santo Nino Maddela, a scattering of wooden shacks in the wooded interior of Luzon, the Philippines' main island. His father had wanted him to become a policeman or a soldier, but after failing his exams twice, Balbero had settled for becoming a lifeguard at a local swimming pool. That hadn't worked out either – a fellow lifeguard had got him fired so he could get a relative hired instead.

Faced with few other options than working on the family farm, he'd signed up with an employment agency whose reps toured Luzon's countryside, offering villagers work abroad. Millions of Filipinos did that every year, taking jobs in every corner of the world. They nursed pensioners in Florida retirement homes, served coffee at Starbucks cafes in Dubai, worked as caterers at US army bases in Afghanistan. They made up one-fifth of the world's merchant sailors. They had a reputation for being diligent and uncomplaining, qualities that put them in demand, but which also led to cases of exploitation. Horror stories would often emerge of housemaids being kept in near-slavery somewhere in the Middle East.

For their own protection, Filipinos who sought work abroad were supposed to register with a government-run welfare office that explained their rights, and gave them a helpline to call. Yet the agency Balbero signed on with made no mention of it. That was why its reps came recruiting in villages like his in the first place. Out in the countryside, people were too desperate for jobs to ask questions.

Balbero signed up for work as a fisherman. Along with four other Filipinos, he was flown first to Mauritius, where they'd had a week's training. It was only then that they learned they'd be heading to the waters off Somalia. A few asked about piracy, but were told not to worry – hijackings only happened to unlicensed cowboys, they were told. Besides, they'd be going nowhere near the Somali coast. One of their new crewmates even reckoned that being hijacked wouldn't be such a bad thing. He claimed to know a sailor who'd been held hostage for three months, spending the entire time lazing in his bunk – better than working 36-hour shifts hauling in tuna. Nobody had been hurt or mistreated, and afterwards, his agency had sent him home with wages for his entire three-year contract.

The crewmate turned out to be talking as much bullshit as the agency. When the *Naham 3* was captured south of the

Seychelles in March 2012, the pirates were brutal from the start. The ship's Chinese captain Chung Hui-de, had thrown a chair at them during the hijacking, to which the pirates replied by shooting him dead on the spot. Balbero, hiding in his room, had heard the gunfire. Minutes later, the pirates had found him too, and made him crawl on his hands and knees past the captain's dead body. He'd spent his first few days as a hostage wearing clothes soaked with the captain's blood.

As the months in captivity had dragged on, it had become clear that the negotiations were not going well.

The *Naham 3*'s Taiwanese owner, 80-year-old Hung Kao-Hsiung, would later tell local media that in late 2012, he'd agreed a ransom deal of $1.3 million, and sent a delegation to Dubai with the money, which he'd secured through a bank loan. He claimed, however, that because of feuding between the hijackers – who he said had five different factions – the go-between appointed to collect the cash never showed up. In June 2013 – fifteen months into the hijacking – his firm had struck a new deal, this time planning to airdrop the ransom into Somalia. Once again it was scuppered by infighting.

Balbero's family had appealed to the Philippines government to get involved, and so had the local branch of MPHRP, the sailor's welfare charity. The government said that since the sailors weren't registered as overseas workers, there was nothing they could do.

For the first year, they'd just about coped. The pirates, having established their authority by murdering the captain, let them roam the ship. They supplemented their diet by catching fish, using home-made fishing rods. The Chinese crewmen were good cooks, capable of turning even the most unpromising catches into something edible. When they briefly hosted the *Albedo* crew after it sank in 2013, and heard their guests' tales of torture, they'd figured things could be much worse.

In time, they were. As on the *Prantalay 12*, they were put on starvation rations, sparking an outbreak of beriberi. It killed a Chinese crewman, swelling his head and neck so wide that the crew thought he looked like a cobra. One desperate Chinese sailor escaped by swimming ashore one night, only to make the mistake of begging for water from a local shepherd. Knowing that the pirates would pay him a bounty, the shepherd pulled a gun on him and handed him back.

Then, in August 2013, the *Naham 3*'s anchor chain snapped, leaving the ship adrift. The crew were transferred to shore, where they began a nomadic life in the bush, sometimes camping in caves, sometimes in thickets. Water had to be brought in by car from a distant village. The pirates limited the hostages to just over a litre of water each per day, barely enough for the human body to survive on. Fights broke out between the Chinese and Indonesian crewmen over who got most. One sailor clubbed another with a home-made axe. Only when a second hostage died from beriberi did the pirates increase the supply.

Often there was so little food that the hostages fended for themselves. Using makeshift traps and slingshots, they caught birds and wildcats. When they could find nothing else, they ate rats. No amount of expertise by the Chinese camp cooks could make rat curry taste good – the pirates wouldn't touch it, but the hostages forced themselves to eat anything that came their way. One Cambodian sailor would even cook up the scorpions that crept into their beds at night.

During the months in the bush, they had little idea of the passage of time. Balbero kept a vague track of the dates by reading the pages of Kenyan newspapers that the pirates' khat supplies came wrapped in. Occasionally they'd have news from home in them.

He read about Typhoon Yolanda, the devastating cyclone that killed more than 6,000 people across the Philippines in late 2013. In early 2016, he learned of the election of the tough-talking Rodrigo 'Dirty Harry' Duterte as president of the Philippines. Duterte came to power on a pledge to wage all-out war on criminals, but his reach didn't extend as far as Somalia. Neither the Philippines government nor the much more powerful Chinese government made any moves to rescue the *Naham 3*.

At one point, the Chinese contingent thought seriously about trying to kill the pirates – with all the knives, blades and clubs they'd made for cooking and chopping wood, they had enough to smash a few skulls and slit a few throats. None had the slightest compunction about doing so; it would have been a pleasure. All that stopped them was the knowledge that the moment they set foot outside camp, they'd be lost in the bush forever.

It was clear to Edwards that if the *Naham 3* hostages stayed captive much longer, there'd probably be more deaths. The stroke victim could die anytime, and if one of the Chinese crew planted an axe in a pirate's head, there'd be a bloodbath. Steed had also heard, via the pirate grapevine, that several of the crew were suicidal. Even if they didn't take their own lives, the longer they spent in that state, the less chance there was of them coming out mentally fit.

Yet the pirates seemed in no hurry for a deal. In the *Albedo* and *Prantalay 12* cases, the commanders had been keen to reach an agreement because the guards were exhausted, and on the point of mutiny. With the *Naham 3*, it was as if they couldn't care less.

Edwards could sense it in how they talked to him. Usually, pirates maintained a modicum of respect, unless things really weren't going their way. With this lot, all he often got was: 'You are shit. Fuck off.' Sometimes, when high on khat, they'd ring up to tell him that 25 times a day – mostly in the small hours when he was trying sleep. Or, on one occasion, while on another job in Afghanistan, where he'd been deployed at short notice to free someone kidnapped by the Taliban.

The irony was that this time round, Edwards actually had decent money to play with. Steed and the lawyers in London had lobbied in every country that had nationals on board the *Naham 3*, asking for contributions to the pirates 'expense fund'. Quite a number of benefactors had pledged to help, as long as their role was kept secret. The owners themselves had also contributed around $300,000. There was now $2 million in the pot – a perfectly respectable pay-out for any pirate gang, especially for a ship like the *Naham 3*.

Once again, the donors' purse-strings had been loosened partly by Steed telling them about the previous two rescues. He was good at playing up to his 'hostage saviour' role, making it a story they wanted to be part of. Not everyone, though, seemed comfortable with his new-found fame. In the spring of 2015, a senior manager at the UN had hauled him in for a meeting. He was upset about an interview Steed had given to the *New Yorker*, a high-brow US magazine, about the operation to free the *Albedo*. It was a well-researched and balanced article, but it had made it clear that the *Albedo*'s release had only come about because money had changed hands. Steed's manager had felt that it suggested the UN was involved in paying ransoms, or at the very least turning a blind eye. He'd summoned Steed to his house one morning. An 'interview without coffee', as they called it. The UN, the manager pointed out, was supposed to be fighting pirates, not paying them.

Steed had argued that publicising his past successes was an essential part of his pitch to donors. An article in a prestige publication like the *New Yorker* spoke far more loudly than a PowerPoint presentation. His superior wasn't convinced. There was already a worry in the UN that Steed had let celebrity go to his head, and was just doing these interviews for self-promotion. He'd sacked Steed on the spot. Officially, it meant the Hostage Support Programme was over – or, at least, the bit that did the most good.

In the end, it hadn't mattered. Steed had found another backer for the programme, a US charity called Oceans Beyond Piracy. He'd simply carried on the work through them, but it had left both him and Edwards dispirited. Here they were, doing their best in very difficult circumstances, taking all the risks on their own back, and this was the thanks they got. For sure, on the days when the *Albedo* and *Prantalay 12* hostages had walked free, the sense of achievement made it all worth it. To see the prisoners' smiles was a joy like no other, and all the sweeter because they'd done it off their own backs, not because someone had paid them to. As the front man for the operation, Steed got constant accolades. On a visit to hospital to get his heart checked, two Somalis had insisted on posing with him for selfies.

For Edwards, though, the novelty was wearing thin. Now it felt like just another job, trying to rescue a bunch of wretches that nobody else gave a shit about, and dealing with a bunch of pirates who seemed deaf to all reason. Normally in these situations, he'd reach up to his bookshelf for his copy of Gerald Hanley's *Warriors*, his original field guide to the Somali mindset. On one page was a quote he found particularly useful: *'If you have the patience and use the slow, steady drip technique, keep your temper, stick to your points, and never let yourself be rushed, you can beat a Somali in argument.'*

That tactic tended to work for Edwards every time, but not now. Perhaps Hanley had never met a Somali who'd told him: 'You're shit, fuck off,' 25 times a day.

Chapter 26

THE ODD COUPLE

Lincolnshire, January 2016

*'Happy are those who dream dreams, and are ready
to pay the price to make the dreams come true.'*
Dr Geoffrey Griffin, founder and principal,
Starehe Boys' School, Nairobi

'Hello, Mr Edwards? My name is Said Osman. I am a spokesman for the community where the hostages of the *Naham 3*
are being held. The community have asked me to try to help.'

Edwards put his phone on loudspeaker and wearily
grabbed a notepad. *Here we go again.* Yet another chancer
wanting to act as a go-between. It happened in every piracy
case. They'd introduce themselves with a load of high-minded,
altruistic guff, then, sooner or later – usually sooner – there'd
be a demand for 'expenses', typically starting at $10,000.
The more pompous the spiel, the higher the figure, usually.
People who described themselves as 'community spokesmen'
or 'humanitarian actors' were often the greediest.

Unfortunately, no matter who they were, you had to hear
them out, because for every dozen who were time-wasters or

fraudsters, there'd be one who could genuinely help. By using clan connections, or by knowing the right palms to grease, they might break a deadlock, persuading some intransigent party to drop their objections to a deal, but they nearly always wanted a fee. In somewhere as poor as Somalia, even philanthropists sometimes had to charge for their services.

'I can help you build up trust with the local community,' Osman continued. 'I am married to a Somali woman from that area, but I myself was born and educated in Kenya. You are British, yes? That is very good. I was educated in a British school in Kenya. It was run by your fellow citizen, Dr Geoffrey Griffin.'

'Sorry, who?'

'You haven't heard of Dr Griffin?'

'Sorry, no.'

'A great man, a great educator. He taught us the value of hard work and service to the community. I love the British people. Kenya was colonised by them, and they gave us our education system. If you are British, I feel I can trust you.'

Flattery will get you nowhere, Edwards thought. A variation, though, on the standard bullshit. This guy had clearly borrowed his script from some *Merchant Ivory* film. Time to call him out.

'Well, Mr Osman, as you know, we British are very keen on fair play. So if you are the spokesman for this community, can you just tell the pirates to let these hostages go? It is quite wrong that they've been held against their will, especially for so long.'

'It is not that easy. There is a lot of distrust in this community because it has long been in conflict. Nobody is sure of right and wrong any more.'

'Maybe. But the fact is that these men have been hostage quite long enough already. If the community wants to help, all it has to do is pressure the pirates to release them. As simple as that. Can I ask, by the way, who put you in touch with me?'

'The community elders. They know I speak good English, so they came to me to see if I could help. I asked them who was representing the hostages' interests, and they gave me your name and that of Mr John Steed.'

'Oh really? And what did these elders have to say about us, may I ask?'

'They say Mr Steed is a big liar, and that you Mr Edwards, are an even bigger liar. I apologise, but this is just their words. They said that you had been talking for a long time about money, but none has ever come.'

'Well, it is right that we have made some offers. Some very generous ones. But we are not going to pay the kind of money that these pirates want. Not in my lifetime. Not in my children's lifetime. Not in my children's children's lifetime.'

'Yes. As I say, the community feel very embarrassed about this. It is a stain on their reputation.'

'Absolutely. So if they feel that bad, why don't they just tell the pirates to release the hostages?

'Well, the majority want that to happen, but a small section of the community has made profit from the pirates, by trading with them and selling them fuel and food. If the pirates are not paid, these people will not get paid either.'

Edwards brought the conversation to a close. This Osman guy certainly sounded educated, but all this 'community' stuff sounded like the usual hypocritical twaddle. The way they tried to spin it, you'd think 'the community' meant the local Women's Institute, plus some nice grandfatherly imams, all singing 'Kumbaya' together. It wasn't like that. 'The community' were as self-interested as the pirates. 'The community' wanted the hostages freed because they wanted the money they were owed. 'The community', in Edwards' opinion, didn't have an altruistic bone in their bodies.

Still, there was no harm in seeing if this Osman character could get somewhere. Edwards was usually wary of encouraging third parties from getting involved. Often, they just complicated matters, swanning around telling everyone they were his personal emissary, making all sorts of promises on his behalf. But in this case, frankly, there was no progress to jeopardise. They hadn't even been able to get a medic in to see the hostages.

'We still cannot pay anything like what the pirates or the community want,' Edwards told Osman. 'If you think you can persuade them of that, Mr Osman, you are welcome to try.'

The next day, Edwards called Osman back and asked if he could provide some bona fides. If he was ever to be used as a go-between, the lawyers in London might want some due diligence checks done. It was their way of saying: *'Prove to us that this isn't just another Captain Birdseye rip-off merchant.'*

It proved unexpectedly straightforward. A lot of go-betweens wouldn't reveal their real identities at all – all you got was a first name, half a dozen mobile numbers, and the details of a bank account in Dubai. With Osman, a detailed CV arrived by email within minutes of Edwards' request. Born in 1976, he'd studied at university in Kenya before moving to

Somalia, teaching in a secondary school in Mogadishu. Then he'd worked for a succession of NGOs, including the medical agency Médecins Sans Frontiers, and a British mine-clearance charity, the Mines Advisory Group. What he seemed proudest of, though, was his secondary school education under this headmaster fellow, Geoffrey Griffin.

Who on earth was he? Edwards Googled Griffin's name, and discovered a minor *éminence grise* in Kenyan educational circles. An ex-colonial army officer, Griffin had set up Starehe Boy's School in the 1950s, aiming it at destitute Kenyan boys. Many were former child-soldiers for the anti-colonial Mau-Mau insurgency, then at its height. The school thrived, with some of its street urchin pupils ending up as cabinet ministers and professors. At his funeral in 1995, Kenya's then president, Mwai Kibaki, described Griffin as a national hero. Osman seemed to go even further than that, quoting the great man's wisdom in the same breath as Shakespeare and John F. Kennedy. Somewhat to Edwards' amusement, he had also formed a similar opinion of Steed, after reading an article about his work freeing the *Albedo* and the *Prantalay 12*.

'This man is a hero, just like my former headteacher,' he told Edwards one day. 'Both of them are great soldiers and philanthropists. This is why I am happy to help in this mission.'

Osman was as good as his word. A few weeks later, he told Edwards that he had arranged to meet with the pirates in a tea house in Galkayo. He would be bringing a respected local imam, Sheikh Abdiweli Ali Elmi, to act as referee. Edwards was impressed, although he warned him to be careful. Many go-betweens, even those who directly represented a pirate clan, were afraid to go anywhere near the pirates themselves, and with good reason. Frequently, there'd be some commander or deputy who was angry, high, or just a plain psychopath. It wasn't unusual for someone to pull a gun, just to show they meant business.

The meeting lasted three stormy hours, much of it taken up by the pirates bad-mouthing Edwards and Steed. Several times, they asked Osman if he was a spy. Nobody, though, had brandished a weapon. By local standards, it was a promising start.

Osman's main day job was as a youth mentor, trying to help jobless youngsters in the coastal villages find work. The idea, he told Edwards, was to stop them being tempted into piracy. Not that that was much of a career option any more. In Hobyo, Eyl and other hijacking havens, bays that once held half a dozen ships each were now empty. There were unlikely to be new arrivals, because every passing ship was now bristling with armed guards. Skiffs that went out on the hunt came back empty-handed and bullet-ridden, if they came back at all.

In the space of just five years, Eyl, Hobyo and a few other small pirate towns had raked in nearly half a billion dollars in ransoms – that was about half of Somalia's annual aid budget, all in hard cash. But in places where mere survival had always been a struggle, where life had to focus on the here and now, nobody had thought to invest for the future. For all the talk of robbing the rich to help the poor, hardly any pirate cash had gone into schools, hospitals, or new businesses that might provide a livelihood. Aside from a few garish villas squatting incongruously among the shacks, there was little to show for the good times. While some of the top players were rumoured to have salted their dollars away in Nairobi or Dubai, a lot had gone on khat parties, prostitutes and fancy SUVs. All that was left was the hangover from the good times.

'The crime rates have soared, and rape and robbery is now a big problem,' Osman told Edwards. 'Most of the aid programmes have shut down because people are too afraid to go anywhere near these towns. These communities there have been as much a victim of these pirates as anyone else.'

'Have they? They have had millions in ransom cash coming in for years.'

'Some have done well, yes, but others haven't. And now they know the good times are over. It is one reason why they want a bigger payment for the *Naham 3*. They know there will be no more ransoms after that.'

'That is not something I can do anything about, I'm afraid.'

'No, but every night you are talking about the suffering of these hostages, and never mentioning the suffering of those in the community.'

Edwards didn't share Osman's sympathy for the locals. In his view, they were treating the *Naham 3* hostages as no different from the camels to be sold in their market. If anything, they valued them rather less. When they sold a herd of camels, they would knock some money off if a couple of animals died. When they sold hostages, they bargained for them as a job lot, whether or not a few had perished in captivity. Edwards always maintained that if there were more fatalities, there'd be no money forthcoming. The reality, though, was that dying hostages put more pressure on him to reach a deal than on the pirates. Still, at no point so far had Osman himself asked Edwards for any kind of payment. His motives seemed to be every bit as honourable as he professed.

'What do you think of him, then?' Edwards asked Steed, who was now also in regular contact with Osman.

'Early days yet, but a lot better than some of the go-betweens I've dealt with.'

'He seems to think the world of you, by the way John. I think he finds me a bit cynical by comparison.'

'Yes, he was saying to me that the pirates and some of the elders had complained that you were a bit brusque!'

'I'm afraid I regard that as part of my job. Plus, I'm a bit jaded – I've been on this job for more than a year now. I feel like I'm the 27th hostage.'

Over the next few months, Osman held more meetings with the pirates and elders, often on his own initiative, and Edwards began to treat him as part of the team. The clearest sign of that was the amount of time they spent arguing. It soon became clear that Osman viewed Edwards rather like Edwards viewed Steed – as a novice in need of gentle guidance. Frequently, he would lecture Edwards on the protocols of Somali culture. It was rude, he said, to talk of the pirates as Muslims, or describe them as part of the community. It was wrong to use 'negative language', or to be 'disrespectful'. At times, Edwards felt like he was in some NGO talking shop with a particularly earnest aid worker – the sort of meeting where lots of nice words were said, but not much got done.

'Osman, I know you think I am blunt sometimes in my manner, but we do need to keep things moving here,' Edwards said. 'Otherwise the hostages will never get released. We will just keep talking.'

'Please understand, Mr Leslie. If I am seen to be arguing too much for your side, they will shoot me. Remember, it is me who is on the ground here, in potential danger.'

There was no disputing that. Already, the pirates had been turning up for meetings at Osman's house uninvited. It was a way of reminding him that they knew where he lived. Sometimes, Osman would excuse himself from the talks altogether for a few weeks, scared that they were getting too heated.

Despite the arguments, a close – if occasionally stormy – rapport gradually formed between Osman and Edwards. They were the odd couple: the seen-it-all, cynical professional, and the proud idealist, answering a noble calling – each thinking the other could be doing things differently. To add to the friction, Osman also seemed convinced that Steed was a wiser operator than Edwards, despite him playing only a backseat role in the *Naham 3* negotiations. He saw Edwards as Steed's incompetent understudy, a blundering Dr Watson to his Sherlock Holmes.

'Mr Steed is a fine military officer,' Osman told Edwards one day, after yet another difference of opinion. 'You should follow his example.'

Edwards didn't take offence. It wasn't the first time, after all, that he'd dealt with enthusiastic amateur negotiators. The difference was that while Osman had been in the game a few months, Edwards had now devoted the best part of three years of his life to rescuing these forgotten ships. Time when he could have been rowing or shooting in the Lincolnshire countryside, or spending time with his family. It didn't always help his mood, at the end of another fruitless day, to have a new cheerful sermon from the late Dr Geoffrey Griffin popping into his email box:

> *'This world is full of people who do their duty half-heartedly, grudgingly and poorly. Don't be like them. And when you have finished your duty, go on to spare some time and talent in service for less fortunate people, not for any reward at all, but because it is the right thing to do.'*

Chapter 27

Pirate Conference Call

Nairobi, 22 October 2016. Four years and seven months since the Naham 3 *hijacking*

John Steed drove through the empty streets, the headlights piercing Nairobi's pre-dawn gloom. At every red traffic light, he glanced round the car, checking yet again that the doors were locked. Nairobi wasn't nicknamed 'Nairobbery' for nothing – carjackings were common, and the route out to Wilson Airport went through some of the dicier parts of town. Not ideal when you had $2.3 million in the boot.

The ransom cash had arrived in Nairobi the day before. After six months of negotiating, during which they'd argued as much with each other as with the pirates, the unlikely negotiating team of Edwards and Osman had finally reached a deal. The handover in Somalia was on for later that day.

The money had been counted up overseas, and a friendly government had brought it into their embassy in Nairobi by diplomatic bags. That was as much help as they were willing to give. From now on, they didn't want to be seen anywhere near it. Getting it across town to Wilson Airport was down to Steed.

He and Edwards, who'd flown in a few days earlier, had agonised over how to do it. In a sane world, they'd have asked for a security escort from Steed's old colleagues at the British embassy. But with Her Majesty's Government's priggishness about being seen to have anything to do with ransoms, that was out of the question. Might as well ask for help shipping a cargo of heroin. Steed had thought about hiring a private Kenyan security company, but again, they'd want to know what was in the bags, and it meant widening the circle of trust. In the end, they'd decided it was easier just to shift the money around themselves. The fewer people who knew, the better. Unless he got robbed, of course, or searched by a nosy policeman at a checkpoint. At which point, he'd once again look like an utter, naive fool. As with so much of this hostage rescue business, the only viable option also happened to be the riskiest – and the daftest-seeming to anyone who didn't know the score. Once again, grim newspaper headlines flashed through his mind: *'Briton robbed of £2.3 million on airport highway', 'Briton in money-laundering probe after traffic police find £2.3 million in his car.'*

The turn-off for Wilson loomed. In the queue at the main vehicle checkpoint, he tried not to look nervous. He had a covering letter from the lawyers in London in case the guards checked his bags, but the Kenyan attitude would likely be to confiscate the cash first and ask questions after, most likely arresting him in the meantime.

Luckily, he'd done a bit of security consultancy work at Wilson a few years ago, and still had his old pass for the staff car park. As predicted, the guard, on the end of a long night shift, didn't notice that it was months out of date.

'Thank you sir, on you go.'

He drove through. So much for all that security advice he'd given them. If he ever needed to raise money for a ransom payment again, perhaps he could start a sideline as a smuggler.

Back at Steed's flat, Edwards was in the 'ops room', ready to supervise the handover. Osman was coming in with an armed escort to take the hostages back to Galkayo. That was the plan, anyway. After all the hurdles just to get this far, nobody expected things to go smoothly.

The deal had actually been reached a few months before, and in the end, the breakthrough hadn't been down to any negotiating masterstroke by Edwards. Instead, it had come after Osman – like Edwards – had finally run out of patience with the pirates. An NGO had offered him a new job, one that would involve him going abroad for six months. He wasn't prepared to put it on hold while the pirates dithered.

'I am leaving Somalia for half a year,' he'd told them. 'I won't be around to help. If you want to keep waiting until I come back, that is your choice. But I would take what is on offer now. There is no big money, no $6 million. I am tired of talking. So is Mr Leslie. Take the offer, or go to hell.'

It did the trick. A meeting was held at the home of Sheikh Abdiweli Ali Elmi, the imam acting as intermediary. Osman and six of the leading pirate commanders and investors attended. They convened a pirate 'conference call' with Edwards in his lounge in Lincolnshire. By midnight, the figure of £2.3 million had been agreed. The sheikh put his moral authority on the line, offering to guarantee good conduct by both sides. He reminded them that it was Ramadan, the holy month, when Muslims were supposed to do good deeds.

That wasn't the only reason the pirates were feeling benign. During the conference call, Edwards had heard a football match being played live on TV. Every now and then, the pirates broke into whoops and cheers. To his astonishment, Osman explained that they were following a game at Leicester City, whose ground was just 30 miles from where Edwards lived. The pirates, one of whom apparently knew someone living in Leicester's small Somali community, were all avid fans of the club, which had celebrated an historic victory three months before. After years languishing in Britain's lower leagues, they had won the Premier League, a feat the bookmakers had put at 5,000–1 against.

During the conference call, the pirates had seemed more excited about the Leicester City game than the prospect of a ransom payment. When Leicester had scored against Hull City, it had taken at least ten minutes for everyone to calm down and focus back on becoming rich. At the end of the conference call, one pirate commander grabbed the phone to exchange matey banter in pidgin English with Edwards. Edwards had played along, pretending he too was an avid Leicester fan. Anything to help seal the deal.

In the end, Hull had triumphed 2–1 that night. But it didn't matter. As Osman joked to Edwards later on: 'Leicester City lost, but you and I won.'

Over following days, a contract had been drawn up, and another proof of life video taken. This time it was done properly, the hostages lined up in front of a large termite mound, one row standing, the other row kneeling in front, like a class photo. To be absolutely sure it was them, Edwards asked for each one to hold up a piece of card with a code number.

After that, things unravelled again. First, one of the greedier pirates had tried to scrap the deal, insisting it wasn't enough. Then, just when they'd organised a handover for early September, an inter-clan gun feud over some camel rustling had led the pirates to put everything on hold.

Finally, by late October, everything seemed to be in place. This time, Edwards arranged for the cash to be dropped by parachute direct to the pirates. It was safer than hauling it through bandit country, and it kept the number of middle-men to a minimum. Hopefully that would reduce the chances of any going missing, as had happened with the *Prantalay 12*.

It still required careful planning. The pilot – chosen this time by the lawyer, Richard Neylon – was to be accompanied by a 'drop expert', who would push the cash out of the plane's loading bay. Edwards knew such a man, an ex-Special Forces operator, who had done lots of ransom drops before, using parachutes designed for base jumpers.

The challenge would be getting the landing spot marked out clearly. The pilot wouldn't have enough fuel to spend much time looking for it. Edwards sent the pirates a cartoon diagram, showing a plane swooping over the landing strip, and explaining how to make sure the strip was visible by lighting a fire with burning tyres. The pirates would park their vehicles in a row nearby. To avoid any passing US spy planes mistaking the whole thing for an Al-Shabaab weapons drop, Steed also notified the US embassy of the plan. Nobody wanted a drone strike wiping everyone out.

The drop was due near a village called Bitaale, a hamlet spread over open red desert about seven hours' drive from

Galkayo. Osman was already headed there with an armed police escort. Edwards had emailed him earlier, advising him to be completely honest if anything went wrong. The reply was robust: '*Of course I will tell you the truth. I'm an anointed agent of Starehe Boys' School. Integrity was given to me long before.*'

The pirates arrived at the drop point several hours early. Osman had drilled them multiple times on the procedure. Every ten minutes, they rang Edwards, excited as schoolboys.

'Shall we light the fire yet, Mr Leslie? Shall we light the fire?'

'Not yet, no. The plane has only just left Nairobi. Wait until I tell you.'

Two hours later, the pilot called to say he was nearing the rendezvous point. The fires were lit.

'Can you spot anything?' Edwards asked him.

'Sure. Best marked drop zone I've ever seen.'

Shortly after, an email arrived from Osman's mobile phone.

Dear Leslie,
I confirm for the charities that the pirates keeping Naham 3 *crew received 2 bags of money by air-drop at agreed location near Bitaale village at 1325 Hrs. I salute the brave air-drop specialist for spirit of community service.*

Now began the anxious wait for the pirates to fetch the hostages. In an ideal world, the pirates would have turned up with the prisoners so that they could be seen and counted before the drop was made. In practice, it hadn't worked like that.

The pirates were already paranoid about the whole thing being an elaborate trap. With 26 people in their custody, it would be hard to make a quick getaway if things went wrong. There was no option but to hope that they honoured their side of the bargain. Four hours later, Edwards got another email from Osman.

Hi Leslie.
Hurray! I have 26 good-looking sea-farers for you! Feel happy. I'm proud to declare true and fair friendship to you.

Edwards had a cup of tea to celebrate. No time for a proper drink right now. They'd done it. *They'd bloody done it.* The last ship, finally out. After the most gruelling bloody negotiations he'd ever done. Or, as Osman would put it in a later email. *'A coalition action platform to persuade the pirates and rogue traders to calm down and accept community-based mediation.'*

The hostages were driven back to Galkayo in a twenty-vehicle convoy. Jubilant at finally getting their cash, the pirates escorted it half the way, letting off streams of celebratory gunfire into thickets where suspected ambushers might lurk. The hostages arrived in Galkayo, only to find the city quaking to the sounds of artillery fire. For years, the tiny town had been divided, Berlin-style, between two rival administrations, one in the south and one in the north, who occasionally waged open warfare. This was one of the conflict's livelier nights. From the upper floors of the Five Star Hotel, where the hostages were billeted, rockets and tracer fire could be seen arcing across the sky. It didn't stop the usual stream of VIPs coming for photo ops with the hostages though. 'Don't worry, this is routine stuff,' breezed one dignitary, noting the hostages' terrified faces as they posed for the cameras. 'Just our hot-blooded ways!'

Two days later, during a lull in the fighting, Steed came in on a UN flight to pick the hostages up. The UN were still willing to lay on transport, despite his fall-out with them, but Edwards was not allowed to accompany him, much to his dismay. He'd been keen to meet Osman and thank him face to face, but the UN felt that the presence of a professional negotiator on the plane would indicate that a ransom had been paid.

As it turned out, nobody was in much doubt about it. Within hours of the hostages' release, the Associated Press newswire ran a piece quoting a *Naham 3* pirate commander as saying that $1.5 million had changed hands. The real figure was $2.3 million, but the commander was probably trying to manage the expectations of his creditors. Asked about the ransom by journalists at Galkayo airport, Steed retreated into UN-bureaucrat babble.

'What I would say is that we got there in the end via the local community,' he beamed. 'The religious leaders put pressure on the pirates. It was a team effort.'

Later, he would tell one journalist that the rescue was 'something that Special Forces from a government would be pretty proud of doing.' It was a bit of a cheesy quote, but it felt true enough. Special Forces had back-up from their governments. His team had been on their own.

As with the *Albedo* hostages, the *Naham 3* crew were still adjusting to freedom. Two days of 'decompression' in a city at war with itself hadn't been much help. On the flight back to Nairobi, Steed tried to raise a cheer as they left Somali airspace, but most of the faces just looked blank. Some didn't seem convinced they were really free.

At Wilson Airport, Steed saw the usual gaggle of diplomats gathered on the tarmac, keen, as ever, to whisk the hostages away, and keen no doubt to take the credit. Even though some of them had done absolutely nothing. The Cambodian embassy, for example, had refused to even issue the sailors with temporary travel documents, insisting that they couldn't do so without proper passport photos. Steed had explained that as the hostages were still prisoners, that was going to be difficult. They still hadn't bent the rules. In the end, the embassy of the Philippines, one of the few that had been helpful, issued the Cambodians with temporary Filipino passports. The Cambodian government, meanwhile, was still refusing to pay for their flights home.

Without warning, a small bus made its way along the tarmac, accompanied by a black van from the Chinese embassy. Several smiling officials appeared. They spoke briefly in Chinese to the group of Chinese crewmen and gestured towards the bus. Steed didn't speak Chinese, but it seemed to translate as 'This way, please gentlemen.' This time he didn't try to object. For all the smiles, he knew there was politics going on behind the scenes. The Chinese knew that the *Naham 3*'s crew included Shen Jui-chang, the elderly sailor from Taiwan who had spoken in the hostage video. Taiwan regarded itself as an independent republic, but Beijing insisted it was still part of China, a view it liked to remind the world of whenever possible. For that reason, the Chinese diplomats didn't want Shen being separated off from the rest of the Chinese contingent, as it would imply de facto recognition of Taiwan's independence. That could be politically embarrassing, especially when there was a waiting press pack inside the airport. So they wanted to take both him and the Chinese sailors with them for now, and make arrangements for him to get back to Taiwan later. It was diplomatic stage management.

The hostages didn't look terribly happy at being whisked away from their comrades without warning. It also broke all the rules in the hostage decompression book, which Steed had spelt out to the various embassies in advance. But the Chinese had helped with some of the logistics of the release, and besides, Beijing was a powerful player in Kenya these days. As an ex-diplomat himself, Steed knew when to hold his tongue. Just as well Edwards wasn't there, he thought. For all his detached veneer, Edwards took hostages' welfare seriously. He'd have sparked an international incident between Britain and China. '*Take your hands off those men! They haven't spent four years kidnapped just to be taken prisoner again by you!*'

In fact, Edwards *was* there. With no need to man the ops room any longer, he'd wandered up to the airport to watch the hostages arrive. By waving around a file marked 'Naham 3 *Hostage Release*' and adopting a brisk, officious manner, he'd bluffed himself airside. Edwards watched from a discreet distance as the hostages disembarked, resisting the temptation to wander over to introduce himself. Plenty of time for that later.

He'd spent a year, a whole year of his life on this case, turning those men from a few ghost-like images on a hostage video back into living, breathing people. Normally, hostage negotiations were a solo performance. This one had been like directing a play, bringing in a whole cast of actors: Osman, the pirates, the sheikh, the elders, the traders, the 'community'. Leicester City, even.

He hadn't been able to write the script. All he'd been able to do was get the actors to improvise, and hope that they'd go for the happy ending, not the tragic one. In the end, this case hadn't just been down to him, but lots of people. Which, in a way, made it all the more of a triumph. Even more than the *Albedo*.

As the hostages headed to the airport terminal, he felt something he'd never experienced before in 25 years of hostage negotiations. He began welling up with tears.

What was the matter with him? Just a change in the body chemistry, he told himself. Like that time he'd suffered chest pains. Only this time, it wasn't brought on by stress building up, but by it ebbing away. Either that, or he was just being a soppy old fool. *Come on Edwards, get a grip.* It was no good, the tears kept coming. People were looking at him and he excused himself, left airside, and found the nearest airport cafe.

'A cup of tea. Actually, make that a large whisky.'

Later, over several glasses of wine at Steed's apartment, he confessed.

'I had a proper emotional wobble at the airport. Very strange.'

'Oh, me too. I was in tears the whole time.'

'Really? I wish you'd told me. I wouldn't have felt so bloody silly.'

When the *Naham 3* sailors arrived home, they had harsh words for the ship's owner, Hung Kao-Hsiung. The *Naham 3*'s Taiwanese chief engineer, Shen Rui-Chang, gave an interview in which he claimed he had been told by the owner that he would be fishing in the Atlantic, not the pirate-infested Indian Ocean. 'He didn't tell me the ship I was going onboard was on the Indian Ocean, if I knew I wouldn't have agreed to go!' he said. 'I knew there were pirates in the area.'

Two days before the kidnapping, he added, the *Naham 3*'s captain had received a fax from the owner telling them to leave the area because of the hijacking risk. However, another employee of the company had then rung to tell them to remain where they were because the fishing was good. 'We caught so much fish there, but we were hijacked by the pirates the same night,' he said.

Hung had tried to keep a low profile during the years of the hijacking, but after Shen's accusations, he eventually broke his silence. The 80-year-old insisted he'd done his best to free the crew, despite being hospitalised with illness several times during the hijacking. In all, the company had spent around £2 million, forcing it into bankruptcy. He also claimed that the firm had warned the *Naham 3*'s captain, Chung Hui-de, repeatedly not to stray into dangerous waters. 'We called the captain six times, saying to leave the area as soon as possible,' he claimed. After shooting the captain dead during the hijacking, the pirates had even tried to ransom out his corpse, demanding $200,000 for his body's return.

In late 2018, the Chinese sailors involved in the hijacking launched a lawsuit against the owner in a Taiwanese court, seeking compensation for mental stress and unpaid wages. The case is still ongoing.

AFTERWORD

In May 2015, I received a letter from a *Daily Telegraph* reader in response to an article I'd written about John Steed. The article told how Steed had secured the release of the *Albedo* and *Prantalay 12*, but was still struggling to find funding for the release of the *Naham 3*. It read:

Ted Phillips
Chelsea
London SW3

Dear Mr Freeman

I saw your article about John Steed and his problems paying off the pirates in Somalia. Some years ago, I discovered a British charity that had been founded centuries ago with the express object of paying the ransoms of Christians who had been taken prisoner by Barbary Pirates.

The Henry Smith Charity is still in existence today. The charity owns the freehold of much of the land in South Kensington. Why hasn't it come forward in these years of piracy? I don't know. When I tried to telephone them recently, they tried to hide the fact that the charity was in existence to pay ransoms for Christians. They spent the money on other things now.

> *If you think you have a chance of squeezing some money out of Smith's charity for the ransom of Christians, I would appreciate hearing from you.'*
>
> *Yours sincerely*
>
> *Ted Phillips*

I was intrigued. Was there really a fund that could have been the answer to Steed's prayers all along? Sure enough, it turned out that the Henry Smith Charity had not merely survived into the modern day, but was now one of Britain's richest grant-making bodies.

A Tudor-era businessman, Smith was one of Britain's first estate agents, a man who grasped the value of land and location. He made a fortune by buying and selling property around London. When he died in 1628, he bequeathed two charitable funds – £1,000 to help the poor, and another £1,000 'for the relief and ransom of poore Captives being slaves under the Turkish pirates'.

The plight of the 'poore Captives' was a fashionable philanthropic cause at the time. Thousands of British sailors were being held in slave camps along the Barbary Coast, often in appalling conditions. Britain's new merchant class – many of them seafarers themselves – considered it their Christian duty to buy them back. In Italy and Spain, special Catholic religious orders, such as the Church of Our Lady of Ransom, were set up for the same purpose.

After the Barbary wars, most such ventures were wound up, but long after his death, Smith's charity continued to make shrewd property investments. In the 1640s, they bought

84 acres of marshy fields west of London. That soggy patch of land is now better known as Kensington.

That gave the charity a large chunk of Britain's most expensive patch of real estate, which it sold in 1995 to the Wellcome Trust, for £280 million. Today it has total endowments worth £800 million, and up to £30 million to give away every year to good causes, 'to honour the spirit of Henry Smith's will and interpret his charitable ethos for our modern society'. All anyone had to do was apply via their website.

'Worth giving them a try, isn't it?' I said to Steed. 'Seems they're tailor-made for your needs.'

It was not to be. It turned out that the charity only funded ventures for UK-based projects. If Steed had needed money to help Girl Guides, asylum seekers, ex-offenders, battered women, underprivileged children, LGBT communities, drug users, or any manner of other British causes, he might have stood a chance. But foreign sailors held prisoner in far-off lands didn't count. Besides, while I had a feeling that Smith himself might have been willing to make an exception, modern charities have rather tighter procedures on what they can do. Even if they'd wanted to help, channelling cash to pirates would surely have broken all kinds of Charity Commission rules.

Still, it showed how the world had changed. In Smith's time, clearly, nobody had hang-ups about paying ransoms at all. It was seen as a legitimate, even noble thing to do. But the defeat of the Barbary pirates coincided with Britain's rise as the world's foremost maritime power. With a global empire to run, a strict no-ransom policy made much more sense. Had His Majesty's Government not enforced this, no district administrator in India or Kenya would have been safe from abduction attempts. It also chimed with Britain's changing religious outlook. Under the puritan zeal of Protestantism, there was a heightened awareness that paying ransoms to criminals was ethically questionable. It was a line that the British government has stuck to to this day.

That is all very morally upright, but in situations like the Somali piracy crisis, it made the work of Steed's hostage rescue programme even harder. When he and the lawyers went cap in hand, it was all too easy for would-be donors to politely turn them down. That meant the sailors on the *Albedo, Prantalay 12* and *Naham 3* spent far longer in captivity than they should have.

Not that they should have had to rely on a retired British colonel in the first place. Others could have come to their rescue long before. Most culpable, of course, are the ships' owners, who Steed believes should never have sent them through such dangerous waters uninsured and unprotected. After all, when their three ships were hijacked, the piracy crisis had already been dominating the news for three years. Could they really have been unaware of the risks?

The owners could also have done more for the hostages' families – not just with hardship payments, but also the simple courtesy of keeping them properly informed. For much of the time, the sailors' families had no real idea of whether their loved ones were even still alive. Nor were much amends made when the sailors finally got home. The most generous payment was for the *Prantalay 12* crew, who got $5,000 each. Given their 1,774 days in captivity, that worked out at $2.81 per day.

Such failings, of course, reflect how the culture of corporate responsibility is still in its infancy in some parts of the world. Companies can still cut corners and get away with it. Those who suffer have little means of redress, especially if they are poor and uneducated.

It's harder to see, though, why governments could not have been more pro-active. After all, by the time Steed got involved, all these ships had been languishing for several years apiece. News of the sailors' plight may not have excited the international media, but shipping ministers in the sailors' own countries were all too aware.

True, matters were complicated by the fact both crews and owners were of multiple nationalities, blurring the lines of responsibility, but was it really beyond the wit of a few shipping ministers to co-ordinate some solution? And might they not, at the very least, have prosecuted the owners if there was evidence of dereliction of duty to their crews? Many of the sailors would dearly like to have their day in court. So far, none have, nor is there any talk of it happening.

Questions might also be asked of the international anti-piracy force, one of the largest peace-time Armadas the world has ever seen. For much of the time that the *Albedo*, *Prantalay 12* and *Naham 3* languished off the Somali coast, naval gunboats were never far away. The British, American and French contingents, and some others, all had Special Forces teams at their disposal, trained to carry out hostage rescue operations. Yet because of the risk of either the troops or the hostages being killed, these forces were generally reserved only for the rescue of their own nationals. It's understandable that Western nations do not lightly risk the lives of their best soldiers, however, given that hardly any of the commercial sailors taken hostage during the Somali piracy crisis were Westerners, it meant the Special Forces were only really there for a select few. Might the anti-piracy commanders not have created a pooled Special Forces rescue team, there to deal with egregious cases? After all, the chances of a bloodbath would have been minimal. Pirates aren't jihadists, eager to die for their cause. Confronted by highly-trained soldiers, most would have given up without a fight. Indeed, many argue that had such a robust approach been taken from the outset, the problem might have ended there and then, sparing thousands of sailors from lengthy hostage ordeals.

Sadly, the ex-naval commanders I have asked about this cite all manner of reasons why a multi-national rescue team wasn't possible. Given the risk to life, permission to carry out rescues would have to be sought first from the hostages' governments – no simple matter with a multi-national crew. There'd be risks of lawsuits and compensation claims if it went wrong. And were such a team on hand, unscrupulous ship owners might have even less incentive to pay a ransom.

Those arguments, though, underline how the West's willingness to commit military force depends on context. Our interventions in Iraq, Syria and Afghanistan have always involved putting troops in harms' way to protect innocent lives abroad. Our leaders even cite it as evidence of their governments' compassion, their willingness to stand up for what is right. Yet for 48 crewmen from the poorer corners of Asia, who sought only to earn a living for their families, no such help was forthcoming. And had a certain ex-colonel not been so lucky with his heart surgery, they might well be stuck there still.

⚓

As I write, more than three years have passed since John Steed, Leslie Edwards and the rest of the hostage rescue team freed the *Naham 3*, the last of the three forgotten vessels. Somali pirates no longer make the headlines much. Now that most commercial ships routinely carry armed guards in the western half of the Indian Ocean, hijackings have all but stopped.

However, the threat hasn't gone away altogether. In ports like Eyl and Hobyo, the same dire poverty that drove people to piracy in the first place still prevails, although there is now talk of building big new ports there that bring real prosperity. In the meantime, though, pirate skiffs still sally forth, hoping for a ship that has got complacent and ignored the warnings to steer clear of the Somali coast. Far from finally taking his retirement, John Steed has just finished helping to free some sailors from the *Siraj*, an Iranian vessel whose crew were hijacked in March 2015. On top of his heart problems, he suffered a minor stroke in 2018, leading friends to urge him yet again to take it easy. He has no plans to listen to them. The sense of reward he gets from helping out, he tells me, isn't one he finds easy to resist.

For the rest of the team, there have been rewards of a different kind. In the Queen's New Year's Honours List at the end of 2016, James Gosling, Richard Neylon's senior partner at lawyers Holman Fenwick Willan, received an OBE. It was in recognition of the firm's pro bono work in helping to free the crews of the *Albedo*, *Prantalay 12*, and *Naham 3*, plus its efforts securing the release of more than 1,750 other piracy victims. It is true that the exact means by which the pirates were persuaded to release all these captives were glossed over somewhat. The award citation, which appeared in a single line entry in *The Gazette*, Britain's official public record, merely stated 'For Services to the Legal Profession and to Maritime Hostages'. Her Majesty's Government, it seems, still doesn't like to mention the 'R' word. Not in official records anyway.

Indeed, Gosling himself was surprised to get anything at all. As he told his local newspaper, the *Saffron Walden Reporter*: 'I really thought what we have been doing wasn't the centre of official approval.'

Why Steed, Edwards and the others did not get recognition is unclear. Her Majesty's Government doesn't discuss its honours decisions. Steed may have been overlooked because he already had an MBE for his work as a UN military observer. As the man who directly negotiated the ransoms, Edwards may have been deemed too close to the money trail. The honours system attracts enough controversy as it is.

Still, the mission itself provided its own rewards. How many people, after all, can justifiably claim to have saved the lives of 48 innocent men? Yes, there are a few: the pioneering heart surgeon, the cancer researcher who has achieved a breakthrough, the soldiers who have distinguished themselves in battle. All of whom will no doubt say: 'Just doing my job.' What makes the work of Steed and his team so unique, though, is that they weren't 'just doing their jobs'. They did what they did entirely unbidden, and often against received wisdom. Steed got involved in ransom talks despite knowing that if it went wrong, the blame might be laid squarely on him, the naive, interfering bureaucrat from the UN. Edwards and Gosling took the decision to cut some of the *Albedo* pirates out of the deal – a gamble that could have looked reckless had it failed. Rather than gongs, they might have faced lawsuits. It's one thing to play the hero when the world expects it. It's another thing to do it at the risk of looking a fool.

In the end, though, the team did get some official recognition, and from an arguably higher authority than Her Majesty's Government. In late 2017, I had the following email from Richard Neylon: *'I thought it might amuse you to know that the work of our "support group"… was "commended" by the United Nations Security Council in* Security Council Resolution 2383, Piracy and Armed Robbery at Sea off the coast of Somalia, *of 7 November 2017.'*

True, in order to find the glowing testimony, I had to delve deep into a twelve-page statement of UN bureaucratese – it wasn't exactly trumpeted to the wider world. But it isn't everyone who gets an endorsement from the body representing all five of the world's pre-eminent nuclear powers, especially if they work from an office in their spare room.

Finally, what of the other characters in this book? It would be impractical to list here how all 48 forgotten hostages have fared since their release. Some of those I interviewed for this book I have lost touch with. Others, despite their ordeal, have had no choice but to return to sea to earn a living, and are incommunicado for long periods. Here, though, is a brief round-up.

Aman Sharma, the Indian sailor on the *Albedo*, is still a merchant sailor. After a few months recovering at home in Kardial, he tired of village life again and signed up once more as an able seaman. This time, though, it was with a reputable outfit: Maersk, the Danish shipping giant. Life with Maersk is more like the merchant sailors' life he first signed up for. The pay is better, and every now and then he posts pictures on

Facebook of some exotic new destination he has visited. He has also worked with seafarer's charities, speaking out about the dangers of piracy, and counselling other piracy victims and their families. When I last spoke to him, he'd been promoted to bosun, and had signed a deal to make a movie about his experience with a Bollywood film maker. He's also got married.

Shahriar Aliabadi, the Iranian bosun on the *Albedo*, remains in high regard among his fellow crewmen for the leadership he showed in the cruellest of circumstances. He returned to Iran, where he still lives, and now works in an insurance firm in Tehran.

Captain Jawaid Khan returned to sea, despite the pleas of his wife and daughters to retire. He prefers not to speak publicly about his ordeal on the *Albedo*. His daughters, Mishal and Nareman, are both now married with children.

Paul Muller, the German who promised Steed $900,000 for the *Albedo*, is still living Ireland. The extradition hearing against him failed, although German prosecutors still have fraud charges issued against him. He protests his innocence.

Omid Khosrojerdi, the owner of the *Albedo*, remains incommunicado. It would appear he has left Malaysia, and may now be back in Iran. My own efforts to track him down through his former business partners have not been successful.

Captain Channarong Navara, skipper of the *Prantalay 12*, returned to Thailand and still lives with his wife in Bangkok.

When I interviewed him for this book in 2016, he told me his story while wearing a T-shirt that claimed, somewhat inappropriately: 'It all happened in Starbucks'. Today he runs a vegetable stall.

Arnel Balbero, the Filipino fisherman who acted as the spokesman for the hostages on the *Naham 3*, is now back living in the Philippines. He has refused to return to seafaring, but has struggled to find a permanent job as of yet. He has, however, recently married and is due to become a father.

Said Osman, the 'community spokesman' who helped Edwards broker the deal for the *Naham 3* hostages, still lives in Somalia. Today, he works as a liaison officer for Galmudug Maritime Police, a new Somali-led anti-piracy force whose jurisdiction includes the port of Hobyo.

Sheikh Abdiweli Ali Elmi, who acted as guarantor for the *Naham 3* deal, was killed by the terrorist group Al-Shabaab in November 2018. Two suicide bombers attacked him at his mosque in Galkayo, killing sixteen other worshippers as they did so. The sheikh had published videos showing him chanting Somali poetry along to music, in defiance of Al-Shabaab's claim that music is un-Islamic.

Hung Kao-Hsiung, the owner of the *Naham 3*, declined to be interviewed.

Leslie Edwards still works as a hostage negotiator. Life is quieter now that the Somali piracy crisis is over, but there are still enough kidnappings around the world to keep him busy.

James Gosling has now retired from shipping law, and is pursuing a lifelong passion to set up his own brewery.

Richard Neylon still works as a lawyer at Holman Fenwick Willan. He and I still meet up occasionally near his offices in the City. These days, though, he no longer has stories of withdrawing millions of dollars from the bank vaults round the corner.

Colin Freeman
London, September 2020

ACKNOWLEDGEMENTS

Writing a book is a long and lonesome task, especially when juggling it with a day job as a freelance hack. So any help one receives from other people is all the more welcome. My first thanks go to John Steed, Leslie Edwards, Richard Neylon and James Gosling, who took me into their confidence and helped me convince myself that there was a book-worthy story to be told. Later on, they patiently dealt with endless follow-up questions, some of which I no doubt asked multiple times. They were also candid about when things went wrong, which I think is certainly to readers' benefit.

Other people who endured lengthy grillings were the hostages themselves, who opened up to a stranger on what can only have been an utterly traumatic experience. Some agreed to speak to me partly because I had languished in pirate custody myself, even though their incarceration was clearly in a different league. So too did Shahnaz Khan and her daughters Mishal and Nareman, whose ordeal – and spirited response – hopefully gives readers some idea of the particular hell that hostages' families endure.

I am also indebted to those who helped me track down the hostages I interviewed: thanks to Roger Harris and Tom Holmer at the London-based International Seafarers' Welfare and Assistance Network, and their colleagues Jun Pablo in the Philippines, Chirag Bahri in India and Apinya Tajit in Thailand. While in Thailand, I was helped out by my old journalist friends Phil Sherwell and Jonathan Miller, of *The Sunday*

Times and Channel Four News respectively, who found me translators and put me up for a few nights (sorry, Phil, by the way, about losing your door keys). For the interviews with the hostages themselves, I had the excellent translation skills of Pailin Wedel in Thailand and Leilani Chavez and Jef Maitem in the Philippines. And for the task of speaking to the ship owners (or at least trying to) I was assisted by fellow journalists Vee Intarakratug in Thailand, Gladys Tsai in Taiwan, Arthur Lim Ling Fong in Malaysia, and Naeim Karimi in Canada. The research for this book involved doing 40,000 miles of travel in all, and the aforementioned people all helped ensure that it went smoothly.

Friends of John Steed were helpful with their time, especially Richard Bailey and Robyn Kriel. In Somalia, Said Osman and Omar Sheikh obliged me on the details of their role in the mission – which, in dealing directly with the pirates on the ground, put them right at the very sharp end. I should also point out that while this book has inevitably focused on some of the rescue mission's central characters, there was an entire cast of other helpful folks, at the UN, Holman Fenwick Willan, the MPHRP. Their contributions are too numerous to mention here, but doubtless helped the mission succeed. As I remember from my own case, hostage operations aren't just about the cloak-and-dagger stuff – there's a devil of a lot of admin and paperwork too.

On the research side, some of the many gaps in my knowledge were filled by Somali analyst Nuradin Dirie and Captain Gerry Northwood, former commander of the UK counter-piracy force off Somalia. On the writing side, Wendy Jones gave some invaluable – if painful – critiques of an early draft. Later versions were read by James Wilson, Ian Evans, Roland

Oliphant, Lisa Mitchell and Zoe Flood, who all made comments that were both useful and (thank God) encouraging. I am indebted also to Ellen Conlon and the rest of the staff at Icon Books – firstly for publishing it, and secondly also for Ellen's diligent editing.

Finally, thanks also to my other half, Jane, for her unwavering support, especially in the early days when all often seemed lost. This was a hard book to write, and without your help, I would never have got this far.